Chamber Music for Solo Voice and Instruments 1960-1989

Kenneth S. Klaus

Chamber Music for Solo Voice and Instruments 1960-1989

An Annotated Guide

Fallen Leaf Press
Berkeley, California

Manufactured in the United States of America
Published by Fallen Leaf Press
P.O. Box 10034
Berkeley, CA 94709 USA

Library of Congress Cataloging-in-Publication Data

Klaus, Kenneth Sheldon, 1952-
Chamber music for solo voice and instruments, 1960–1989: an annotated guide / [Kenneth S. Klaus].
p. cm.
Includes indexes.
ISBN 0-914913-30-1
1. Songs with instrumental ensemble—20th century—Bibliography. 2. Sacred songs with instrumental ensemble—20th century—Bibliography. I. Title
ML128.S3K55 1994
016.7832--dc20 94-31680
CIP
MN

The paper used in this book meets the minimum requirements of the American National Standard for Information Services—Permanence of Paper for Printed Library Materials, ANSI Z39.48-1984.

Contents

To Darlene

Preface

This book is the result of an expansion of research done for my doctoral dissertation at Louisiana State University. I found works cited in this study in music publishing company catalogs, various lists of composers' works, and in several music libraries. Much of the music I investigated was obtained from publishers "on approval." Some scores were purchased, but a majority of the scores were found in the Music Division of the Library of Congress and in other music libraries such as Louisiana State University, Florida State University, University of North Texas, and Southern Methodist University.

Numerous persons at music libraries have been helpful but none more so than Charles L. Sens, reference librarian in the Music Division of the Library of Congress. He has truly gone well beyond the call of duty.

While some publishing companies ignored my requests for scores for examination, several companies were most helpful. These companies include C.F. Peters Corporation, Boosey & Hawkes, European American, MMB Music, Heinrichshofens Verlag, Theodore Presser, Berandol Music, Faber Music, Arsis Press, E.C. Schirmer, Transcontinental Music, United Music Publishers, Tonos International, Art Masters Studios, Chantry Music Press, Oxford University Press, Broude Bros., and John Shepard Music Press. Dale Music Company of Silver Spring, Maryland also granted courtesies to me.

As far as individuals are concerned, the list would be too long to mention everyone. However there are several persons whom I must mention including my loving wife, Darlene, who has constantly supported my endeavors as well as typed the original dissertation; my mother, Marian Klaus Moles, who has provided much support for me in many significant ways; Gayle M. Ross for word processing and typesetting; Andy Dahm for word processing; Douglas Leedy for proof reading and preparing the instrumental index; Professor Jimmy Landry, Nicholls State University Department of Engineering and Technology and Dr. Ted

Mims, Nicholls State University Department of Computer Science for converting computer discs; Mrs. Shirley Lasseigne and Mrs. Connie Doran, former secretaries in the Nicholls State University Department of Music have been most helpful in preparing a multitude of correspondence; Dr. Otis B. Wheeler, Professor Emeritus of English at Louisiana State University for providing the computer on which the original dissertation was written; my late father, Dr. Kenneth Blanchard Klaus, who was such a profound influence in my life both musically and otherwise; the late Dr. Earl Redding and also Professor Dallas Draper, my major professors at LSU; and last but certainly not least, Mrs. Ann Basart of Fallen Leaf Press who believed in me and very patiently awaited the arrival of my manuscript.

Introduction

Music for solo voice and small instrumental ensemble, relatively uncommon during the late eighteenth and nineteenth centuries, has come into its own again in the twentieth century. The present bibliography provides a guide to recent works in this rich repertory, listing published original music for solo voice and instrumental chamber ensemble written between 1960 and 1989.

For the purpose of this bibliography, "chamber music for solo voice and instruments" refers to works for solo voice with instrumental ensemble accompaniment—not necessarily one player per part, but no more than a total of twenty players. The accompaniment may consist of any combination of any instruments, or even of only one instrument as long as it is not a keyboard instrument, guitar, or harp. A second vocal part is considered an accompaniment if it truly serves as one or has a minor role in the piece (such as the boy soprano in George Crumb's *Ancient Voices of Children*).

This book does not include: works with an accompaniment of keyboard, guitar, harp, or electronic tape alone; excerpts from larger works such as operas or oratorios, unless they have been published separately; works with orchestra, chamber orchestra, or choral accompaniment; arrangements of pre-existing works; or works for solo voice and string orchestra that would not function well for string quartet or quintet.

The bibliography is divided into sections according to voice type: soprano, mezzo soprano, alto, tenor, baritone and bass, medium voice, and countertenor and miscellaneous. Under each section pieces are listed in alphabetical order by composer. Information about each work includes, as available, the composer's name and dates; the title of the work and date of composition; the author and/or source of the text; the publisher, place of publication, and catalog number; the voice type and instruments required for performance; the level of difficulty of the voice and instrumental parts; the vocal range; the language of the text; the duration; and occasional comments.

Although Reginald Smith Brindle has claimed that medium voices are in the greatest demand because of the wide ranges common in new music, more than half of the scores I examined (over seven hundred works by more than five hundred composers) were for soprano. The number of works scored for baritone, mezzo-soprano, or medium voice totalled slightly more than half the number for soprano.

The pieces listed here are uncommonly diverse in styles and technique. Several use aleatoric or improvisatory elements, among them Morton Feldman's *The O'Hara Songs,* Witold Lutosławsky's *Paroles Tissées*, and Serge Garant's *Phrases I.* Many are serially oriented. Harrison Birtwistle uses microtones in his *La Plage*, as does Roman Vlad in his *immer wieder.* Metric modulation appears in *A Prayer for Jerusalem*, by Richard Wernick, and in *A Mirror On Which To Dwell*, by Elliott Carter. Alison Bauld indicates durations in her *Egg* by spatial time, and other examples of graphic notation may be found in works by Toru Takemitsu, Jacob Druckman, Hans Zender, Cornel Ţăranu, Henry Górecki, and others. Sprechstimme is a fairly common device, used by Birtwistle, Roman Haubenstock-Ramati, Jere Hutcheson, Oliver Knussen, and Ronald Perea, among others.

Composers have made extensive use of percussion instruments for accompaniment, often using instruments that have originated in the music of Asia, Africa, or Latin America. They also use non-standard ensembles to accompany the voice; string quartets and woodwind quintets are not as common as are ensembles with a diverse assortment of instruments.

New music, with its new techniques for voice and instruments, is often difficult to perform, and learning it may require more work and dedication than learning traditional music. For example, in a work with extremely wide leaps that must be executed quickly such as Betsy Jolas's *Quatuor II* the singer has no time to stop and "think" the next pitch before it is time to sing it. Many of the works listed here have continuously high tessituras or extreme ranges; some were written for specific singers who have remarkable abilities. One must be careful when selecting from this repertoire.

Under the guidance of a competent teacher, however, an advanced student can conquer many of the obstacles found in these pieces. Working out rhythmic difficulties can make a musician more competent, and practicing complex vocal lines can further develop a singer's ear. Singers and teachers of voice could profitably explore this new literature for solo voice and chamber ensemble, and it is the aim of this book to help them do so.

Guide to Use

The bibliography is divided into sections according to voice type: soprano, mezzo soprano, alto, tenor, baritone and bass, medium voice, and countertenor and miscellaneous. Within each section, pieces are listed in alphabetical order by composer. Information about each work includes, as available, the composer's name and dates; the title of the work and date of composition; the author and/or source of the text; the publisher, place of publication, and catalog number; the voice type and instruments required for performance; the level of difficulty of the voice and instrumental parts; the vocal range; the language of the text; the duration; and occasional comments.

If the composer did not indicate a voice type, I have suggested one, in parentheses:

For Voice (soprano or tenor), clarinet in B♭, and piano.

Instruments listed in parentheses indicate doublings where the performer plays more than one instrument:

Trumpet I (bongos with yarn mallets)

Foreign names of instruments have been translated into common English usage.

The term "white score" is defined as a score in which rests of one-measure duration or longer are represented by blank spaces.

The system employed for pitch and octave designation of vocal ranges is contra C C c c′ c″ c″ c‴ where middle "C" is designated c′.

Copyright ownership changes from time to time; therefore, some works may not be published now by the company listed. Other works that at one time were available for purchase are now available only as rental material. Some works are permanently or temporarily out of print. The status of each work may be ascertained by consulting a music dealer or the publisher.

Chamber Music for Solo Voice and Instruments 1960-1989

Soprano

001
Adler, Samuel (b. 1928)
Canto V (1970)
I. The Importance of Poetry or The Coming Forth from Eternity into Time
II. If Causality is Impossible, Genesis is Recurrent
Text: Hyam Plutzik
Publisher: New York: Carl Fischer © 1978
Series: Carl Fischer facsimile edition
For: Soprano, flute, cello, and 3 percussion players.
Percussion instrumentation: 3 glockenspiels, 3 vibraphones, xylophone, 3 triangles, snare drum, large tam-tam, and 3 pairs of finger cymbals.
Difficulty: Voice: very difficult; Instruments: difficult
Vocal range: c′ - d^{b}‴
Language: English

002
Aitken, Hugh (b. 1924)
Cantata IV (1980)
I. Desnuda está la Tierra (Antonio Machado)
II. Mi Bufón (Antonio Machado)
III. ¡Oh tarde luminosa! (Antonio Machado)
IV. Pegasos (Paul Verlaine)
V. El sol es un Globo de Fuego (Antonio Machado)
VI. Campo (Antonio Machado)
Publisher: New York: Oxford University Press
For: Soprano, flute, oboe, cello, and double bass.
Difficulty: Voice: difficult; Instruments: difficult
Vocal range: a - a″
Language: Spanish

003
Albert, Stephen (b. 1941)
To Wake the Dead: Six Sentimental Songs and an Interlude after Finnegan's Wake
Text: James Joyce
Publisher: New York: Carl Fischer, © 1980 05084
For: Soprano, flute (alto flute), clarinet in B^{b} (bass clarinet), violin (viola), cello, piano, and harmonium (played by an assistant to the pianist).
Difficulty: Voice: *; Instruments: *
Vocal range: *
Duration: 25:00
*Comments: Score not examined.

004
Alemann, Eduardo A. (b. 1922)
Sueños Grises (1978)
Text: Composer
I. Ocaso
II. Ensueño
III. Réprobo
Publisher: Darmstadt: Tonos - 10512
For: Voice (soprano), violin, clarinet in B^{b}, cello, and piano.
Difficulty: Voice: difficult; Instruments: difficult
Vocal range: c′ - c‴
Language: Spanish
Duration: 9:45

005

Anderson, Thomas Jefferson (b. 1928)

Variations on a Theme by M.B. Tolson: Cantata

Text: M.B. Tolson

Publisher: New York: American Composers Alliance, 1969

For: Soprano, violin, cello, alto saxophone, trumpet in B^b, trombone, and piano.

Difficulty: Voice: *; Instruments: *

Vocal range: *

Language: English

Duration: 16:00

*Comments: Score not examined.

006

Anhalt, Istvan (b. 1919)

Foci (1969)

Text: Composer

Publisher: Scarborough, Ontario: Berandol Music

For: Soprano, flute, clarinet in B^b (bass clarinet), trombone, violin, cello, 2 double basses, 2 keyboard players (piano, electric organ, celesta, electric harpsichord), and tapes (3 recorders, 4 operators), 2 very small mouth organs, and percussion (2 players).

Percussion instrumentation: 1 vibraphone, 1 glockenspiel, 1 set of tubular bells, crotales, 4 tam-tams (2 medium, 1 large, 1 very large), 3 Javanese gongs (or other objects with similar sounds), 1 small Indian handbell, 1 middle sized elephant bell, 3 suspended cymbals (large, medium, small), 1 small rivet cymbal, 1 sleigh bell chain (with at least 25 bells), water-gong (large or medium), timpano (medium range), 2 bongos, 1 conga, 2 tom-toms, 3 timbales, 1 tenor drum, 1 bass drum, 5 or 6 tunable small drums, tambourine, 1 pair of sand blocks, castanets, washboard (glass) of about 10 to 12 inches, cardboard box filled with peas, güiro, 2 claves, 1 heavy wooden hammer, about 5 lbs. of broken glass, 1 brick-lined shallow box of about 3 x 3 feet, 2 marimbas, 2 sets of temple blocks (5 each), 1 ratchet, 4 maracas, 3 triangles (large, medium, small), 1 set of bamboo chimes, and 1 set of glass chimes.

Difficulty: Voice: very difficult; Instruments: very difficult

Vocal range: b^b - $a^{b''}$

Language: English and phonemes

Duration: 31:00

Comments: Singer does not begin until page 89 of score in section 9, which is entitled "Testimony."

007

Antoniou, Theodore (b. 1935)

For Ernst (© 1986)

Publisher: Newton Centre, MA: Margun Music

For: Soprano, flute, trumpet, trombone, piano, violin, cello, double bass, and percussion (optional).

Difficulty: Voice: *; Instruments: *

Vocal range: *

Language: *

Duration: 2:20

*Comments: Score not examined.

008

Applebaum, Edward (b. 1937)

The Garden (1981)

Text: Composer

Publisher: Saint Louis: MMB Music

For: Soprano (finger cymbals), flute (piccolo, 2 small bells struck with plastic beater), alto flute (2 small bells struck with plastic beater), clarinet in B^b (bass clarinet, 2 small bells struck with plastic beater), violin, cello, and percussion (one player).

Percussion instrumentation: Tubular bells, vibraphone, crotales, triangles, and glockenspiel.

Difficulty: Voice: difficult; Instruments: difficult

Vocal range: a^b - a″

Language: English

Comments: Contains unmetered sections.

009

Arandia-Navarro, Jorge (b. 1929)

Intemperancias (1962)

I. Esquema
II. Transformación Birrítmica
III. El Canto Aciago
IV. Secuencia

Text: William Shakespeare

Publisher: Washington, D.C.: Pan American Union 55-16

For: Voice (soprano), flute (piccolo), bass clarinet, trumpet in C, trombone, and percussion.

Percussion instrumentation: Vibraphone, xylophone, timpani, 5 cowbells (G-E-F-F-A), afochê [or small maraca], caxixi [or large maraca], pratinella [or tambourine], high-sounding gong, low-sounding gong, and large suspended cymbal.

Difficulty: Voice: very difficult; Instruments: difficult

Vocal range: g - c‴

Language: English

010

Argento, Dominick (b. 1927)

To be sung upon the Water: Barcarolles and Nocturnes (1972)

I. Prologue: Shadow and Substance
II. The Lake at Evening
III. Music on the Water
IV. Fair is the Swan
V. In Remembrance of Schubert
VI. Hymn Near the Rapids
VII. The Lake at Night
VIII. Epilogue: De Profundis

Text: William Wordsworth

Publisher: New York: Boosey & Hawkes BH.BK.794

For: High voice (soprano or tenor), piano, and clarinet in B^b (bass clarinet).

Difficulty: Voice: difficult; Instruments: difficult

Vocal range: c′ - b^{b}″

Language: English

Duration: 24:10

011

Auric, Georges (1899-1983)

Imaginées VI (1973)

Text: none

Publisher: Paris: Salabert

For: Voice (soprano or oboe), flute, clarinet in A, violin I, violin II, viola, cello, double bass, and piano.

Difficulty: Voice: difficult; Instruments: difficult
Vocal range: e′ - b″
Language: none - no phonemes given
Comments: Voice is treated as instrument.

012

Bach, Eric

Romance de la Peña Negra (1975)

(Balladen om dem sorte sorg)

Text: Federico García Lorca, Translated by Iljitsch Johansen
Publisher: Egtved, Denmark: Musikhojs Kolens © 1975
For: Soprano, flute, 2 violins, viola, cello, and double bass.
Difficulty: Voice: *; Instruments: *
Vocal range: *
Language: Danish
Duration: *
*Comments: Score not examined.

013

Bainbridge, Simon (b. 1952)

People of the Dawn (1975)

Text: based on Navajo creation myth
Publisher: London: United Music Publishers © 1977
For: Soprano (2 tam-tams, finger cymbals), clarinet in B^b I (soprano saxophone), clarinet in B^b II (bass clarinet), piano (celesta, 2 tam-tams), and percussion.
Percussion instrumentation: Glockenspiel, 4 Chinese tom-toms, 4 tuned Burmese gongs (optional), vibraphone, and marimba.
Difficulty: Voice: very difficult; Instruments: difficult
Vocal range: b^b - d‴
Language: Navajo

014

Bank, Jacques (b. 1943)

Minutes of Lives (1982)

I. Introduction
II. Song I - The Lady Jordan
III. Interlude I
IV. Song II - Thomas Goffe
V. Interlude II
VI. Song III - Eleanor Radcliffe
VII. Interlude III
VIII. Song IV - Sir Walter Raleigh
IX. Interlude IV
X. Song V - Mr. Rushworth
XI. Interlude V
XII. Song VI - Sir Thomas More

Text: John Aubrey
Publisher: Amsterdam: Donemus
For: Soprano and four clarinets in B^b (first clarinet doubles on clarinet in E^b).
Difficulty: Voice: very difficult; Instruments: very difficult
Vocal range: c′ - c‴ plus highest and lowest note possible
Language: English
Duration: 35:00
Comments: Clarinetists must hum while playing.

015

Barab, Seymour (b. 1921)

Airs and Fancies (© 1988)

I. Music, When Soft Voices Die (Percy Bysshe Shelley)
II. The Oocuck (Justin Richardson)
III. Weep You No More, Sad Fountains (Anonymous)

IV. Bread and Butter (William Makepeace Thackeray)
V. Five Reasons (On a round by Henry Purcell)
VI. Autumn Song (Dante Gabriel Rossetti)
VII. Why Does (S)He So Long Delay? (Thomas Moore)

Publisher: New York: Galaxy Music - 1.3011
Series: Contemporary Art Song Series
For: High voice (soprano or tenor), violin, cello, and harpsichord or piano.
Difficulty: Voice: moderately difficult; Instruments: moderately difficult
Vocal range: c$^{\#}$′- a^{b}″
Language: English

016

Barab, Seymour (b. 1921)

Bagatelles (© 1979)

I. Prelude (voice tacet)
II. Roundelay
III. Pure
IV. The Fly
V. If Love Were What the Rose Is
VI. Tom
VII. The Owl
VIII. The Pigtail

Text: Composer
Publisher: New York: Galaxy Music 1.2877.7
For: Soprano or tenor, recorder, and guitar.
Difficulty: Voice: moderate; Instruments: moderate
Vocal range: d′ - a″
Language: English

017

Barab, Seymour (b. 1921)

Moments Macabres (© 1981)

I. Old Roger
II. Down by the Green Wood Shady
III. The Walk
IV. A Man of Words and not of Deeds
V. Gypsies in the Wood
VI. Elegy for Frederick the Great
VII. Mama had a Baby

Text: *The Oxford Book of Light Verse*
Publisher: Galaxy Music: New York 1.2882.7
For: Voice (soprano or tenor), flute, oboe, clarinet in B^b, violin I, violin II, viola, and cello.
Difficulty: Voice: moderately difficult; Instruments: moderately difficult
Vocal range: e′ - b″
Language: English

018

Barraqué, Jean (1928-1973)

Chant après chant (1966)

Text: Composer and Hermann Broch
Publisher: Florence: Aldo Bruzzichelli
For: Voice (soprano or tenor), piano, and percussion (6 players).
Percussion instrumentation: 2 crotales, tubular bells, 5 chromatic cowbells, 2 triangles, 12 Turkish suspended cymbals, 2 crash cymbals, 2 Chinese cymbals, sizzle cymbal, 4 tam-tams (high, medium, low, very low), 12 Thailand gongs, 2 tambou-

rines, snare drum, 3 Brazilian snare drums, 6 tom-toms (high to low), 2 congas, 2 bongos, 2 timbales, 3 tablas (high, medium, low), 6 temple blocks (high to low), frame of snare drum, bass drum with pedal, tenor drum, 4 timpani (2 with tuning keys and 2 with pedals), 6 temple blocks (high to low), 9 mokubios (low to very high), 5 claves (low to high), 3 maracas (low, medium, high), cabaça, güiro, 3 xylorimbas, 3 vibraphones, marimba, and 2 glockenspiels.
Difficulty: Voice: difficult; Instruments: difficult
Vocal range: $c^{\#\prime}$ - $d^{\#}$
Language: French
Duration: 23:00
Comments: Note extreme range.

019
BARRY, GERALD (B. 1913)
Things that gain by being Painted (1977)
Text: Composer
Publisher: New York: Oxford University Press
For: Female singer (soprano), speaker, cello, and piano.
Difficulty: Voice: difficult; Instruments: difficult
Vocal range: b^{b} - $b^{\#\prime\prime}$
Language: English

020
BASART, ROBERT (1926-1993)
Serenade (1967)
Text: None
Publisher: Berkeley, CA: Fallen Leaf Press
Series: Fallen Leaf Publications in Contemporary Music, No. 18
For: Soprano, flute, clarinet in B^{b}, piano, and tape.
Difficulty: Voice: difficult; Instruments: difficult
Vocal range: b - b″
Language: Phonemes (indicated by composer)
Duration: 10:00
Comments: A male voice may not be substituted.

021
BAULD, ALISON (B. 1944)
One Pearl (1973)
Text: Composer
Publisher: Borough Green, Kent, England: Novello
For: Soprano and string quartet.
Difficulty: Voice: moderately difficult; Instruments: moderate
Vocal range: b - a″
Language: English
Duration: 16:00
Comments: Note markings in vocal part for various effects.

022
BEDFORD, DAVID (B. 1937)
Music for Albion Moonlight (1965)
I. "So it ends"
Interlude I
II. "If we are to know where we live"
Interlude II
III. "Lament for the makers of songs"
Interlude III
Text: Kenneth Patchen
Publisher: London: Universal Edition UE 14162 L © 1966

For: Soprano, flute, clarinet in B^b, violin, cello, Hohner alto-Melodica, and piano.
Difficulty: Voice: very difficult; Instruments: difficult
Vocal range: b - $b^{b''}$
Language: English
Comments: Somewhat aleatoric.

023
BEDFORD, DAVID (B. 1937)
That white and radiant Legend (1966)
Text: Kenneth Patchen
Publisher: London: Universal Edition UE 14208L
For: Soprano, reader, flute, oboe, clarinet in B^b, bassoon, violin, viola, cello, and double bass.
Difficulty: Voice: difficult; Instruments: difficult
Vocal range: c′ - $b^{b''}$
Language: English
Duration: 12:15

024
BENSON, WARREN (B. 1924)
Nara (1970)
I. Song - Response
II. Song - Response (voice tacet)
III. Consequent Response (voice tacet)
IV. Song - Response (voice tacet)
V. Wind Chimes in a Temple Ruin
Text: Earle Birney
Publisher: Carl Fischer: New York
For: Soprano, flute, piano, and percussion (2 players).
Percussion instrumentation: 8 high pitched drums (Moroccan clay drums if possible), 2 small tom-toms, large tam-tam, 3 timpani, maraca, Japanese temple gong or chime tuned to A=440, small muted gong, whip, large bass drum, and jaw bone.
Difficulty: Voice: moderately difficult; Instruments: moderate
Vocal range: a - b″
Language: English
Duration: 16:00

025
BERGER, JEAN (B. 1909)
Diversion for Three (© 1986)
I. Prelude (voice tacet)
II. What one may and may not call a woman (Anonymous)
III. Thee and I (John Ray)
IV. Patience (Robert Dodsley)
V. Postlude (voice tacet)
Publisher: Denver: John Sheppard Music Press
For: Voice (soprano or tenor), flute, and piano.
Difficulty: Voice: moderate; Instruments: moderately difficult
Vocal range: b - $b^{b''}$
Language: English

026
BHATIA, VANRAJ (B. 1927)
Kinguri-Vali (1960) (The Toy-Seller)
Text: Based on a poem by Gautam Mishra
Publisher: New York: Oxford University Press
For: Soprano, violin, and piano.
Difficulty: Voice: very difficult; Instruments: difficult
Vocal range: a - e‴
Language: Hindi (pronunciation guide and English translation provided).
Duration: 10:00

027
BIALAS, GÜNTER (1907 - 1992)
Haiku - Folge I (1972)
I. Ein Mensch und eine Fliege
II. Wintermond I, II, III
III. Ein kleines Mädchen
IV. Der grosse Buddha
V. Nach dem Essen
VI. Wir schliefen alle
VII. Die Nachtigall, o je!
VIII. Das Loch in der Tür
Text: Translated from traditional Japanese by Dietrich Krusche
Publisher: Kassel: Bärenreiter BA6157
For: Soprano and flute.
Difficulty: Voice: moderately difficult; Instrument: difficult
Vocal range: $d^{\#\prime}$ - b''
Language: German

028
BILUCAGLIA, CLAUDIO
Lied (1974)
Text: Composer
Publisher: Milan: Suvini Zerboni S.8127 Z.
For: Soprano, flute, oboe, trumpet in C, vibraphone, tubular bells, suspended cymbals, piano, violin I, violin II, viola, and cello.
Difficulty: Voice: extremely difficult; Instruments: difficult
Vocal range: b - $b^{b''}$
Language: Italian
Duration: 15:00

029
BINKERD, GORDON (B. 1916)
Secret-Love (© 1977)
Text: John Dryden
Publisher: New York: Boosey & Hawkes BH.BK.780
For: Voice (soprano), cello, and harp.
Difficulty: Voice: moderate; Instruments: moderate
Vocal range: e' - $a^{b''}$
Language: English

030
BIRTWISTLE, HARRISON (B. 1934)
Cantata (1969)
Text: Composer, (tombstone inscriptions, translations from Sappho, and The Greek Anthology)
Publisher: London: Universal Edition UE 15344L
For: Soprano, flute (piccolo), clarinet in B^b, violin (viola), cello, piano (celesta), and glockenspiel.
Difficulty: Voice: difficult; Instruments: difficult
Vocal range: a - $b^{b''}$
Language: English
Duration: 11:00
Comments: Use of some graphic notation; white score.; sprechstimme.

031
BIRTWISTLE, HARRISON (B. 1934)
Entr'actes and Sappho Fragments (1964)
Text: Sappho
Publisher: London: Universal Edition UE 12948L
For: Soprano, oboe, harp, viola, violin, flute, and percussion.
Percussion instrumentation: claves, tambourine, maracas, and 5 suspended cymbals.
Difficulty: Voice: very difficult; Instruments: difficult
Vocal range: c' - b''

Language: humming, phonemes, and English
Comments: Use of quarter tones.

032
Birtwistle, Harrison (b. 1934)
Songs by Myself (1986)
I. O light set the flame in amber...
II. I lean against a shade...
III. Cold statements...
IV. Steps...
V. This silence before light
Text: Composer
Publisher: London: Universal Edition UE17918
For: Soprano, flute (alto flute), piano, vibraphone, violin, viola, cello, and double bass.
Difficulty: Voice: difficult; Instruments: difficult
Vocal range: c′ - b″
Language: English
Duration: 10:00

033
Blackwood, Easley (b. 1933)
La Voyage à Cythère
My Heart fluttered joyously like a Bird, Op. 20 (1966)
Text: Charles Baudelaire/English translation by the composer, but to be sung in the original French
Publisher: New York: G. Schirmer 46355
For: Soprano, flute, piccolo (flute), oboe (English horn), clarinets in A and E^{b}, bass clarinet, bassoon, trumpet in C, horn, trombone (tenor and bass), and double bass.
Difficulty: Voice: difficult; Instruments: difficult
Vocal range: c′ - b^{b}″
Language: French
Duration: 14:00

034
Blake, David (b. 1936)
In Praise of Krishna (1973)
Text: translated from the Bengali by Edward C. Dimock and Denise Levertov
Publisher: Borough Green, Kent, England: Novello 89 0069 08
For: Soprano, flute (alto flute), clarinet in A, bass clarinet, horn, harp, violin, viola, cello, and double bass.
Difficulty: Voice: moderately difficult; Instruments: moderately difficult
Vocal range: b^{b} - b″
Language: English
Duration: 24:00

035
Bloch, Augustyn (b. 1929)
Medytacje (1961)
(Meditations)
I. ____________
II. Ustanie wesele bębnów (The mirth of Tabrets ceaseth)
II. Daj mi poznać Panie (Lord, make me to know)
Text: Isaiah 24, Psalm 39
Publisher: Warsaw: P W M 5069
For: Soprano, organ, and percussion (1 player).
Percussion instrumentation: vibraphone, 3 wood drums (soprano, alto, tenor), snare drum, bass drum, 3 suspended cymbals (soprano, tenor, bass), 3 tom-toms (small, medium, large), and tam-tam.

Difficulty: Voice: extremely difficult, especially movement I; Instruments: moderately difficult
Vocal range: b^b - $e^{b'''}$
Language: Polish (English and German translations provided for performance)
Duration: 9:00
Comments: No text in movement I; white score.

036
Blume, Joachim
Hymnus (1973)
Text: Walther Bulst
Publisher: Wolfenbüttel: Möseler
For: Soprano and percussion.
Percussion instrumentation: small cymbal, medium cymbal, sizzle cymbal, large cymbal, 4 temple blocks, and 4 tom-toms.
Difficulty: Voice: difficult; Instruments: moderately difficult
Vocal range: b^b - d'''
Language: Latin
Duration: 6:00

037
Boehmer, Konrad (b. 1941)
Je Vis - Je Meurs (1980)
I. Scorpio
II. Triste Aventure
III. Bien je mourrois
IV. Martyre
V. Je Fuis
VI. Lute, Compagnon
VII. Je Vis - Je Meurs
Text: Louïze Labé
Publisher: Darmstadt: Tonos 7268
For: Soprano, flute and percussion.
Percussion instrumentation: vibraphone, xylophone, 2 bongos, 2 tom-toms, 3 woodblocks, 2 Chinese cymbals, and 2 gongs.
Difficulty: Voice: very difficult; Instruments: very difficult
Vocal range: b - b''
Language: Italian, French

038
Boehnlein, Frank (b. 1945)
From the J.C. Penney Catalog Spring and Summer 1973 (1973)
I. What Do the Symbols Mean?
II. What Is Mailable and What Is Not? (spoken)
III. The Weight Loser's Bra and Girdle with Expand-a-Thigh
IV. Penney's Fine Quality Underwear...Greater Comfort and Roominess for Men with Average Builds
V. Penney's Helps You Work at Getting the Body You Want (spoken)
VI. If You Can Count, You Can Play! (spoken)
Text: from the same
Publisher: Pendleton, OR: Manuscript Publications
For: Soprano, flute, clarinet in B^b, oboe, bassoon, trumpet in C, horn, trombone, 4 violins, 2 violas, 2 cellos, timpani, and trap set.
Difficulty: Voice: moderate; Instruments: moderate
Vocal range: b - a''
Language: English
Comments: Humorous.

039
Boesmans, Philippe (b. 1936)
Upon la mi (1971)
Text: Composer

Publisher: Paris: Jobert
For: Voice (soprano or tenor), (bass drum lying down, brush, 2 ball bearings, glass chimes siren), horn, flute (piccolo), whistle, clarinet in B^b, harp (siren), piano, violin I, violin II, viola, cello, double bass (siren), and percussion (2 players).
Percussion instrumentation: (I) 2 temple blocks, snare drum, tenor drum, 2 bongos, bass drum lying down, 2 cymbals (large and small), bass drum with pedal, tam-tam, triangle, wood chimes, and whip; (II) temple blocks, bongos, 2 tom-toms, 2 timbales (small and large) [timpani], cymbal [medium], marimba, cog rattle, anvil, glass chimes, and triangle.
Difficulty: Voice: very difficult; Instruments: very difficult
Vocal range: a - b$^{b''}$
Language: English
Duration: 16:00

040

Bondon, Jacques (b. 1927)

Les Monts de l'étoile (1980)

I. Ohé Mistral
II. La source
III. L'enfant du garlaban
IV. Prière
V. La glace et le soleil

Text: Nicole Ciravegna
Publisher: Paris: Max Eschig M.E.8437
For: Soprano, string quartet, and piano.
Difficulty: Voice: moderately difficult; Instruments: moderately difficult
Vocal range: e' - a''
Language: French
Duration: 23:00

041

Borg, Kim (b. 1919)

Ophelia Sings, Op. 16 (1974)

I. How should I your true-love know...
II. To Morrow is Saint-Valentine's Day
III. They Bore Him Barefaced

Text: William Shakespeare
Publisher: Copenhagen: Engstrom & Sødring E&S.532
For: Soprano, flute, and viola.
Difficulty: Voice: difficult; Instruments: difficult
Vocal range: g - c'''
Language: English

042

Bortolotti, Mauro (b. 1926)

Contre 2–Vocalizzo (1967)

Text: Composer
Publisher: Milan: Ricordi 131889
For: Voice (soprano or mezzo soprano), piano, trombone, violin, clarinet in B^b, and double bass.
Difficulty: Voice: very difficult; Instruments: moderately difficult
Vocal range: f - e'''
Language: Latin, English, German, Italian, and French
Duration: 11:00
Comments: Text is in several languages and varies from word to word or phrase to phrase; note extreme range.

043

Bosco, Gilberto (b. 1946)

Dedica (1982)

Text: Gaspara Stampa
Publisher: Milan: Suvini Zerboni S. 9165 Z.
For: Soprano, flute, clarinet in B^b, and horn.
Difficulty: Voice: difficult; Instruments: difficult
Vocal range: c′ - a^{b}″
Language: Italian

044
BOUCOURECHLIEV, ANDRÉ (B. 1925)
Grodek d'après Georg Trakl (1963, rev. 1969)
Text: Georg Trakl
Publisher: London: Universal Edition UE 15 841 LW
For: Soprano, flute, and percussion (3 players).
Percussion instrumentation: (I) vibraphone, 4 temple blocks, 2 timpani, bass drum, 2 tam-tams, and 2 triangles; (II) 12 crotales (chromatic scale), glockenspiel, 3 timpani, snare drum, 4 gongs (soprano, alto, tenor, bass), and tam-tam; (III) vibraphone, 4 temple blocks, 2 timpani, bass drum, 2 tam-tams, and 2 triangles.
Difficulty: Voice: moderately difficult; Instruments: difficult
Vocal range: c′ - c‴
Language: German

045
BOZAY, ATTILA (B. 1939)
Papirszeletek, Op. 5 (1962) (Paperslips)
I. Engedj (Let me...)
II. Éjszaka (Night)
III. Kisfiú (The Little Boy)
IV. Mese (Fairy-Tale)
Text: Miklós Radnóti
Publisher: Budapest: Editio Musica. Sole Agent: New York: Boosey & Hawkes Z4683
For: Soprano, clarinet in B^b, and cello.
Difficulty: Voice: moderately difficult; Instruments: moderate
Vocal range: b - a″
Language: Hungarian
Duration: 5:50

046
BREDEMEYER, REINER (B. 1929)
Zum 13. 7. (1976)
Text: Arnold Schoenberg
Publisher: Leipzig: Peters 9618
For: Soprano, clarinet in E^b, alto saxophone, and percussion.
Percussion instrumentation: tiefes Metall [deep], vibraphone, helles Metall [bright], and tubular bells.
Difficulty: Voice: difficult; Instruments: moderately difficult
Vocal range: a - a″
Language: German
Comments: Almost entire piece in Sprechstimme.

047
BREHM, ALVIN (B. 1925)
Cycle of Six Songs (© 1976)
I. Fable (English translation by Roy Campbell)
II. Night (Engish translation by Jaime Angulo)
III. Adam (English translation by Roy Campbell)
IV. The Little Mute Boy (English translation by W.S. Merwin)
V. He Died at Dawn (English translated by Greville Texidor)

VI. Song of the Barren Orange Tree (English translation by W.S. Merwin)
Text: Federico García Lorca.
Publisher: Melville, NY: Edward B. Marks/Belwin-Mills M839
For: Soprano, string quartet, double bass, and woodwind quintet.
Difficulty: Voice: difficult; Instruments: difficult
Vocal range: c♯′ - a″
Language: English
Duration: 16:40

048
Brenet, Therèse (b. 1935)
Hommage à Signorelli (1967)
I. Les morts ressortant
II. Interlude (voice tacet)
III. Morts purifiés
Text: P. J. Jouve
Publisher: Paris: Rideau Rouge R630 RC
For: Soprano, piano, ondes martenot, and percussion (2 players)
Percussion instrumentation: 6 bongos, 4 temple blocks, 4 tom-toms, 2 small snare drums, 1 tenor drum, 5 timbales, 2 bass drum, 3 suspended cymbals, 4 tam-tams, 1 vibraphone, tambourine, 1 snare drum, gong, and xylophone.
Difficulty: Voice: very difficult; Instruments: moderately difficult
Vocal range: c♯′ - c‴
Language: French
Duration: 16:00
Comments: High tessitura.

049
Bresgen, Cesar (1913-1988)
Les Consolations (1978)
I. Millstätter Blutsegen (12th century)
II. Immensegen (10th century)
III. Stummensegen (11th century)
Text: Benedictions from the Middle Ages
Publisher: Vienna: Doblinger 08 872
For: Soprano, cello, and organ.
Difficulty: Voice: moderately difficult; Instruments: moderate
Vocal range: c′ - a♭″
Language: German

050
Bresgen, Cesar (1913-1988)
Trois Chants pour Signare (1977)
I. Je t'ai accompagnée
II. Une main de lumière
III. Je t'ai filé une chanson
Text: Leopold Sédar Senghor
Publisher: Bad Schwalbach: Gravis EG1456
For: Soprano, flute, and harp.
Difficulty: Voice: difficult; Instruments: difficult
Vocal range: d′ - g♯″
Language: French
Comments: Score is facsimile of composer's manuscript and is somewhat difficult to read.

051
Brettingham Smith, Jolyon (b. 1949)
Dancing Days, Op. 13 (1975)
Text: William Butler Yeats
Publisher: Berlin: Bote & Bock B&B22 673(1293)
For: Soprano (tambourine), flute (piccolo, alto flute, bass flute), oboe, clarinet in B♭, horn, trum-

pet in B^b with wa-wa and plunger mutes, harp, piano, string quartet, and percussion (3 players).

Percussion instrumentation: marimba, vibraphone, claves, castanets, 2 snare drums, 2 glass chimes (small, high-pitched), sizzle cymbal, 4 tom-toms, sleigh bells, suspended cymbals, tam-tam, glockenspiel, woodblocks, maracas, whip, xylophone, temple blocks, Chinese cymbal, güiro, and bongos.

Difficulty: Voice: extremely difficult; Instruments: very difficult

Vocal range: g* - d‴

Language: English

Duration: 13:00

Comments: White score.

052

Bruno, Carlo

Tre Sonetti (© 1967)

I. Assai mi son comerta, amore mio
II. Quando Dio Messer
III. Dovun que vo, o vegno o volgo giro

Text: Composer

Publisher: Milan: Curci E.8813C

For: Soprano, flute, 2 clarinets in B^b, horn, bassoon or trombone, piano, violin, and 2 cellos.

Difficulty: Voice: difficult; Instruments: moderately difficult

Vocal range: d′ - c‴

Language: Italian

053 - MOVED TO TENOR

054

Bussotti, Sylvano (b. 1931)

Il nudo: quattro frammanti da "Torso" (1964)*

Text: Composer

Publisher: Celle: Hermann Moeck 5021

For: Soprano, piano, and string quartet.

Difficulty: Voice: extremely difficult; Instruments: very difficult

Vocal range: g - c‴

Language: Italian

Comments: Extreme use of avant-garde idioms; performers also need to be well versed in graphic notation. *From the opera *Torso*, but also intended to be performed separately, if desired.

055

Butler, Martin (b. 1960)

Three Emily Dickinson Songs (1985)

I. The Summer lapsed Away
II. There came a Wind
III. To make a Prairie

Text: Emily Dickinson

Publisher: Oxford: Oxford University Press ISBN 0-19-362227-0

For: Soprano, clarinet in B^b, and piano.

Difficulty: Voice: difficult; Instruments: difficult

Vocal range: b - a″

Language: English

Duration: 9:00

056

Cacioppo, George (b. 1926)

Bestiary I: Eingang (1961)

Text: Rainer Maria Rilke

Publisher: New York: Music for Percussion E-86-18

For: Soprano, piano, vibraphone, celesta, and percussion (4 players).
Percussion instrumentation: (I) glockenspiel, finger cymbals, 3 triangles, pair of maracas, and the inside of a piano; (II) pair of maracas, 2 gongs (large and small), and 3 temple blocks; (III) 3 suspended cymbals, 3 tom-toms, 2 congas, bongos, and bass drum; (IV) pair of claves, woodblocks, and pair of maracas.
Difficulty: Voice: difficult; Instruments: difficult
Vocal range: b - f#′
Language: German
Duration: 7:00
Comments: White score.

057

CACIOPPO, GEORGE (B. 1926)

Time on time in Miracles (© 1969)
Text: None
Publisher: Don Mills, Ontario: BMI Canada
For: Soprano, 2 horns, trombone, bass trombone, cello, piano, and percussion.
Percussion instrumentation: 2 tam-tams, suspended cymbal, claves, tom-toms, and woodblock.
Difficulty: Voice: difficult; Instruments: difficult
Vocal range: g - a″
Language: specified phonemes
Comments: White score; graphic notation; use of microtones.

058

CAPDENAT, PHILIPPE (B. 1934)

"Croce e Delizia..." (1972)
Text: Composer
Publisher: Paris: Amphion
For: Soprano (small cymbal), flute (piccolo), clarinet in B♭, violin, cello, prepared piano, and electronic tape.
Difficulty: Voice: extremely difficult; Instruments: very difficult
Vocal range: d′ - d♭‴
Language: Italian
Comments: Soprano tessitura is very high. Requires considerable vocal agility because of rapid passages.

059

CARR, PETER

Two Songs for Quintet (© 1977)
I. Strings by the River
II. A Song
Text: Joyce Shelley
Publisher: Paigles, England: Anglian ANMS 36
For: Soprano and string quartet.
Difficulty: Voice: moderately difficult; Instruments: moderately difficult
Vocal range: c′ - a″
Language: English

060

CARTER, ELLIOTT (B. 1908)

A Mirror on Which to Dwell (1976)
I. Anaphora
II. Argument
III. Sandpiper
IV. Insomnia
V. View of the Capitol
VI. O Breath
Text: Elizabeth Bishop

Publisher: New York: Associated AMP 7701
For: Soprano, flute (piccolo and alto flute), oboe (English horn), clarinet in B^b (clarinet in E^b and bass clarinet), piano, violin, viola, cello, double bass, and percussion (1 player).
Percussion instrumentation: vibraphone, bass drum, marimba, large suspended cymbal, 4 bongos, triangle, and snare drum.
Difficulty: Voice: difficult; Instruments: very difficult
Vocal range: b - b″
Language: English
Duration: 19:30

061

Casagrande, Alessandro

A Saffo (© 1972)
Text: Sappho
Publisher: Milan: Carisch S.p.A. 21902
For: Soprano, flute, cello, and celesta.
Vocal range: d - g′
Difficulty: Voice: moderate; Instruments: moderate
Language: Italian

062

Casken, John (b. 1949)

Firewhirl (1980)
Text: George MacBeth
Publisher: London: Schott ED11491
For: Soprano, flute, clarinet in B^b, horn, bassoon, violin, viola, and cello.
Difficulty: Voice: very difficult; Instruments: very difficult
Vocal range: a - c‴
Language: English
Duration: 16:00
Comments: Use of quartertones.

063

Castiglioni, Niccolò (b. 1932)

A Solemn Music II (1963) (new version 1965)
Text: John Milton
Publisher: Mainz: Ars Viva AV 77
For: Soprano, flute (piccolo), 3 clarinets in E^b, trumpet in B^b, harp, piano, 4 violins, 3 violas, 2 cellos, double bass, and percussion.
Percussion instrumentation: vibraphone, marimba, xylophone, 5 bottles, pair of cymbals, 3 suspended cymbals, blocked cymbals, tam-tam, and glockenspiel.
Difficulty: voice: very difficult; instruments: very difficult
Vocal range: a - c#‴
Language: English
Duration: 14:00

064

Chance, Nancy (b. 1931)

Dark Song (1970)
Text: Composer
Publisher: New York: Seesaw
For: Soprano, 2 flutes, 2 clarinets in B^b, 2 horns, harp, guitar, piano, and percussion (5 players).
Percussion instrumentation: temple blocks, mokubios, glockenspiel, triangle, large suspended cymbal, 3 tom-toms, 2 gongs, 2 bongos, small suspended cymbal, 2 woodblocks, 30 inch timpano, 28 inch timpano, 2 maracas, tam-tam, castanets, tenor drum, brass wind chimes,

crotales, marimba, and vibraphone.
Difficulty: Voice: moderately difficult; Instruments: moderate
Vocal range: a - a″
Language: English

065
CHANCE, NANCY (B. 1931)
Duos I (1975)
Text: none
Publisher: New York: Seesaw
For: Soprano, flute, and finger cymbals.
Difficulty: Voice: moderately difficult; Instruments: moderately difficult
Vocal range: b - a″
Language: phonemes

066
CHANCE, NANCY (B. 1931)
Edensong (1973)
Text: Elizabeth Barrett Browning
Publisher: New York: Seesaw
For: Soprano, flute, clarinet in B^b, cello, harp, vibraphone, marimba, and percussion.
Percussion instrumentation: 3 tom-toms (graduated in pitch), 2 suspended cymbals (high and low), 2 woodblocks, brass wind chimes, gong, 2 triangles, and crotales (A^b, A, B^b, B).
Difficulty: Voice: difficult; Instruments: difficult
Vocal range: a^b - b^{b}″
Language: English
Comments: Dry (breath only) flutter tongue required for all performers; fast tremolo and various trills required for singer.

067
CHANCE, NANCY (B. 1931)
Three Poems by Rilke (1966)
I. O dieses ist das Tier...
II. Nur wer die Leier...
III. Ein Gott vermags...
Text: Rainer Maria Rilke
Publisher: New York: Seesaw
For: Soprano, flute, English horn, and cello.
Difficulty: Voice: moderately difficult; Instruments: moderately difficult
Vocal range: a^b - b^{b}″
Language: German

068
CIRONE, ANTHONY J. (B. 1941)
5 Items (© 1973)
I. At the Pinnacles
II. The Triple Refrain at Yang-Kuan Pass–after Wang Wei
III. Spring in Nak Yang
IV. ___________
V. To a Gikuyu Musician
Text: Lou Harrison
Publisher: Menlo Park, CA: Cirone
For: Soprano and percussion quintet.
Percussion instrumentation: glockenspiel, vibraphone, suspended cymbals, finger cymbal, triangle, timpani, gong, 4 tom-toms, temple blocks, trap set, woodblocks, timbales, bongos, mbira [small African instrument with plucked tongues of metal or wood on a wooden resonator], and brake drums.
Difficulty: Voice: very difficult; Instruments: difficult
Vocal range: b^b - b″
Language: English

069
Clayton, Laura (b. 1943)
Cree Songs to the Newborn
I. All the Warm Nights...
II. I'm no Owl...
III. There's Things I Do...
IV. If I popped out of the Snow...
Text: Cree Indian stories gathered and translated by Howard Norman
Publisher: New York: Peters 66845
For: Soprano, 2 flutes, 2 cellos (2 maracas - high and low), double bass, celesta, harp, and percussion (2 or more players).
Percussion instrumentation: xylophone, 30-inch timpani, crotales, 2 suspended cymbals, temple block, 2 triangles, vibraphone, small snare drum, tambourine, and wood chimes.
Difficulty: Voice: very difficult; Instruments: difficult
Vocal range: a - c‴
Language: Cree Indian or English
Duration: 15:00

070
Connolly, Justin (b. 1933)
Poems of Wallace Stevens I, Op. 9 (1967)
I. Tattoo
II. Anecdote of the Prince of Peacocks
III. The Snow Man
Text: Wallace Stevens
Publisher: Borough Green, Kent, England: Novello 89-0089-02
For: Soprano, flute (piccolo), clarinet in B^b (bass clarinet), trumpet in C, viola, vibraphone, celesta, and harp.
Difficulty: Voice: very difficult; Instruments: difficult
Vocal range: g - c‴
Language: English
Duration: 13:30
Comments: White score; rhythmic complexities.

071
Connolly, Justin (b. 1933)
Poems of Wallace Stevens II, Op. 14 (1970)
I. Earthly Anecdote
II. The Place of the Solitaires
III. Life Is Motion
Text: Wallace Stevens
Publisher: Borough Green, Kent, England: Novello © 1982 17 0310 02
For: Soprano, flute (piccolo), clarinet in B^b (bass clarinet), trumpet in C, viola, vibraphone, celesta, and harp.
Difficulty: Voice: * ; Instruments: *
Vocal range: *
Language: English
Duration: 13:00
*Comments: Score not examined.

072
Connyngham, Barry (b. 1944)
Bashō (1980)
I. Bell Tones
II. So Still...
III. Song of the Cuckoo...
IV. Hawk's Eyes...
V. Lightning Gleam...
VI. Old Pond...
VII. On a journey...
Text: Haiku by Matsuo Bashō
Publisher: Australia: Universal Edition UE29239A
For: Soprano, alto flute (piccolo), bass clarinet (clarinet in B^b), trombone, piano, cello, and percussion.

Percussion instrumentation: gong, tam-tam, crotales, vibraphone, triangle, xylophone, bass marimba, hi-hat, cymbals, bass drum, tubular bells, sticks, etc., and double-bass bow.
Difficulty: Voice: very difficult; Instruments: very difficult
Vocal range: f# - b″
Language: Japanese and English
Duration: 20:00
Comments: White score; vocal effects.

073
Consoli, Marc-Antonio (b. 1941)
Tre Canzoni (1976)
I. Run, Little Child...
II. To a Butterfly with Hurt Wings...
III. Daffodils, Lilies, Almond, and Apple Blossoms...
Text: Composer
Publisher: New York: American Composers Alliance
For: Soprano, flute, and cello.
Difficulty: Voice: moderately difficult; Instruments: difficult
Vocal range: c#′ - ab″
Language: English
Comments: White score.

074
Crumb, George (b. 1929)
Ancient Voices of Children (1970)
I. El niño busca su voz (The little boy was looking for his voice) (English translation by W. S. Merwinns)
II. Me he perdido muchas veces por el mar (I have lost myself in the sea many times) (English translation by Stephen Spender and J. L. Gili)
III. ¿De dónde vienes, amor, mi niño? (From where do you come, my love, my child?) (English translation by J. L. Gili)
IV. Todas las tardes en Granada, todas las tardes se muere un niño (Each afternoon in Granada, a child dies each afternoon) (English translation by J. L. Gili)
V. Se ha llenado de luces mi corazón de seda (My heart of silk is filled with lights) (English translation by Edwin Honig)
Text: Federico García Lorca
Publisher: New York: Peters 66303
For: Soprano (2 mounted glockenspiel plates [with brass beaters], and cardboard speaking tube), boy soprano (cardboard speaking tube), oboe (small harmonica), mandolin (3 mounted crotales with brass beaters, fine quality saw, and bass or cello bow, and glass rod and metal plectrum), harp, electric piano [amplified grand piano] (fine quality toy piano and 5/8 inch chisel), and percussion (3 players).
Percussion and other instrumentation: (I) large tam-tam, pair of finger cymbals, 1 mounted antique cymbal, tambourine, single timbale (creole), marimba (also played by percussion II), 2 maracas, tubular bells, very small suspended triangle, and large suspended cymbal; (II) medium

size tam-tam, 4 tunable tom-toms, large suspended cymbal, tenor drum, 2 maracas, tubular bells, and sleigh bells; (III) small tam-tam, pair of Tibetan prayer stones, claves, vibraphone, 1 large pedal timpano, 2 mounted crotales, 1 mounted glockenspiel plate, sleigh bells, 2 maracas, large suspended cymbal, and 5 Japanese (bowl-shaped) temple bells.

Difficulty: Voice: extremely difficult; Instruments: extremely difficult

Vocal range: g - c‴

Language: Spanish (English translation provided but is not meant to be sung)

Duration: 27:00

Comments: Read performance notes carefully.

075

Crumb, George (b. 1929)

Lux aeterna: For Five Masked Musicians (1971)

Text: Requiem Mass

Publisher: New York: Peters 66495

For: Soprano, bass flute (soprano recorder), sitar, and percussion (2 players).

Percussion instrumentation: 3 timpani, large cymbal with flattened dome, 2 large suspended cymbals, large tam-tam, tubular bells, 2 Indian drums, 2 double bass bows (for bowed tam-tam harmonics), crotales, small tam-tam, vibraphone, pair of finger cymbals, bell tree, and 3 Indian elephant bells.

Difficulty: Voice: very difficult; Instruments: difficult

Vocal range: g - b^{b}″

Language: Latin

Duration: 15:00

Comments: Requires certain theatrical effects including black masks. A solo dancer is optional.

076

Crumb, George (b. 1929)

Madrigals, Book I (1965)

I. Verte desnuda es recordar la tierra

II. No piesan en la lluvia, y se han dormido

III. Los muertos llevan alas de musgo

Text: Federico García Lorca

Publisher: New York: Peters 66460

For: Soprano, vibraphone, and double bass.

Difficulty: Voice: difficult; Instruments: difficult

Vocal range: g - a″

Language: Spanish (pronunciation guide provided)

Duration: 9:00

Comments: Vocal line requires dexterity, control, and a finely tuned ear. White score.

077

Crumb, George (b. 1929)

Madrigals, Book II (1965)

I. Bebe el agua tranquila de la canción añeja

II. La muerte entra y sale de la taberna

III. Caballito negro

Text: Federico García Lorca

Publisher: New York: Peters 66459

For: Soprano, alto flute (flute and piccolo), and percussion (1 player).

Percussion instrumentation: crotales, glockenspiel, 2 timpani, and marimba.
Difficulty: Voice: extremely difficult; Instruments: difficult
Vocal range: $g^{\#}$ - a''
Language: Spanish (pronunciation guide provided)
Duration: 6:30
Comments: Vocal line requires dexterity, control, and a finely tuned ear. White score.

078

Crumb, George (b. 1929)

Madrigals, Book III (1969)

I. La noche canta desnuda sobre los puentes de marzo
II. Quiero dormir el sueño de las manzanas
III. Nana, niño, nana del caballo grande que no quiso el agua

Text: Federico García Lorca
Publisher: New York: Peters 66460
For: Soprano, harp, and percussion (1 player).
Percussion instrumentation: vibraphone, bongos, 3 timbales (high, medium, and low), and very small suspended triangle.
Difficulty: Voice: extremely difficult; Instruments: difficult
Vocal range: $a^{\#}$ - $b^{b''}$
Language: Spanish (pronunciation guide provided)
Duration: 7:30
Comments: Vocal line requires dexterity, control, and a finely tuned ear. White score.

079

Crumb, George (b. 1929)

Madrigals, Book IV (1969)

I. ¿Por qué nací entre espejos?
II. Tu cuerpo, con la sombra violeta de mis manos, era un arcángel de frío
III. ¡La muerte me está mirando desde las torres de Córdoba!

Text: Federico García Lorca
Publisher: New York: Peters 66461
For: Soprano, flute (piccolo and alto flute), harp, double bass, and percussion (1 player).
Percussion instrumentation: glockenspiel, marimba, 2 suspended cymbals (1 large and 1 small), glass chimes, and tubular bells.
Difficulty: Voice: extremely difficult; Instruments: difficult
Vocal range: a - c'''
Language: Spanish (pronunciation guide provided)
Duration: 9:00
Comments: Vocal line requires dexterity, control, and a finely tuned ear. White score.

080

Crumb, George (b. 1929)

Night Music I (1963)

I. Notturno I (voice tacet)
II. Notturno II (voice tacet)
III. La luna asoma
IV. Notturno IV (voice tacet)
V. Gacela de la terrible presencia
VI. Noturno VI (voice tacet)
VII. Noturno VII (voice tacet)

Text: Federico García Lorca
Publisher: Melville, NY: Mills Music: Belwin-Mills 90164
For: Soprano, piano (celesta), and 2 percussionists.
Percussion instrumentation: glockenspiel, xylophone, 1 large pedal timpano, tenor drum, 1

large suspended cymbal, 3 mounted crotales, 3 detached crotales, marimba, vibraphone, 1 very small triangle, 3 bongos, low pitched bell, 3 tam-tams (13", 20", and 36"), and a large tub of water.
Difficulty: Voice: moderately difficult; Instruments: difficult
Vocal range: approximately a - a″
Language: Spanish
Duration: 18:00
Comments: Soprano must approximate pitch contour; use of quarter tones.

081
Dallapiccola, Luigi (1904-1975)
Commiato (1972)
I. O fratel nostro, che se' morto
II. O fratel nostro, la cui fratellanza
Text: attributed to Brunetto Latini
Publisher: Milan: Suvini Zerboni S.7526Z.
For: Soprano, flute I, flute II (piccolo), sopranino clarinet in E^b, clarinet in B^b, bass clarinet, bassoon, horn, trumpet in C, harp, celesta (piano), marimba (vibraphone), violin, viola, cello, and double bass.
Difficulty: Voice: difficult; Instruments: difficult
Vocal range: a - c‴
Language: Italian
Duration: 14:00

082
Dallapiccola, Luigi (1904-1975)
Quattro Liriche di Antonio Machado (1964)
I. La primavera è giunta
II. Ieri sognai che vedevo
III. Signor, già mi strappasti
IV. La primavera è giunta
Text: Antonio Machado
Publisher: Milan: Suvini Zerboni S.6332Z.
For: Voice (soprano or tenor), flute, oboe, sopranino clarinet in E^b, clarinet in B^b, bassoon, horn, trumpet in C, celesta, vibraphone, marimba, harp, violin I, violin II, viola, cello, and double bass.
Difficulty: Voice: difficult; Instruments: moderately difficult
Vocal range: b^b - $c^{b'''}$
Language: Italian
Duration: 7:00

083
Đạo, Nguyên-Thiên (b. 1940)
Nhớ (© 1971)
Text: Nguyên Đinh Thi
Publisher: Paris: Salabert MC509
For: Soprano, cello, five double basses (one a 5-string), and percussion (percussion instrumentation not made clear).
Difficulty: Voice: very difficult; Instruments: difficult
Vocal range: b - c‴ plus lowest and highest note possible
Language: Vietnamese
Comments: Graphic notation; exact pitches not notated in instrumentation or vocal part for part of the piece. Use of quartertones; vocal part at times in alto clef; white score.

084
Darvas, Gábor (b. 1911)
Medália (© 1969)
Text: Attila József

Publisher: Budapest: Editio Musica Z 10088
For: Soprano, piano (harpsichord and celesta), percussion, and electronic tape.
Percussion instrumentation: triangle, 3 crotales, 3 cowbells, 3 suspended cymbals, 2 tam-tams, 2 side drums (with and without snare), tenor drum, 2 bongos, 3 tom-toms, 2 timpani, bass drum, glockenspiel, tubular bells, xylophone, and vibraphone.
Difficulty: Voice: very difficult; Instruments: very difficult
Vocal range: b^b - b″
Language: Hungarian
Duration: 10:00
Comments: Performance must be prerecorded on tape.

085

Davidovsky, Mario (b. 1934)
Romancero (1983)
I. Morenica a mi me llaman
II. ¡Arriba canes, Arriba!
III. Seguidillas
IV. Triste estaba el Rey David
Text: popular Spanish poetry
Publisher: New York: Peters
For: Soprano, flute, clarinet in B^b, violin, and cello.
Difficulty: Voice: very difficult; Instruments: difficult
Vocal range: b^b - $b^{b\prime\prime}$
Language: Spanish
Comments: English translation provided.

086

Davies, Peter Maxwell (b. 1934)
Anakreontika (1976)
Texts: late ancient Greek in the style of Anacreon
Publisher: London: Chester JWC 55315
For: Soprano, alto flute, cello, harpsichord, and percussion.
Percussion instrumentation: glockenspiel, marimba, 2 woodblocks (small and very small), and tambourine.
Difficulty: Voice: very difficult; Instruments: difficult
Vocal range: g - b″
Language: Ancient Greek (pronunciation guide provided)
Duration: 15:00

087

Davies, Peter Maxwell (b. 1934)
Offenbarung und Untergang (1966 Rev. 1980)
(Revelation and Fall)
Text: Georg Trakl
Publisher: London, New York: Boosey & Hawkes © 1971 B+H 20648
For: Soprano, flute (piccolo), oboe, clarinet in B^b (bass clarinet), bassoon, horn, trumpet in B^b, trombone, harp, solo string quartet, and percussion (3 players).
Percussion instrumentation: (I) 2 flatstones, 2 woodblocks, school dulcimer, bass drum, cymbals, metal cylinder with protruding rods, anvil, guard's whistle, metal claves, knife-grinder, 3 small timpani, small cymbal, large cymbal, snare drum, and tenor drum; (II) very small cymbal, large cymbal, small woodblock, ratchet, metal disc, glockenspiel, and piano (with action removed); (III) small metal claves, very large claves, plate glass (for smashing), rattle,

ratchet, 2 whips, bass drum, and handbells in D^b.
Difficulty: Voice: extremely difficult; Instruments: difficult - some passages very difficult
Vocal range: f - $e^{b'''}$
Language: German
Duration: 25:00
Comments: Soprano required to shout through a megaphone. Note extreme range.

088
Davis, Sharon (b. 1937)
Suite of Wildflowers, Op. 1 (© 1981)
I. Indian Paintbrush
II. Cactus Flower
III. Lupine
IV. Mimulus (Monkey Flower)
Text: Composer
Publisher: Los Angeles: Avant Music; Sole Agent: Western International Music AV208
For: Soprano, flute, oboe, violin, cello, and piano.
Difficulty: Voice: difficult; Instruments: difficult
Vocal range: b^b - $c^{b'''}$
Language: English

089
De Bohun, Lyle (b. 1927)
Songs of Estrangement (© 1975)
I. Snow Has Lain
II. Flowers Fall
III. Death Has Risen
IV. Love is a-borning
Text: Composer
Publisher: Washington, D.C.: Arsis Press
For: Soprano and string quartet.
Difficulty: Voice: moderate; Instruments: moderate
Vocal range: c′ - g″
Language: English

090
De Jong, Conrad (b. 1934)
Hist Whist (1969)
Text: e. e. cummings: POEMS
Publisher: New York: G. Schirmer
For: Voice (soprano or tenor), flute, viola, and percussion.
Percussion instrumentation: 2 bongos, 2 tom-toms, timpani, 2 triangles, and 1 large suspended sizzle cymbal.
Difficulty: Voice: difficult; Instruments: moderately difficult
Vocal range: d′ - $a^{b''}$
Language: English
Duration: 3:05

091
Del Tredici, David (b. 1937)
I Hear an Army (1964)
Text: James Joyce: No. 36 from *Chamber Music*
Publisher: New York: Boosey & Hawkes H.P.S. 810
For: Soprano and string quartet.
Difficulty: Voice: very difficult; Instruments: difficult
Vocal range: g - d‴
Language: English
Duration: 13:00
Comments: A conductor is recommended.

092
Del Tredici, David (b. 1937)
Syzygy (1966)
I. Ecce Puer
II. Nightpiece
Text: James Joyce
Publisher: New York: Boosey & Hawkes © 1974 H.P.S. 812

For: Soprano, horn, and chamber orchestra.
Solo group: soprano (amplified), horn, and tubular bells with extended range.
Chamber orchestra instrumentation: piccolo I (alto flute), flute (piccolo II), oboe I (English horn II), English horn I (oboe II), clarinet I in B^b, clarinet II in B^b (clarinet in A and bass clarinet), bassoon I (contrabassoon), bassoon II, trumpet I in C, trumpet II in C, solo violin I, solo violin II, solo viola I, solo viola II, solo cello, and solo double bass (5-string or with e-string extension).
Difficulty: Voice: very difficult; Instruments: difficult
Vocal range: e^b - d‴
Language: English
Duration: 26:00
Comments: Extreme vocal range.

093

Del Tredici, David (b. 1937)

Vintage Alice: (Fantascene on A Mad Tea-Party) (1972)

Text: Composer, from Lewis Carroll
Publisher: New York: Boosey & Hawkes H.P.S. 818
For: Soprano (amplified), folk group, and chamber orchestra.
Folk group instrumentation: 2 soprano saxophones, mandolin, tenor banjo, and accordion.
Chamber orchestra instrumentation: piccolo (flute), oboe, sopranino clarinet in E^b, bassoon, trumpet in C, 2 horns, trombone, 3 timpani, crash cymbals, whip, violin I, violin II, viola, cello, and double bass.
Difficulty: Voice: difficult; Instruments: difficult
Vocal range: a - e‴
Language: English
Duration: 28:00
Comments: Extremely high tessitura. Parts available on rental.

094

Denis, Didier D. (b. 1947)

!!! Trois...Partout

Text: Composer
Publisher: Paris: Rideau Rouge R960RC
For: Soprano, ondes martenot, piano, percussion (1 player), and 2 tape recorders.
Percussion instrumentation: xylophone, vibraphone, glockenspiel, güiro, triangle, 3 temple blocks (high, medium, low), bongo (low), 4 suspended cymbals, 1 cymbal beater, 1 gong, and 2 tam-tams.
Difficulty: Voice: difficult; Instruments: moderate
Vocal range: g$^\#$ - a″
Language: French
Duration: 17:03
Comments: Rhythmic difficulties.

095

Denisov, Edisson Vasil'evich (b. 1929)

Blätter (© 1979)

I. Begegnung
II. Einsicht
III. Blätter
IV. Wohin
V. Das Ende

Text: Francisco Tanzer
Publisher: Hamburg: Hans Sikorski 2294

For: Soprano, violin, viola, and cello.
Difficulty: Voice: difficult; Instruments: difficult
Vocal range: b - b″
Language: German
Comments: Use of quarter tones.

096

Denisov, Edisson Vasil'evich (b. 1929)
Ital'ianskie Pesni (1964) © 1973 (Chansons Italiennes)
I. Ravenna (Ravenna)
II. Florentsiya (Florenz)
III. Venetsiya (Venedig)
IV. Uspenie (Himmelfahrt)
Text: Aleksandr Blok
Publisher: Budapest: Editio Musica Z.6847
For: Soprano, flute, violin, horn, and harpsichord.
Difficulty: Voice: difficult; Instruments: moderately difficult
Vocal range: f# - c#‴
Language: Russian (German also given for performance)
Comments: Free tempo in III.

097

Denisov, Edisson Vasil'evich (b. 1929)
Plachi (Les Pleures) (Klagelieder) (Laments) (1966)
I. Fragend
II. Benachrichtigung
III. Klagelied beim Hineintragen des Sarges
IV. Klagelied beim Hinaustragen es Sarges
V. Klagelied auf dem Weg zum Friedhof
VI. Klagelied beim Hinablassen des Sarges
Text: 6 Russian folk legends
Publisher: Vienna: Universal Edition © 1972 UE14138 Sole agent: Eurpoean American
For: Soprano, 3 percussion players, and piano.
Percussion instrumentation: timpani, 3 bongos, tenor drum, medium gong, 10 bells, (f′ - e″), vibraphone, xylophone, 2 woodblocks, Charleston [pedal cymbal, predecessor of the hihat], triangle, marimba, claves, 4 temple blocks, 3 suspended cymbals (high, medium, and low), and tam-tam (large).
Difficulty: Voice: difficult; Instruments: difficult
Vocal range: a♭ - c#‴
Language: Russian
Duration: 16:00

098

Denisov, Edisson Vasil'evich (b. 1929)
Solntse Inkov (Die Sonne der Inkas) (1964)
I. Preludium (voice tacet)
II. Trauriger Gott
III. Indermedium (voice tacet)
IV. Roter Abend
V. Das verfluchte Wort (voice tacet)
VI. Fingerchenlied
Text: Gabriela Mistral
Publisher: London: Universal Edition UE 13597 LW ©1971
For: Soprano, 3 speakers, flute, oboe, clarinet in B♭, trumpet in B♭, horn, violin, cello, 2 pianos, and percussion (2 players).
Percussion instrumentation: vibraphone, marimba, tubular bells, 2 wood drums, 3 suspended cymbals, tam-tam, 3 tom-toms, and timpani.

Difficulty: Voice: very difficult; Instruments: difficult
Vocal range: b - $c^{\#'''}$
Language: Russian (German translation provided for performance); original Spanish poems printed as text.
Duration: 18:00

099
Diemente, Edward (b. 1923)
Forms of Flight and Fancy (1973)
I. Flight to Cleveland
II. Sarah Plays
III. Hearts Win
IV. Cloudwalk
Text: Composer
Publisher: Baltimore: Smith Publications
For: Soprano and brass quintet [trumpet I in B^b (bongos with yarn mallets), trumpet II in B^b (finger cymbal with metal beater, woodblock with wood stick), horn (three India bells - high, medium, low, suspended symbal), trombone (timbales, high and low), and tuba (maraca)].
Difficulty: Voice: difficult; Instruments: difficult
Vocal range: b - $b^{b''}$
Language: English

100
Diemer, Emma Lou (b. 1927)
Four Poems by Alice Meynell (1976)
I. Chimes
II. Renouncement
III. The Roaring Frost
IV. The Fold
Text: Alice Meynell
Publisher: New York: Carl Fischer 05029
For: Soprano (or tenor) and chamber ensemble.
Instrumentation: ensemble not clearly defined in piano/vocal score but includes violin I, violin II, viola, cello, flute, piano, harpsichord, harp, and vibraphone.
Difficulty: Voice: moderate; Instruments: moderate
Vocal range: $c^{\#'}$ - $b^{b''}$
Language: English

101
Dimov, Bojidar (b. 1935)
Incantationes II (1967)
Text: Georg Trakl, multilingual text from various sources
Publisher: Munich: Edition Modern M1374E
For: Soprano, flute, trumpet in B^b, 2 violins, harp, 3 loudspeakers with microphones, and percussion (2 players).
Percussion instrumentation: (I) various large bells, (hung up, as quickly as possible, Indian), triangle, Alpine meadow bell, cymbals, crotales, bongos, bass drum, timpani, and tubular bells; (II) large suspended cymbal, and large tam-tam.
Difficulty: Voice: difficult; Instruments: difficult
Vocal range: e' - b''
Language: Hebrew and other languages
Comments: Graphic notation; use of quarter tones.

102
Dinerstein, Norman (1937-1982)
Four Settings (1961)
I. Dying
II. The Bustle in a House
III. Apparently with no Surprise
IV. I died for Beauty
Text: Emily Dickinson
Publisher: New York: Boosey & Hawkes B.Ens.183
For: Soprano and string quartet.
Difficulty: Voice: moderately difficult; Instruments: moderately difficult
Vocal range: g - $b^{b''}$
Language: English
Duration: 13:00

103
Dobos, Kálmán (b. 1931)
Villanások (1963)
(Flashes)
I. Az Ébredés Partjáig (Until the Shores Waking)
II. Clown
Text: Éva Stetka (English translation by Agnes of Gergely)
Publisher: Budapest: Editio Musica Z. 5128
For: Soprano, violin, cello, and piano.
Difficulty: Voice: moderately difficult; Instruments: moderately difficult
Vocal range: $d^{b'}$ - $a^{\#''}$
Language: Hungarian (English translation provided for performance)
Duration: 5:35

104
Downes, Andrew (b. 1950)
Lost Love (1977)
I. The Walk
II. Lost Love
III. A Night in November
IV. Last Love Word
Text: Thomas Hardy
Publisher: West Midlands, England: Lynwood Music Photo Editions
For: Soprano, flute or tenor recorder, harpsichord, and cello.
Difficulty: Voice: moderately difficult; Instruments: moderately difficult
Vocal range: c' - g''
Language: English

105
Dreyfus, George (b. 1928)
From Within, Looking Out (1962)
I. (Voice tacet)
II. I live all alone...
III. Most tender things...
Text: Composer
Publisher: Melbourne: Allan's Music. Sole Agent: London: Schott
For: Soprano, flute, viola, celesta, and vibraphone.
Difficulty: Voice: very difficult; Instruments: difficult
Vocal range: b - c'''
Language: English

106
Du Bois, Rob (b. 1934)
Pour faire chanter la Polonaise (1965)
Text: Composer
Publisher: Amsterdam: Donemus
For: Soprano, flute, and 3 pianos.
Difficulty: Voice: difficult; Instruments: moderately difficult
Vocal range: d' - $b^{b''}$
Language: French

Comments: White score; speaking part for singer.

107

Eberhard, Dennis (b. 1943)

Parody

Publisher: Newton Centre, MA: Margun Music

For: Soprano, flute (piccolo), clarinet in B^b (bass clarinet), trombone, violin, cello, piano (celesta), and percussion (3 players).

Percussion instrumentation: (I) Vibraphone, marimba, crotales, maracas, tam-tam, 5 Alpine meadow bells, 4 tom-toms, 2 gongs, tubular bells; (II) tam-tam, 3 gongs, crotales, 5 Alpine meadow bells, 3 suspended cymbals (large one with sizzles), sleigh bells, maracas, wind chimes, 4 tom-toms; (III) Bass drum, 4 tom-toms, bongos, glockenspiel, suspended cymbal, 5 Alpine meadow bells, lion's roar, trap set, hi-hat, sleigh bells, 5 temple blocks, and claves.

Difficulty: Voice: very difficult; Instruments: difficult

Vocal range: g - c‴

Language: English

Duration: 10:00

Comments: Use of spatial and metrical time; some new notation; white score.

108

Ehle, Robert C. (b. 1939)

Algorhythms (©1972)

I. Electronic Song Cycle
II. Illusion
III. Precision
IV. Architecture

Text: Composer

Publisher: New York: Carl Fischer

For: Soprano, prepared piano, clarinet in B^b, and double bass.

Difficulty: Voice: difficult; Instruments: difficult

Vocal range: b - b^{b}″

Language: English

Comments: All instruments and the singer are to be miked.

109

Emmer, Huib (b. 1951)

Le Rebelle (1976)

Text: Charles Baudelaire

Publisher: Amsterdam: Donemus

For: Soprano, piano, oboe, clarinet in A, clarinet in B^b, tenor saxophone, trombone, 2 horns, 2 violins, viola, 2 cellos, 2 double basses, and percussion (4 players).

Percussion instrumentation: (I) bongos; (II) woodblock and 2 tom-toms; (III) snare drum; (IV) small, medium, and large drums, tam-tam, timpano, and bass drum.

Difficulty: Voice: difficult; Instruments: moderately difficult

Vocal range: c′ - b″

Language: French

Duration: 15:00

110

Erickson, Robert (b. 1917)

The Idea of Order at Key West (1979)

Text: Wallace Stevens

Publisher: Baltimore: Smith Publications

For: Soprano, flute, sopranino clarinet in E^b (bass clarinet), trumpet in B^b, viola, and cello.
Vocal range: g - b$^{b''}$
Difficulty: Voice: difficult; Instruments: difficult
Language: English

111
Fegers, Karl
Sechs kleine Weisen (1960)
I. Der Floh
II. Die Seifenblase
III. Der Funke
IV. Die Feder
V. Der Stein
VI. Das Samenkorn
Text: Joachim Ringelnatz
Publisher: Mainz: Schott B142
For: Voice (soprano or tenor), 2 soprano recorders, and percussion.
Percussion instrumentation: hand drum, triangle, xylophone, metallophone, glockenspiel, and timpani.
Difficulty: Voice: moderate; Instruments: moderate
Vocal range: c$'$ - g$''$
Language: German

112
Felciano, Richard (b. 1930)
The Angels of Turtle Island (1971)
Text: phonemes
Publisher: Boston: E.C. Schirmer ECS 2533 (© 1984)
Series: ECS Mixed Media Series, 697
For: Soprano, flute, violin, percussion, and live electronics.
Percussion instrumentation: tom-toms, glass chimes, suspended finger cymbal, timpani, snare drum, glockenspiel, tubular bells, tam-tam, small and large cymbals.
Difficulty: Voice: moderate; Instruments: difficult
Vocal range: e$'$ - c$''$
Language: Phonemes
Duration: 14:00
Comments: Use of spatial time; some graphic notation; performers must read notes carefully.

113
Feldman, Morton (1926-1987)
For Franz Kline (1962)
Text: none
Publisher: New York: Peters P6948
For: Soprano, violin, cello, horn, tubular bells, and piano.
Difficulty: Voice: moderately easy; Instruments: easy
Vocal range: b^b - a$^{b''}$
Language: none - no indication of phonemes
Comments: The duration of each sound after simultaneous beginning is left to the singer and each instrumentalist.

114
Feldman, Morton (1926-1987)
Rabbi Akiba (1963)
Text: none
Publisher: New York: Peters P6957
For: Soprano, flute, English horn, horn, trumpet in B^b, trombone, tuba, piano (celesta), cello, double bass, and percussion (1 player).
Percussion instrumentation: tubular bells, crotales (F, F$^\#$, G, A^b), timpani, large tenor drum, large

bass drum, extra-large tom-tom, and maracas.
Difficulty: Voice: moderately difficult; Instruments: easy
Vocal range: b^b - a″
Language: none - no indication of phonemes
Comments: Vocal line treated as instrumental part.

115

Feldman, Morton (1926-1987)

Vertical Thoughts 3 (1963)

Text: Composer
Publisher: New York: Peters P6954
For: Soprano, flute, horn, trumpet in B^b, trombone, tuba, piano (celesta), violin, cello, double bass, and percussion (2 players).
Percussion instrumentation: large vibraphone, tubular bells, timpani, extra large tom-tom, large gong, and antique cymbal (A).
Difficulty: Voice: easy; Instruments: moderately easy
Vocal range: d#″ is the only pitch sung
Language: English

116

Feldman, Morton (1926-1987)

Vertical Thoughts 5 (1963)

Text: Composer
Publisher: New York: Peters P6956
For: Soprano, violin, tuba, celesta, and percussion (1 player).
Percussion instrumentation: large bass drum, timpani, large tom-tom, and antique cymbal.
Difficulty: Voice: easy; Instruments: easy
Vocal range: g#″ is the only pitch sung
Language: English

117

Fennelly, Brian (b. 1934)

Songs with Improvisation (© 1970)

I. crazy jay blue)
II. the sky was
III. off a pane) the
IV. Interlude
V. Beautiful
VI. un (bee) mo
VII. pity this busy monster, manunkind

Text: e. e. cummings
Publisher: New York: American Composers Alliance
Series: Composers Facsimile Edition
For: High voice (soprano), clarinet in B^b, and piano.
Difficulty: Voice: very difficult; Instruments: very difficult
Vocal range: d#′ - a″
Language: English
Duration: 20:20
Comments: Use of Sprechstimme; approximated pitches.

118

Foss, Lukas (b. 1922)

Time Cycle (1960)

Chamber version by the composer (1961)

I. We're Late (W. H. Auden)
II. When the Bells Justle (A. E. Housman)
III. Sechzehnter Januar (Franz Kafka)
IV. O Mensch, gib Acht (Friedrich Nietzsche)

Publisher: New York: Carl Fischer © 1964
For: Soprano, clarinet in B^{b}, cello, piano (celesta), and percussion.
Percussion instrumentation: medium timpano, vibraphone, xylophone, tubular bells ($F^{\#}$, $G^{\#}$, A, B, C), antique cymbal (E^{b}) (mounted and struck with heavy brass thimble), pair of bongos, 3 temple blocks, high and medium woodblocks, one suspended cymbal, gong, tambourine, bass drum, and triangle.
Difficulty: Voice: very difficult; Instruments: very difficult
Vocal range: b - c'''
Language: English (I and II) and German (III and IV)
Duration: 22:00

119
Foss, Lukas (b. 1922)
Thirteen Ways of Looking at a Blackbird (1978)
Text: Wallace Stevens
Publisher: New York: Pembroke. Sole Agent: Carl Fischer PCB 114 © 1980
For: Soprano or mezzo-soprano, piano, flute, 2 tape recorders (for echo effect) and percussion.
Percussion instrumentation: (plays inside piano) tape-covered triangle beaters, 2 cowbells, 2 bowls, Superball mallet, flexatone, and Jew's harp.
Difficulty: Voice: difficult; Instruments: very difficult
Vocal range: b^{b} - $a^{b''}$
Language: English
Duration: 17:00

120
Fouillaud, Patrice (b. 1949)
Le Chant de l'Absence (1983)
Text: Composer
Publisher: Durand SA Editions Musicales
For: Soprano, flute, bass clarinet, violin, viola, cello, piano, harpsichord, celesta, and percussion.
Percussion instrumentation: vibraphone, xylorimba, 3 cymbals, 3 Thailand gongs, 2 tam-tams, crotales, jeux de tubes, 2 timbales, 3 tom-toms, and bass drum.
Difficulty: Voice: very difficult; Instruments: very difficult
Vocal range: b - $d^{\#'''}$
Language: French
Duration: 20:00

121
Fowler, Jennifer (b. 1939)
Voice of the Shades (1977)
Text: Composer
Publisher: Australia: Universal Edition UE29200A
For: Soprano, oboe or clarinet in B^{b}, and violin (see comments).
Difficulty: Voice: very difficult; Instruments: difficult
Vocal range: b - $b^{b''}$
Language: pronounced as English (some use of IPA)
Duration: about 15:00
Comments: Many combinations of instruments may be used including 2 trumpets in B^{b} and oboe or clarinet in B^{b}; or oboe or clarinet, and flute (alto flute); or clarinet, oboe, and violin or flute (alto flute). Read performance notes carefully.

122
Garant, Serge (1929-1986)
Anerca (1961 rev. 1963)
I. (voice tacet)
II. Arise from rest...
III. Great Sea Sends Me Drifting
Text: Knud Rasmussen
Publisher: Don Mills, Ontario: BMI Canada
For: Soprano, flute, clarinet in B^b, bassoon, violin, viola, cello, harp, and percussion.
Percussion instrumentation: 1 snare drum, 2 tom-toms, suspended cymbal, crotales, Japanese temple bells, vibraphone, Chinese bell tree, 2 woodblocks, 2 temple blocks, and many other instruments at the discretion of the musician.
Difficulty: Voice: difficult; Instruments: moderately difficult
Vocal range: b - b″
Language: English
Duration: 9:00
Comments: Voice must change timbre.

123
Gaslini, Giorgio (b. 1929)
Magnificat (1963)
Text: Luke 1:46-55
Publisher: London: Universal Edition UE 13589 mi © 1970
For: Soprano, alto saxophone, double bass, and piano.
Difficulty: Voice: moderate; Instruments: moderate
Vocal range: d′ - e″
Language: Latin

124
Geissler, Fritz (1921-1984)
Nachtelegien (1969)
I. Den des Mondes...
II. (Intermezzo I)
III. Abende meiner lage...
IV. (Intermezzo II)
V. Silberne Gefilde
Text: Arnold Zweig: *Jahresringe*
Publisher: Leipzig: Peters 9143
For: Soprano, flute, alto flute, bass clarinet, harpsichord, vibraphone (tom-toms), violin, viola, cello, and double bass.
Difficulty: Voice: difficult; Instruments: difficult
Vocal range: c′ - b^{b}″
Language: German

125
Gideon, Miriam (b. 1906)
Wing'd Hour (© 1985)
I. Silent Noon (Dante Gabriel Rossetti)
II. My Heart Is Like a Singing Bird (Christina Rossetti)
III. Interlude (voice tacet)
IV. Autumn (Walter de la Mare)
Publisher: New York: Peters 67031
For: High voice (soprano or tenor), flute, oboe, vibraphone, violin, and cello.
Difficulty: Voice: difficult; Instruments: difficult
Vocal range: e′ - a″
Language: English
Duration: 10:00

126
Gilbert, Anthony (b. 1934)
Inscapes, Op. 26 (1975) (rev. 1981)
I. Walked Up the Valley...
II. I Was Looking at High Waves
III. This Day and May 11

IV. We have had other such Afternoons

Text: Gerard Manley Hopkins

Publisher: London: Schott ED11417 © 1983

For: Soprano, reader, two reed players (clarinet in B^b, soprano saxophone, bass clarinet), and percussion (one player).

Percussion instrumentation: vibraphone, glockenspiel, marimba, lujon with plates, timpani, tam-tam, sizzle cymbal, 4 drums, 2 temple blocks, harmonica, maracas, güiro, and Radha Krishna bell.

Difficulty: Voice: very difficult; Instruments: difficult

Vocal range: g - c‴

Language: English

Duration: 30:00

Comments: Use of spatial time.

127

Ginastera, Alberto (1916-1983)

Cantata para América Mágica Op.27 (1961)

I. Preludio y Canto a la Aurora (Prelude and Song of Dawn)

II. Nocturno y Canto de Amor (Nocturne and Love Song)

III. Canto para la Partida de los Guerreros (Song for the Warrior's Departure)

IV. Interludio fantástico (Fantastic interlude)

V. Canto de Agonía y Desolación (Song of Agony and Desolation)

VI. Canto de la Profecía (Song of Prophecy)

Text: Mercedes de Toro "inspired by antique pre-Colombian texts"

Publisher: Buenos Aires: Barry. Sole Agent: New York: Boosey & Hawkes

For: Dramatic soprano and percussion (16 players).

Instrumentation: timpani I; timpani II; drums I (small, medium, and large Indian drums); drums II (snare drum without snares), tenor drum, bass drum, also small sistrum; 6 temple blocks of different sizes; small, medium, and large suspended cymbals, 2 crashing cymbals, and 2 cowbells; small, medium, and large tam-tams; Percussion I: 2 pairs of crotales, small suspended cymbal, 2 bongos, tubular bells, small triangle, reco-reco [like a güiro but made of bamboo], small high claves, small maracas, and chocallo [Latin American metal shaker]; Percussion II: güiro, triangle, bass drum (very low), and low claves; Percussion III: small and medium maracas, 2 clashing cymbals, 1 metalic sistrum, 1 sea shell sistrum, small triangle, sleigh bells, and pair of stones; large xylophone; marimba; glockenspiel; celesta; piano I; and piano II.

Difficulty: Voice: very difficult; Instruments: difficult

Vocal range: g - c‴

Language: Spanish (English provided for performance)

Duration: 25:00

Comments: Extended b″ for soprano in movement III.

128
GLOBOKAR, VINKO (B. 1934)
Accord (1966)
Text: none
Publisher: Frankfurt: Henry Litoff. Sole Agent: New York: Peters 5976
For: Soprano, flute, trombone with F valve, cello, electric organ with 2 manuals, and percussion (1 player).
Percussion instrumentation: bongos, snare drum without snares, 2 tom-toms, timpano (A), pair of maracas, wood-block, 5 temple blocks, triangle, large gong, pair of cymbals, hi-hat, 4 cowbells, 1 tubular bell (e′), set of glass chimes, set of wind chimes, set of wood chimes, vibraphone, and marimba.
Difficulty: Voice: very difficult; Instruments: very difficult
Vocal range: employs highest note possible and lowest note possible
Language: phonemes
Comments: Uses graphic notation; most pitches, especially for the vocal part, are not definitely notated. Rhythmic difficulty.

129
GÓRECKI, HENRYK MIKOŁAJ (B. 1933)
Genesis, Op. 19, No. 3 (1963)
Text: Composer
Publisher: Warsaw: P W M © 1966
For: Soprano, metal percussion (13 players), and 6 double basses.
Percussion instrumentation: 12 anvils, 16 cymbals, 4 gongs, 12 triangles, 4 tam-tams, and tubular bells.
Difficulty: Voice: moderately difficult; Instruments: moderately easy
Vocal range: d′ - a″ and highest note possible
Language: Polish
Comments: Graphic notation.

130
GÓRECKI, HENRYK MIKOŁAJ (B. 1933)
Monologhi, Op. 16 (1960)
Text: Composer
Publisher: Warsaw: P W M 4783
For: Soprano, 2 harps, bells, vibraphone, marimba, 6 suspended cymbals, 3 tam-tams, and 3 gongs.
Difficulty: Voice: difficult; Instruments: difficult
Vocal range: c′ - c#‴
Language: Polish
Duration: 17:00

131
HALFFTER, CRISTOBAL (B. 1930)
Noche Pasiva del Sentido (1970)
Text: San Juan de la Cruz
Publisher: Vienna: Universal Edition UE 15634
For: Soprano, percussion (2 players), and 5 microphones, 4 tape recorders, and 1 potentiometer (piano is considered a percussion instrument and is played by Percussion I).
Percussion instrumentation: (I) piano, 2 suspended cymbals (high and low), high gong, high tam-tam, handbell, sizzle cymbal, and tumbler; (II) 3 crotales (high, low, middle), vibraphone, 2 tam-tams (high, low), 2 gongs (high, low), 1 tubular bell (b♭′), 2 suspended cymbals (high, low),

sizzle cymbal, tumbler, handbell, and triangle.
Difficulty: Voice: very difficult; Instruments: moderate
Vocal range: g - b″, also highest note possible
Language: Spanish
Comments: Graphic notation.

132
Hampton, Calvin (1938-1984)
The Labyrinth: Vague Is the Silence (© 1976)
Text: Michael Abreu
Publisher: New York: McAfee Music
For: Soprano and saxophone quartet.
Difficulty: Voice: difficult; Instruments: difficult
Vocal range: b - e‴
Language: English

133
Harrex, Patrick (b. 1946)
Sonata (© 1969)
I. In Just
II. Who knows if the moon's
III. Because it's and (listen)
Text: e. e. cummings
Publisher: London: Ars Viva
For: Voice (soprano or tenor), flute, and percussion (1 player).
Percussion instrumentation: 2 woodblocks, 2 triangles, suspended cymbal, 3 temple blocks, maracas, snare drum without snares, crotales, and claves.
Difficulty: Voice: difficult; Instruments: moderately difficult
Vocal range: c′ - a^{b}″
Language: English

134
Hartley, Walter S. (b. 1927)
A Psalm Cycle (1967)
I. O God, Thou art my God... (Psalm 63:1-5)
II. Help, Lord...(Psalm 12:1-4, 9a)
III. Give Sentence with Me... (Psalm 43:1-3)
IV. I waited patiently for the Lord...(Psalm 40:1-4)
V. I Will magnify Thee...(Psalm 145:1-3, 8-10, 21)
Publisher: Bryn Mawr, PA: Tenuto Publications. Sole Agent: Theodore Presser © 1970 T100
For: Medium-high voice (soprano), flute, and piano.
Difficulty: Voice: moderately difficult; Instruments: moderately difficult
Vocal range: c$^{\#}$′ - a″
Language: English
Duration: 13:30

135
Hartwell, Hugh (b. 1945)
Resta di Darmi Noia (© 1978)
Text: from Carlo Gesualdo Principe di Venosa
Publisher: Toronto: Berandol Music BER 1743
For: Soprano, flute (alto flute, bass flute), piano.
Difficulty: Voice: moderately difficult; Instruments: moderately difficult
Vocal range: b^{b} - c″
Language: Italian
Comments: Some Sprechstimme.

136

HAUBENSTOCK-RAMATI, ROMAN (B. 1919)

Credentials or Think, Think Lucky (1961)

Text: Samuel Beckett *Waiting for Godot*

Publisher: Vienna: Universal Edition UE 13676 © 1963

For: Voice (any, but soprano most effective), piano, celesta, vibraphone (tubular bells), violin, clarinet in B^b, trombone, and percussion (2 players).

Percussion instrumentation: (I) hi-hat, 3 tom-toms, conga, bongos, temple blocks, woodblocks, xylorimba, 4 suspended cymbals (1 with sizzles), medium gong, large tam-tam, and pair large maracas; (II) same as I except pair small bongos, 5 cowbells, glockenspiel, small gong, medium tam-tam, and pair small maracas.

Difficulty: Voice: moderately difficult; Instruments: moderately difficult

Vocal range: varies

Language: English

Comments: Few pitches notated but no clef; the sounds singer makes are all approximations as indicated in score. Use of Sprechstimme.

137

HAUBENSTOCK-RAMATI, ROMAN (B. 1919)

Mobile for Shakespeare (1960)

Text: William Shakespeare Sonnets 53 & 54

Publisher: Vienna: Universal Edition UE 13421

For: Soprano or mezzo soprano, piano (celesta), and percussion (3 players).

Percussion instrumentation: 4 woodblocks, 2 bongos, 2 temple blocks, 4 tom-toms (large to small), hi-hat, 2 cymbals (medium & large), tam-tam (large), vibraphone, marimbaphone, crotales, castanets, and maracas (large).

Difficulty: Voice: difficult; Instruments: difficult

Vocal range: g - c‴

Language: English

Duration: 6:00

Comments: Aleatoric elements; free tempo; text not printed on score (piece consists of several areas--each area in the singer's part corresponds to one line (10 syllables of a Sonnet.) Note extreme range.

138

HAWKINS, JOHN (B. 1944)

Three Cavatinas (1967)

I. Lillac star bird (Walt Whitman)

II. A star lit or a moon (William Butler Yeats)

III. Loneliness moans like a fog (William S. Burroughs)

Publisher: Don Mills, Ontario: BMI Canada

For: Soprano (bamboo chimes and maracas), violin, cello, vibraphone, and celesta (sand blocks).

Difficulty: Voice: difficult; Instruments: difficult

Vocal range: b^b - $b^{b''}$ ($c^{\#'''}$ optional)

Language: English
Duration: 7:00

139
Hayakawa, Masaaki (b. 1934)
Four Little Poems: Progressive Muscular Distrophy (1975)
I. Someday, somewhere (Sayoko Fukuda)
II. Sunset (Hiroshi Kiyohara)
III. Darkness (Sadayuki Koyama)
IV. I will give you dreams (Keichi Ueda)
Text: "Musical settings of poems written by victims of muscular dystrophy."
Publisher: Tokyo: Japan Federation of Composers JFC-7511
For: Voice (soprano or mezzo-soprano), saxophone quartet, harp, and percussion (1 player).
Percussion instrumentation: 3 triangles, suspended cymbal, tam-tam, bass drum, glockenspiel, and vibraphone.
Difficulty: Voice: moderately difficult; Instruments: difficult
Vocal range: d′ - g#″
Language: Japanese (English translation provided for performance)
Duration: 9:23

140
Hekster, Walter (b. 1937)
A Song of Peace (1979)
Text: Composer
Publisher: Amsterdam: Donemus
For: Voice (soprano or tenor), sopranino clarinet in E♭ (clarinet in B♭, and bass clarinet), alto saxophone, cello, and percussion (1 player).
Percussion instrumentation: vibraphone, maracas, 10 suspended cymbals, high suspended cymbal (scrape with metal object on cymbal), bamboo chimes, and water gong (raise and lower small tam-tam in a tub of water).
Difficulty: Voice: difficult; Instruments: difficult
Vocal range: b♭ - a″
Language: English
Comments: Some speaking parts.

141
Hekster, Walter (b. 1937)
Songs of all Seasons (1983)
I. Frühlingsnacht (Su Dung-Po)
II. Sommerliche Freuden auf dem Lande (Fan Tscheng-Da)
III. Herbstlied (Lu-Yu)
IV. Improvisation an einem Wintertag (Oschang-Le)
Text: Su Schi
Publisher: Amsterdam: Donemus
For: Soprano, flute (alto flute, piccolo), double bass, harp, and percussion.
Percussion instrumentation: small woodblock, medium split drum, 3 log drums, tabla, 4 tom-toms, tambourine, 2 suspended cymbals, Javanese gong, tam-tam, glockenspiel, vibraphone, marimba, and tubular bells.
Difficulty: Voice: difficult; Instruments: moderately difficult
Vocal range: b♭ - b♭″
Language: German
Duration: 11:00 - 12:00

142
HEMPEL, CHRISTOPH (B. 1946)
Sketch (1978)
Text: Composer
Publisher: Wolfenbüttel: Möseler M59.420
For: Soprano, accordion, and percussion.
Percussion instrumentation: vibraphone, xylophone, 2 cymbals, 2 tom-toms, 2 bongos, 5 temple blocks, triangle, and Ping-Pong ball (to drop on vibraphone).
Difficulty: Voice: very difficult; Instruments: very difficult
Vocal range: g - a″
Language: German
Comments: Use of pitch approximations, Sprechstimme; speaking part for singer.

143
HENZE, HANS WERNER (B. 1926)
Being Beauteous (1963)
Text: Arthur Rimbaud: *Illuminations*
Publisher: Mainz: Schott. Sole Agent: New York: Associated © 1964 5035
For: Coloratura soprano, harp, and 4 cellos.
Difficulty: Voice: very difficult; Instruments: moderate
Vocal range: b - $f^{b'''}$
Language: French
Duration: 14:30

144
HIBBARD, WILLIAM (B. 1939)
Ménage (1974)
Text: none
Publisher: [n.p.]: Lingua Press
For: Soprano, trumpet in B^b, and violin.
Difficulty: Voice: very difficult; Instruments: very difficult
Vocal range: $c^{\#'}$ - b″
Language: phonemes
Duration: 8:30
Comments: Employs no text, only vocal timbres indicated by the International Phonetic Alphabet.

145
HILLER, LEJAREN (1924 - 1994) AND BAKER, ROBERT (B. 1933)
Computer Cantata (1963)
Text: Lee S. Hultzén, Joseph Allen, Jr., Murray Miron, Jr. with the ILLIAC electronic digital computer.
Publisher: Byrn Mawr, PA: Theodore Presser 416-41070
For: Soprano, flute, bass clarinet, trumpet in B^b, horn, violin, viola, guitar, 2-channel tape recorder (electronic sounds produced on Theremin), and percussion.
Percussion instrumentation: snare drum, cymbal, tambourine, castanets, tabor, maracas, bass drum, tam-tam, glockenspiel, and xylophone.
Difficulty: Voice: very difficult; Instruments: very difficult
Vocal range: a - a″
Language: computer generated
Duration: 22:39
Comments: "The text consists of five successive stochastic approximations to spoken English. These phonemes were generated from analytical data on speech...." Score, text, and music on tape "composed" by the MUSICOMP program.

146

Hodkinson, Sydney (b. 1934)

ARC (1969)

Text: phonemes

Publisher: New York: American Composers Alliance

For: Soprano, flute (piccolo, whip), piano, and percussion (2 players).

Percussion instrumentation: (I) vibraphone, glockenspiel, 2 woodblocks (small & medium), 2 cymbals (medium & large), 2 log drums (medium & large), mounted güiro, ratchet, wood table, 4 cowbells (high to low), 2 iron pipes, chocalho, sistrum, 3 tom-toms, bass drum, 2 maracas (large & small), Sarna bells, milk bottle (one gallon), police whistle, metal cricket,cardboard tube, large sheet of plate glass with hammers and metal container (II) marimba, crotales, gong, 3 cymbals (very small, very large, medium sizzle), claves, wood chimes, large woodblock, castanets, toy piano, mounted sandpaper block, sheet of stiff brown wrapping paper, sheet of cellophane, 2 conga drums, 2 timbales, cabaça, 4 brake drums, 2 iron pipes, 1 cowbell (large), lujon, vibraslap, glass chimes, cardboard tube, and police whistle.

Difficulty: Voice: extremely difficult; Instruments: very difficult

Vocal range: $g^{\#}$ - $d^{b'''}$

Language: phonemes

Comments: Read performance notes very carefully. Various vocal effects required including shrieking on highest note possible. Vocalist must make a pre-performance tape (see performance notes at back of score).

147

Holliger, Heinz (b. 1939)

Vier Miniaturen (1962-3)

I. Doppel-Herzkanon
II. Carillon
III. Bicinium
IV. Double

Text: Composer

Publisher: Mainz: Schott 41261

For: Soprano, oboe d'amore, celesta, and harp.

Difficulty: Voice: very difficult; Instruments: very difficult

Vocal range: $g^{\#}$ - $c^{\#'''}$

Language: German

Duration: 7:40

Comments: Note extreme range.

148

Holloway, Robin (b. 1943)

Divertimento, No.3, Op. 33a "Nursery Rhymes" (1977)

I. Overture and Theme-riddles
II. Going along
III. Dialogue
IV. Ickle Ockle
V. Third Egg-Riddle and Answer
VI. Finale

Text:Oxford Dictionary of Nursery Rhymes

Publisher: London: Boosey & Hawkes B&H 20497

For: Soprano and woodwind quintet [flute (piccolo), oboe, clarinet in A, bassoon, and horn].

Difficulty: Voice: difficult; Instruments: difficult

Vocal range: b - b″

Language: English

Duration: 25:00

149
Holten, Bo (b. 1948)
Sonata (1976)
Text: Composer
Publisher: Copenhagen: Wilhelm Hansen WH 29413
For: Soprano, violin, and cello.
Difficulty: Voice: very difficult; Instruments: very difficult
Vocal range: c′ - c‴
Language: phonemes
Duration: 13:00

150
Hopkins, Bill (b. 1943)
Two Pomes (1964)
I. She weeps over Rahoon
II. On the beach at Fontana
Text: James Joyce *Pomes Penyeach*
Publisher: London: Universal Edition UE 14204 L
For: Soprano, trumpet in C, harp, viola, and bass clarinet.
Difficulty: Voice: difficult; Instruments: difficult
Vocal range: b - d″
Language: English

151
Hovhaness, Alan (b. 1911)
Hercules Op. 56, No. 4 (© 1966)
Text: Composer
Publisher: New York: Peters 66025
For: Soprano and violin.
Difficulty: Voice: moderate; instrument: moderate
Vocal range: b^{b} - $b^{b\prime\prime}$
Language: English

152
Hovhaness, Alan (b. 1911)
Saturn, Op. 243 (© 1971)
I. Prelude
II. Titan, Moon of Saturn
III. Orb Mysterious
IV. Saturn, Celestial Globe
V. O Lost Note
VI. My Hymn
VII. Giant Globe
VIII. Vision of Saturn
IX. On Wings of a Soundless Note
X. What is Universe?
XI. Intermezzo
XII. Harp of Saturn
Text: Composer
Publisher: New York: Peters 66440
For: Soprano, clarinet in B^{b}, and piano.
Difficulty: Voice: moderately easy; Instruments: moderate
Vocal range: d′ - $b^{b\prime\prime}$
Language: English
Duration: 24:30

153
Huber, Klaus (b. 1924)
Senfkorn (1975)
Text: Ernesto Cardenal, Psalm 36, Isaiah 11:6-7, Bach Cantata 159
Publisher: Munich: Ricordi Sy. 2347
For: Boy soprano, oboe, violin, viola, cello, and harpsichord.
Difficulty: Voice: moderately difficult (for a child); Instruments: difficult
Vocal range: d′ - e″
Language: German, with English, French, Italian, and Spanish translations.
Comments: Singer has more speaking parts than singing. The spoken texts should be delivered in the vernacular of the period.

154
Hudes, Eric
Romancero a la Muerte de Federico García Lorca (Rev. 1976) (© 1970)
Text: Leopoldo Urrutia de Luis, translation by Sylvia Townsend Warner
Publisher: Braintree, Essex, England: Anglian
Series: Anglian New Music Series, ANMS 48a
For: Soprano, flute, clarinet in B^b, viola, and guitar.
Difficulty: Voice: moderately difficult; Instruments: moderately difficult
Vocal range: c#′ - a″
Language: English
Comments: Piano-vocal score examined only.

155
Huggler, John (b. 1928)
Bittere Nüsse (1975)
I. In Gestalt eines Ebers
II. Eine Hand
III. Psalm
Text: Paul Celan
Publisher: New York: Peters 66680
For: Soprano, flute, clarinet in B^b (bass clarinet), violin, viola, and cello.
Difficulty: Voice: very difficult; Instruments: difficult
Vocal range: g# - e‴
Language: German
Duration: 8:03
Comments: Use of unusual meters; very high tessitura; note extreme range.

156
Hundziak, Andrzej (b. 1927)
Liryki, do Tekstów Safony. (1963)
I. Oto rozkwita mi
II. Mateńko moja słodka
III. Hymenaon!
Text: Sappho translation by Janina Brzostowska
Publisher: Warsaw: P W M 5764
For: Soprano, flute, trumpet in B^b, viola, cello, harp, celesta, xylophone, vibraphone, tavoletta [small table struck with a hammer], and 3 bongos.
Difficulty: Voice: difficult; Instruments: difficult
Vocal range: c′ - d‴
Language: Polish
Duration: 10:12

157
Hutcheson, Jere (b. 1938)
Passing Passing Passing (1977)
Text: Richard Heraty *Telephone Pole*
Publisher: New York: Seesaw
For: Soprano, clarinet in B^b, trombone, cello, and piano.
Difficulty: Voice: difficult; Instruments: difficult
Vocal range: b^b - c‴(also highest note possible "and a very low note.")
Language: English
Duration: 22:00
Comments: Some use of speech, Sprechstimme, and some graphic notation.

158
Ivey, Jean Eichelberger (b. 1923)
Solstice (1977)
I. At half-past night

II. There in the desert
III. We have marked every day
Text: Composer
Publisher: New York: Carl Fischer
For: Soprano, flute, piccolo, piano, and percussion (1 player).
Percussion instrumentation: finger cymbals, small tam-tam, glockenspiel, claves, triangle, and tambourine.
Difficulty: Voice: moderately difficult; Instruments: difficult
Vocal range: b^b - a″
Language: English
Duration: 13:00

159

IVEY, JEAN EICHELBERGER (B. 1923)

Three Songs of Night (1971)

I. The Astronomer (Walt Whitman)
II. I dreamed of Sappho (Richard Hovey)
III. Heraclitus (Callimachus - translation by William Cory)
Publisher: New York: Carl Fischer
For: Soprano, alto flute, clarinet in B^b, viola, cello, piano, and electronic tape (2 channel, 7½ ips).
Difficulty: Voice: difficult; Instruments: difficult
Vocal range: c′ - a″
Language: English
Duration: 14:00-15:00

160

JAMES, THOMAS S. (B. 1937)

Four Poems of Michael Fried (1973)

I. Falling Asleep
II. (Voice tacet)
III. Your Voice
IV. The Black Shag
V. (Voice tacet)
VI. The Flash of Lightning
Text: Michael Fried
Publisher: Hillsdale, NY: Boelke-Bomart BB26
For: Soprano, flute, clarinet in B^b, bass clarinet (with extension), violin, viola, and cello.
Difficulty: Voice: difficult; Instruments: difficult
Vocal range: b^b - b^{b}″
Language: English
Duration: 6:00

161

JENEY, ZOLTÁN (B. 1943)

Cantos para todos (1983)

I. Correspondencia (Millán Gonzalo)
II. El traslado (Millán Gonzalo)
III. No agonizo (anonymous)
Publisher: Budapest: Editio Musica Z.12737
For: Soprano, flute, clarinet in B^b, trumpet in B^b, viola, marimba, harp, and celesta.
Difficulty: Voice: difficult; Instruments: difficult
Vocal range: a - a″
Language: Spanish

162

JIRÁSEK, IVO (B. 1920)

Portrét Ženy (1975)

Text: none
Publisher: Prague: Panton P1760
For: Soprano, flute, bass clarinet, vibraphone, and piano.
Difficulty: Voice: very difficult; Instruments: very difficult
Vocal range: g - a″
Language: phonemes
Duration: 15:00

163

Jolas, Betsy (b. 1926)

Quatuor II (1964)

Text: none

Publisher: Paris: Heugel © 1970 H.E. 32 116

For: Coloratura soprano, violin, viola, and cello.

Difficulty: Voice: extremely difficult; Instruments: difficult

Vocal range: a - f‴

Language: phonemes

Duration: 15:30

Comments: The singer must have vocal agility and an extraordinary ear; wide leaps.

164

Karpman, Laura

Matisse and Jazz (1987)

I. The Airplane
II. (Blue) Forms
III. Tango
IV. Pierrot's Funeral
V. Lagoon
VI. Jazz

Text: Composer

Publisher: Saint Louis: Étoile Music. Sole Agent: Saint Louis: Norruth Music NRM 87002

For: Voice (soprano), soprano saxophone (alto saxophone), piano, and percussion.

Percussion instrumentation: snare drum, triangle, bongos, cowbell, shaker, woodblock, vibraphone, güiro, cymbals (large, medium, and small), tom-toms, crotales, wind chimes, maraca, bamboo chimes, caxixi, and hi-hat.

Difficulty: Voice: difficult; Instruments: difficult

Vocal range: f - $b^{b‴}$

Language: English

165

Karpman, Laura

Stanzas for Music (© 1986)

I. Stanzas for Music
II. On My Wedding Day
III. So We'll Go No More A-Roving

Text: Lord Byron

Publisher: Saint Louis: Norruth Music. Sole Agent: Saint Louis: MMB Music

For: Soprano or tenor, flute (piccolo), English horn, bass clarinet, marimba, harpsichord, violin, viola, and double bass.

Difficulty: Voice: very difficult; Instruments: difficult

Vocal range: b^b - b″

Language: English

166

Keller, Ginette (b. 1925)

Graphiques (1971)

I. Pointilles
II. Courbes
III. Spirales
IV. Arabesques

Text: none

Publisher: Paris: Editions Françaises de Musique-Technisonor EFM-1694

For: Soprano, flute (piccolo), clarinet in B^b (bass clarinet), horn, violin, viola, cello, piano, and percussion (1 player).

Percussion instrumentation: vibraphone, glockenspiel, glass chime, crotales, 3 woodblocks, 3 tom-toms, tam-tam, and 3 cymbals (Chinese, medium, and large).

Difficulty: Voice: difficult; Instruments: difficult

Vocal range: b^b - c‴
Language: phonemes
Comments: White score.

167
Kelterborn, Rudolf (b. 1931)
Consort-Music (1975)
Text: none
Publisher: Berlin: Bote & Bock B&B22682 (1260)
For: Soprano, flute (alto flute, piccolo), clarinet in B^b (bass clarinet), violin, viola, cello, double bass, and percussion (1 player).
Percussion instrumentation: vibraphone, xylophone, 3 suspended cymbals, 3 tom-toms, 4 woodblocks, 4 temple blocks, crotales, 2 snare drums, and tam-tam.
Difficulty: Voice: very difficult; Instruments: very difficult
Vocal range: d′ - b″
Language: phonemes
Duration: 10:00
Comments: Improvisatory section for voice; some aleatoric sections.

168
Keulen, Geert van
Three Poems by James Joyce (1984)
I. On the Beach at Fontana
II. Watching the Needleboats at San Sabba
III. Nightpiece
Text: James Joyce
Publisher: Amsterdam: Donemus
For: Soprano, flute (alto flute and piccolo), clarinet in A (bass clarinet), violin, double bass, harp, vibraphone (tam-tam), mandolin, and guitar.
Difficulty: Voice: very difficult; Instruments: very difficult
Vocal range: $c^{\#\prime}$ - $c^{\#\prime\prime\prime}$
Language: English
Duration: 13:00

169
Killmayer, Wilhelm (b. 1927)
Altissimu (1969)
Text: St. Francis of Assisi
Publisher: Mainz: Schott ED 7303
For: Soprano, tenor recorder, bongo, 3 tom-toms and timpano.
Difficulty: Voice: moderate; Instruments: moderate
Vocal range: $e^{b\prime}$ - a″
Language: Italian
Duration: 7:00

170
Killmayer, Wilhelm (b. 1927)
Blasons: Anatomiques du corps féminin (1968)
I. Tetin refaict (Clément Marot)
II. Ongle, qui tranches (Gilles Daurigny)
III. A layne chaulde (Anonymous)
IV. Genoilsans os (Lancelot Carle)
V. O doulce main (Claude Chappuys)
VI. Ô lieu solacieulx (Anonymous)
Publisher: Mainz: Schott, New York: Schott © 1969 6114
For: Soprano, clarinet in A, violin, cello, and piano.
Difficulty: Voice: very difficult; Instruments: easy
Vocal range: g - c‴
Language: French
Duration: 14:00

Comments: Vocal tremolo; extended difficult unaccompanied sections.

171

Knussen, Oliver (b. 1952)

Océan de terre, Op. 10 (1973, rev. 1976)

Text: Guillaume Apollinaire *Caligrammes*

Publisher: London: Faber Music. Sole Agent: New York: G. Schirmer 1985 F0583

For: Soprano, flute (alto flute), clarinet in B^b (bass clarinet), piano (celesta, small temple block, maracas), violin, cello, double bass, and percussion (1 or 2 players).

Percussion instrumentation: vibraphone, glockenspiel, tubular bells, suspended cymbal, smallish gong, 2 tam-tams (large and very large), xylophone, small woodblock, medium size temple block, claves, whip, maracas, and 2 small tom-toms.

Difficulty: Voice: very difficult; Instruments: very difficult

Vocal range: b^b - $b^{b''}$

Language: French

172

Knussen, Oliver (b. 1952)

Rosenkranz Lieder, Op. 9 (1972) (Rosary Songs)

I. An die Schwester (To my sister)
II. Nähe des Todes (Nearness of Death)
III. Amen

Text: Georg Trakl

Publisher: London: Faber Music F0540

For: Soprano, clarinet in B^b, viola, and piano.

Difficulty: Voice: difficult; Instruments: difficult

Vocal range: b^b - d'''

Language: German

Duration: 14:00

Comments: Use of Sprechstimme; rhythmic freedom in song II.

173

Knussen, Oliver (b. 1952)

Trumpets, Op. 12 (1975)

Text: Georg Trakl

Publisher: London: Faber Music. Sole Agent: New York: G. Schirmer © 1978 F 0541

For: Soprano and 3 clarinets in B^b.

Difficulty: Voice: difficult; Instruments: difficult

Vocal range: a - c'''

Language: German (An English translation by the composer is included but not meant to be sung)

Duration: 4:00

174

Koch, Frederick (b. 1924)

Monadnock Cadenzas and Variations (1971)

Variations 1-5, & 7 (voice tacet)
Variations 6 & 8 (voice and instruments)
Cadenzas at beginning and end of piece (voice tacet)

Text: none

Publisher: New York: Seesaw

For: Voice: (soprano or tenor), clarinet in B^b, trumpet in B^b, vibraphone, violin I, violin II, viola, cello, double bass, electronic tape, and percussion.

Percussion instrumentation: vibraphone, snare drum, woodblocks, suspended cymbal, and wind chimes.
Difficulty: Voice: difficult; Instruments: difficult
Vocal range: c′ - g#″
Language: phonemes
Comments: Some aleatoric elements.

175
Koering, René (b. 1940)
Ci - Gî T I (1963) [Claude Debussy]
Text: Composer
Publisher: Berlin: Ahn & Simrock: A&S 399
For: Soprano (claves), harpsichord, (suspended cymbal), harp I (tom-tom), harp II (yutone xylophone), violin, flute (claves and suspended cymbal), celesta (2 woodblocks), piano I (cymbals, woodblocks, snare drum, claves), and piano II.
Difficulty: Voice: moderate; Instruments: difficult
Vocal range: c#′ (parlando) - highest note possible
Language: French
Duration: 4:00
Comments: Soprano part is very brief and occurs at the end of the piece.

176
Koering, René (b. 1940)
Suite Intemporelle (1960)
Text: Composer
Publisher: Berlin: Ahn & Simrock A&S 359
For: Soprano, flute, violin, cello, vibraphone, marimba, double bass, piano, celesta, harmonium, and speaker.
Difficulty: Voice: difficult; Instruments: difficult
Vocal range: a# - a″
Language: French

177
Kolb, Barbara (b. 1939)
Chansons bas (1966)
I. Le Cantonnier
II. La Femme de l'ouvrier
III. Le Marchand d'ail et d'oignong
IV. Le Vitrier
V. Interlude (voice tacet)
VI. Le Crieur d'imprimés
VII. La Marchande d'habits
Text: Stéphane Mallarmé
Publisher: New York: Carl Fischer
For: Lyric soprano, harp and percussion (2 players).
Percussion instrumentation: (I) 3 suspended cymbals, glass chimes, xylophone, snare drum, tenor drum, and 5 temple blocks. (II) glockenspiel, vibraphone, bongos, 2 woodblocks (high, medium high), 3 suspended cymbals (high, medium, deep), and small and large timpani.
Difficulty: Voice: very difficult; Instruments: difficult
Vocal range: b♭ - b″
Language: French
Duration: 6:30
Comments: Some Sprechstimme.

178
Kolb, Barbara (b. 1939)
Songs Before an Adieu (1979)
I. The Sentences (Robert Pinsky)
II. now i lay (e. e. cummings)

III. Cantata (Howard Stern)
IV. Gluttonous Smoke (Vasko Popa)
V. L'adieu (Guillaume Apollinaire)

Publisher: New York: Boosey & Hawkes BH.BK.822
For: Soprano, flute (alto flute), and guitar.
Difficulty: Voice: difficult; Instruments: difficult
Vocal range: a - a″
Language: English except for "L'Adieu" which is in French.
Duration: 18:00

179
Kolinski, Mieczyslaw (1901-1981)
Lyric Sextet (© 1978)

I. Ernste Stunde (Rainer Maria Rilke)
II. Con Sordino (Hermann Hesse)
III. Naechtlicher Weg (Scholz)
IV. Mein Liebeslied (Else Lasker-Schüler)
V. Letzte Bitte (Otto Julius Bierbaum)

Publisher: Toronto: Berandol Music BER 1738
For: Soprano, flute, and string quartet.
Difficulty: Voice: moderately difficult; Instruments: moderate
Vocal range: $e^{b}{}'$ - $b^{b}{}''$
Language: German

180
Kotoński, Włodzimierz (b. 1925)
Aeolian Harp (1973)

Text: none
Publisher: Celle: Hermann Moeck 5147
For: Soprano (small cymbal, optional plucked instrument); Instrumentalist I: alto recorder, autoharp and Jew's harp; Instrumentalist II: autoharp, dulcimer, Jew's harp, crotales, and small bell; Instrumentalist III: guitar, electric bass, and lute; Instrumentalist IV: electric organ (with 2 manuals and pedals), and optional plucked instrument.
Difficulty: Voice: difficult; Instruments: difficult
Vocal range: b - $a^{b}{}''$
Language: phonemes
Duration: 25:00
Comments: White score; graphic notation. Read performance notes carefully; some quartertones for singer. Each performer also has a microphone and an audio mixer coupled with a preamplifier.

181
Kounadis, Argyris (b. 1924)
Quattro Pezzi (© 1965)

I. "Schläferung" auf Spielplan zu dem Namen Agis
II. Ostinato-Funèbre (voice tacet)
III. Variations (voice tacet)
IV. Scherzo auf Tanz

Text: Hans Magnus Enzensberger
Publisher: Rodenkirchen/Rhein: P. J. Tonger 1366 PJT © 1967
For: Soprano, flute, cello, and piano.
Difficulty: Voice: difficult; Instruments: difficult
Vocal range: b^{b} - $b^{b}{}''$
Language: German

182

KRIST, JOACHIM

Ave Dies (© 1978)

I. Die dunkelste Blume...
II. Die Welt ist stark...
III. Alles Lebendige stirbt...
IV. Der Welt Gerechtigkeit...
V. Wann wird kommen der Wind...
VI. Wundersamen Ring...
VII. Du ludest mich...
VIII. Die Erde schläft...
IX. Ich möchte die leeren...

Text: Hildegard Krist
Publisher: Munich: Edition Modern M2071E
For: Soprano, viola, cello, clarinet in B^b, and double bass or electric bass.
Difficulty: Voice: very difficult; Instruments: very difficult
Vocal range: f - e‴
Language: German
Comments: Use of quartertones and Sprechstimme. Note extreme range.

183

KRIVITS͡KIĬ, DAVID ITS͡KHOKOVICH

Osennie Peĭzazhi (© 1977)

I. Recitativo I (voice tacet)
II. Pod Dozhdem
III. Osennee Utro
IV. Recitativo II (voice tacet)
V. Poslednie Kann'i
VI. Recitativo III (voice tacet)

Text: N. Zabdotskogo
Publisher: Moscow: Sovyetski Kompozitor c3956k
For: Voice (soprano), clarinet in B^b, viola, and harp.
Difficulty: Voice: moderately difficult; Instruments: moderately difficult
Vocal range: c′ - b^{b}″
Language: Russian
Duration: 10:30

184

KROPFREITER, AUGUSTINUS FRANZ (B. 1936)

In Memoriam (1963)

I. Herbstlied
II. Lösch mir die Augen aus...
III. Jetzt reifen shon die roten Berberitzen...
IV. O Herr...
V. In diesem Dorfe...

Text: Rainer Maria Rilke
Publisher: Vienna: Doblinger © 1966 (Bernhard Herzmansky) D.11.400
For: Soprano, flute, viola, and cello.
Difficulty: Voice: moderately difficult; Instruments: moderate
Vocal range: c′ - a^{b}″
Language: German

185

KUPFERMAN, MEYER (B. 1926)

A Crucible for the Moon: Cantata (1986)

I. Moon-Red Canyon Sky...
II. Are There No Memories...
III. Smoke...

Text: Composer
Publisher: Rhinebeck, NY: Soundspells Productions 86005
Series: Virtuoso Editions. 86005
For: High soprano, alto saxophone, and percussion (7 players).
Percussion instrumenation: (I) xylophone, 5 temple blocks, crotales, low cymbal, small tom-tom, vibraslap, and camel bells; (II) vibraphone, 5 tuned drums, tenor drum, cabaça, gourd, medium cymbal, and squeeze

drum; (III) bells, snare drum, bass drum, maracas, rosewood sticks, and high cymbals; (IV) marimba, bass drum, triangle, finger cymbal, bell tree, ratchet, whip, agogo bells, wooden chimes, and small tambourine; (V) Balinese gong, tam-tam, sizzle cymbal, cowbell, claves, glass chimes, tambourine, bass drum, sleigh bells, woodblock, and Swanee whistle; (VI) tubular bells, bass drum, brake drum, castanets, bongos, flexatone, and metal wind chimes; (VII) timpani.

Difficulty: Voice: difficult; Instruments: difficult

Vocal range: a - c‴

Language: English

Duration: 17:00

Comments: Alto saxophone and singer should be amplified with standing microphone.

186

Kurtág, György (b. 1926)

Messages of the Late R. V. Troussova: 21 poems by Rimmy Dalosh, Op. 17 (1980)

I. Loneliness
II. A Little Erotic
III. Bitter Experience - Delight and Grief

Text: Rimma Dalosh

Publisher: Budapest: Editio Musica 2.12021

For: Soprano, oboe, clarinets in A, B^b, and E^b, horn, mandolin, harpsichord, harp, piano, celesta, vibraphone, xylophone, bells, violin, viola, double bass and percussion.

Percussion instrumentation: triangle, suspended cymbals, cymbals, 4 gongs, tom-tom, metal block, maracas, woodblock, breaking of a glass, glass chimes, snare drum, Basque drum, and bass drum.

Difficulty: Voice: very difficult; Instruments: very difficult

Vocal range: g - $d^{b'''}$

Language: Russian, with English, French, and Hungarian translations.

Duration: 26:15

187

Kurtág, György (b. 1926)

Erinnerung an einen Winterabend Op. 8 (1969)

I. Az órák most hozzák alakját...
II. Vártalak...
III. Menynyi út van...
IV. Isten veled...

Text: Pál Gulyás

Publisher: Vienna: Universal Edition UE 15907

For: Soprano, violin, and cymbal (pitched with pedal).

Difficulty: Voice: moderately difficult; Instruments: difficult

Vocal range: f - $g^{\#''}$

Language: Hungarian (German translation by Géza Engl provided for performance.)

188

Lechner, Konrad (b. 1911)

Cantica I (1965)

Text: Giacopone da Todi

Publisher: Cologne: Hans Gerig HG550

For: Soprano, piano, guitar, bass clarinet, horn, violin, cello, and percussion (1 player).
Percussion instrumentation: temple blocks, maracas, hi-hat, sizzle cymbal, 3 suspended cymbals, tam-tam, bongos, tom-tom, snare drum, and bass drum.
Difficulty: Voice: very difficult; Instruments: difficult
Vocal range: f# - b♭″
Language: Latin
Duration: 9:00

189
Leedy, Douglas (b. 1938)
Three Medieval English Lyrics (1979)
I. My Lief is Faren in Londe
II. The Corpus Christi Carol
III. I Sing of a Maiden
Text: Medieval English
Publisher: Oceanside, OR: Harmonie Universelle
For: Soprano and alto recorder.
Difficulty: Voice: difficult; Instrument: Very difficult
Vocal range: c′ - a″
Language: English
Duration: 7:30

190
Leeuw, Charles van der (b. 1952)
Voices in the Dark (1979)
Text: Oscar Wilde, Walt Whitman, F.H.A.R. Paris 1971, Thomas Jefferson, Karl M. Bowman, Bertolt Brecht, and William Blake.
Publisher: Amsterdam: Donemus
For: Soprano, flute, clarinet in B♭, soprano saxophone, alto saxophone, tenor saxophone, 2 horns, 2 trumpets in B♭, 2 trombones, electric bass and piano.
Difficulty: Voice: moderate; Instruments: moderate
Vocal range: c′ - f″
Language: English and French
Duration: 15:00
Comments: Some texts spoken.

191
LeFanu, Nicola (b. 1947)
The Old Woman of Beare (1981)
Text: adapted by composer from a 9th-10th century Irish Poem
Publisher: Borough Green, Kent, England: Novello 89 0131 07 © 1984
For: Soprano, flute, oboe, clarinet in B♭, bassoon, horn, trumpet in B♭, trombone, harp, violin, viola, cello, and percussion (2 players).
Percussion instrumentation: hourglass drum, 6 tom-toms (small to large), bongos, 2 bass drums (small and large), maracas, and claves.
Difficulty: Voice: difficult; Instruments: difficult
Vocal range: f - c‴
Language: English
Duration: 18:00
Comments: Composer intends for soprano to be aided by "unobtrusive" amplification.

192
LeFanu, Nicola (b. 1947)
The Same Day Dawns: Fragments from a Book of Songs (1974)
I. The Still Drone
II. Sanderlings
III. Horses

IV. O my Lord jasmine
V. Oriole
VI. How can one ever know
VII. When
VIII. Paradise
IX. Dumuzi mourned
X. Oriole
XI. O my Lord jasmine
XII. The windsleeps
XIII. Greenfinch
XIV. Sanderlings
XV. The still Drone

Text: Translation from poems in Tamil, Chinese, Japanese, Kannada, and Akkadian.
Publisher: Borough Green, Kent, England: Novello
For: Soprano, alto flute (flute), bass clarinet (clarinet in B^b), violin, cello, and percussion (1 player).
Percussion instrumentation: squeeze drum [African hour glass], suspended cymbals (small and medium), vibraphone, marimba, bongos (low), tuned bells or crotales, and Korean temple gongs (tuned).
Difficulty: Voice: very difficult; Instruments: difficult
Vocal range: g - a″
Language: English
Duration: 18:00
Comments: One section is aleatoric.

193
Legley, Vic (b. 1915)
Zeng, Op. 63 (1965)
I. Ik predik de moeraskoorts
II. In het boek der dagen
III. In het oog van vulkanen
IV. Mensen staan als bomen
V. Steden verteren ons zachtaardig
VI. Ik wil verstenen
VII. Teken voor mij een boom in het water

Text: Jos Vandeloo
Publisher: Brussels: Ce Be De M
For: Soprano and string quartet.
Difficulty: Voice: moderately difficult; Instruments: moderately difficult
Vocal range: b - a″
Language: Dutch
Duration: 17:00

194
Levinas, Michael
Voix dans un vaisseau d'airain "Chants en escalier"
Text: none
Publisher: Paris: Salabert E.A.S. 17307
For: Soprano, flute, horn, piano, and 2 synthesizers.
Difficulty: Voice: very difficult; Instruments: moderately difficult
Vocal range: e - b″ (also highest note possible)
Language: phonemes
Comments: High tessitura.

195
Lieuwen, Peter
Star (1986)
Text: Joanie Whitebird
Publisher: Saint Louis: Norruth Music NRM 87007
For: Soprano, cello, piano, and percussion.
Percussion instrumentation: (1 or 2 players) 1 double bass bow for arco playing, glockenspiel, suspended cymbal, vibraphone,

bass drum, 2 tom-toms, marimba, wind chimes (ceramic, glass, or metal), crotales, and gong.
Difficulty: Voice: very difficult; Instruments: difficult
Vocal range: b - c‴
Language: English
Duration: 8:35
Comments: Some use of spatial time. Speaking and whispering sections for singer. Pianist needs 1 large heavy book (approximately 13 inches long) or other weight suitable for holding down designated keys.

196

Lloyd, Jonathan (b. 1948)
Musices Genus (© 1981)
Text: Composer
Publisher: London: Boosey & Hawkes
For: Female voice (soprano) (upright piano), alto flute (crotale), clarinet in B^b (bass clarinet and crotale), violin (viola and crotale), viola (crotale), cello (crotale), acoustic guitar (electric guitar and banjo), electric organ (celesta and crotale), 3 buskers [itinerant entertainers] (ukulele, clarinet in B^b, and bass drum/cymbals), and percussion.
Percussion instrumentation: Lion's roar, low tam-tam, small bell tree, 9 tuned gongs (a - g′), 2 hi-hat cymbals, bass drums with pedal, 9 small tuned drums ($e^{b\prime}$ - d″), vibraphone, marimba, police whistle, and water gongs.
Difficulty: Voice: difficult; Instruments: difficult
Vocal range: a - e‴ plus highest note possible
Language: Latin and English
Comments: Theatrical effects required. Singer must play piano at times. Use of quartertones, vocal effects, and pitch approximations.

197

Lombardi, Luca (b. 1945)
Tui-Gesänge (1977)
I. Eröffnung
II. Behauste und Unbehauste
III. Wie wird man tui
IV. Von Generation zu Generation
V. Rückversicherung
VI. Sonett von den Ungleichheiten
VII. Sonett von den Hemmenden Begierden
VIII. Von der Potenz Früher und Heute
IX. Rechtspflege
X. Lob, Lohn, und Preis
XI. Kunst des Unterscheidens
XII. Tui-Kreislauf
Text: Albrecht Betz
Publisher: Milan: Suvini Zerboni S. 8397 Z.
For: Soprano, flute (piccolo and alto flute), clarinet in B^b (bass clarinet and contrabass clarinet), piano, violin, and cello.
Difficulty: Voice: very difficult; Instruments: difficult
Vocal range: g - b″
Language: German (with Italian translation)

198

Lorenzini, Danilo
Tre liriche Han (1970)

I. La chiara luna...
II. Lungi brilla...
III. Passando il fiume...

Text: Giorgia Valensin
Publisher: Milan: Suvini Zerboni S.7256Z.
For: Soprano, flute, vibraphone (triangle, medium suspended cymbal, tambourine), celesta, harp, violin I, violin II, viola, and cello.
Difficulty: Voice: moderately difficult; Instruments: moderately difficult
Vocal range: c′ - g″
Language: Italian
Duration: 7:00

199

Lothar, Mark (1902-1985)

Acht Haiku, Op. 85 (1976)

I. Verzauberter Garten
II. Spiel des Windes
III. Schauen wir nach den Sternen
IV. Der Mond
V. Und wieder kreisen hoch die Vögel
VI. Der Läufer
VII. Das Versöhnliche
VIII. Gehen und Kommen

Text: Günther Klinge
Publisher: Winterthur, Switzerland: Amadeus GM697
For: Soprano, flute, viola, piano, and percussion.
Percussion instrumentation: vibraphone, finger cymbal, 2 triangles (small and medium), glockenspiel, xylophone, three cymbals (high, medium, low), 4 bongos, and 3 tom-toms (high, medium, low).
Difficulty: Voice: difficult; Instruments: difficult
Vocal range: d♯′ - a″
Language: German

200

Lumsdaine, David (b. 1931)

Annotations of Auschwitz (1964, rev. 1970)

Text: Peter Porter
Publisher: Australia: Universal Edition UE 29040A
For: Soprano, flute (bass flute), trumpet in C, horn, violin, cello, and piano.
Difficulty: Voice: difficult; Instruments: difficult
Vocal range: f - b″
Language: Latin and English
Duration: 15:00
Comments: White score.

201

Lutyens, Elisabeth (1906-1983)

The Valley of Hatsu-Se, Op. 62 (1965)

I. Fuyu-Komori (Anonymous 6th cent. A.D.)
II. Uguisu no (Nakatsukasa)
III. Koye tayezu (Fujiwara No Okikaze)
IV. Hana wa ne ni (Emperor Sutoku)
V. Nake ya, nake (Sone Yoshitada)
VI. Usu-zumi ni (Tsumori Kunimoto)
VII. Awa-yuki no (Yakamochi)
VIII. Futari-yukedo (Princess Daihaku)

Publisher: London: Olivan
For: Soprano, flute, clarinet in B♭, piano, and cello.

Difficulty: Voice: very difficult; Instruments: difficult
Vocal range: g# - c#‴
Language: Japanese (Romanized); English translation by Eiko Nakamura
Duration: 10:00
Comments: Score is difficult to read (composer's autograph); note extreme range.

202
McNeil, Jan Pfischner (b. 1945)
Three Preludes to the Aureate Earth (1974)
I. Come, fill the cup
II. I sometimes think
III. Into this universe
Text: The Rubaiyat of Omar Khayyam (translation Edward FitzGerald)
Publisher: New York: Carl Fischer (Carl Fischer Facsimile Edition)
For: Soprano and 6 instruments (any C, B♭, or F instruments).
Difficulty: Voice: difficult; Instruments: difficult
Vocal range: b - a″
Language: English
Duration: 16:30
Comments: Whole piece is aleatoric.

203
McTee, Cindy (b. 1953)
Songs of Spring and the Moon (1983)
Text: Sappho
Publisher: Saint Louis: Norruth Music. Sole Agent: Saint Louis: MMB Music
For: Soprano, flute (wine glass), clarinet in B♭ (wine glass), piano, violin (crotales C#, E♭, G♭, A), and percussion (2 players).
Percussion instrumentation: (I) vibraphone (double bass bow), tubular bells, and medium and large suspended cymbals; (II) medium and large suspended cymbals, glockenspiel, tubular bells (shared with Percussion I), autoharp, tambourine, triangle, and timbale.
Difficulty: Voice: difficult; Instruments: difficult
Vocal range: c′ - b″
Language: English
Duration: 11:00

204
Manneke, Daan (b. 1939)
Chant and Madrigal (1983)
I. Prelude
II. Song
III. Sinfonia
IV. Chant and Madrigal
V. Interlude with air
VI. Epitaph (in memoriam Joris Schram)
Text: James Joyce
Publisher: Amsterdam: Donemus
For: Soprano, flute, oboe, clarinet in B♭, bassoon, horn, piano, 2 violins, viola, cello, and double bass.
Difficulty: Voice: difficult; Instruments: difficult
Vocal range: g# - g″
Language: English
Duration: 3:15
Comments: Use of Sprechstimme. "Epitaph" is published as a separate score.

205
MANNEKE, DAAN (B. 1939)
Song (1983)
There's Music along the River
Text: James Joyce
Publisher: Amsterdam: Donemus
For: Soprano, flute, clarinet in B^b, piano, violin, cello, and double bass.
Difficulty: Voice: difficult; Instruments: difficult
Vocal range: b^b - $a^{b''}$
Language: English
Duration: 5:30

206
MAROS, RUDOLF (B. 1917)
Két Sirató (1963)
I. Öles bokrok közt lépeget...
II. Az idök folyama...
Text: Sándor Weöres
Publisher: Budapest: Editio Musica Z.4557
For: Soprano, alto flute, harp, piano, and percussion (2 players).
Percussion instrumentation: (I) bass drum, suspended cymbals, bell, xylophone, 2 bongos, soprano triangle, maracas, and metal blocks 1 & 2; (II) tam-tam 1 & 2, vibraphone, alto triangle, suspended cymbals, and metal blocks 3 & 4.
Difficulty: Voice: difficult; Instruments: moderately difficult
Vocal range: a - d^b
Language: Hungarian (German translation by Imre Ormay provided for performance)

207
MAROS, RUDOLF (B. 1917)
Strófák (Strophes) (1977)
Text: György Fütó
Publisher: New York: Southern
For: Voice (soprano or tenor), vibraphone, and harp.
Difficulty: Voice: difficult; Instruments: difficult
Vocal range: e' - $a^{b''}$
Language: Hungarian

208
MATSUDAIRA, YORITSUNÈ (B. 1907)
Roei Jisei (© 1974)
Text: Composer
Publisher: Milan: Suvini Zerboni S.7146Z.
For: Voice (soprano), flute, oboe, whip, marimba, vibraphone, harp, piano, and four violins.
Difficulty: Voice: difficult; Instruments: difficult
Vocal range: b^b - $b^{b''}$
Language: Japanese
Comments: Vocal effects required, especially changing speed of vibrato. Text is spread out vowel by vowel so that much of the text is unintelligible.

209
MAW, NICHOLAS (B. 1935)
La Vita Nuova (© 1979)
I. Sonetto (Guido Cavalcanti)
II. Madrigale (Matteo Boiardo)
III. Tacciono i boschi (Torquato Tasso)
IV. Madrigale (Michelangelo)
V. Il sogno (Gaspara Stampa)
Publisher: London: Boosey & Hawkes 20493
For: Soprano, flute (piccolo), oboe (English horn), clarinet in B^b, horn, harp, 2 violins, viola, and cello.

Difficulty: Voice: very difficult; Instruments: difficult
Vocal range: c′ - c‴
Language: Italian with English translation
Duration: 26:00

210
Mayer, William (b. 1925)
Eight Miniatures (1967)
I. Outrageous Love (composer)
II. Deeply Down (Elizabeth Aleinikoff)
III. Land of Dead Dreams (Alfred Noyes)
IV. Fireworks: Syllables and Sounds (composer)
V. Prophetic Soul (Dorothy Parker)
VI. Isn't There Some Mistake? (composer)
VII. "...for no man" (composer)
VIII. Résumé (Dorothy Parker)
Publisher: Bryn Mawr, PA: Theodore Presser 416-41096
For: Soprano, flute (piccolo), trumpet in C, violin, cello, harmonium, and percussion.
Percussion instrumentation: xylophone, glockenspiel, gong, timpani, bass drum, bongos, castanets, triangle, snare drum, ratchet, sandpaper blocks, and suspended cymbal.
Difficulty: Voice: difficult; Instruments: difficult
Vocal range: c′ - b^{b}″
Language: English
Duration: 6:00

211
Mayer, William (b. 1925)
Two News Items (1972)
I. Hastily formed Contemporary Music Ensemble reveals Origins
II. Distraught Soprano undergoes unfortunate Transformation
Text: Composer
Publisher: Bryn Mawr, PA: Theodore Presser 416-41095
For: Soprano, flute, piccolo, trumpet in C, violin, cello, piano, and percussion.
Percussion instrumentation: snare drum, timpani, cymbals, glockenspiel, bass drum, xylophone, and vibraphone.
Difficulty: Voice: difficult; Instruments: difficult
Vocal range: a - $a^{\#}$″
Language: English
Duration: 4:00

212
Mellers, Wilfrid (b. 1914)
Rose of May (1964)
I. Invocation
II. Ballad I
III. Ballad II
IV. Ballad III
Text: William Shakespeare
Publisher: London: Novello
For: Soprano, speaker, flute, clarinet in B^{b}, and string quartet.
Difficulty: Voice: difficult; Instruments: difficult
Vocal range: g - b^{b}″
Language: English

213
Métral, Pierre
Caprisme (1968)
Introduction
I. Pour le "Legato"
Interlude I

II. Pour le "Staccato"
Interlude II
III. Pour les "Intervalles"

Publisher: Darmstadt: Tonos 7238

For: Soprano, guitar, and 3 percussionists.

Percussion instrumentation: (I) vibraphone, 2 bongos, 4 woodblocks, and castanet; (II) vibraphone, marimba, 2 timbalettes, woodblock, and güiro; (III) 4 tom-toms, 3 cymbals, cowbells, 2 timbalettes, claves, maracas, 2 tumbas, and 3 tam-tams.

Difficulty: Voice: extremely difficult; Instruments: very difficult

Vocal range: f# - d‴

Language: none

Comments: Apparently singer is to choose phoneme on which to sing.

214

Meyer, Krzysztof (b. 1943)

Liryki (Lyrics), Op. 9 (1963)

I. Pieśni rezygnaji i zapreczenia (Songs of Resignation and Denial) (Jadwiga Szczeblowska)
II. Quartettino, Op. 16 (Julian Tuwim)
III. 5 utworów kameralnych (5 Chamber Pieces) (no text), Op. 18

Publisher: Cracow: P W M 6798 © 1969

For: Soprano, violin, piano, flute, cello, clarinet in B^b, and viola.

Difficulty: Voice: difficult; Instruments: difficult

Vocal range: a^b - b^{b}″

Language: Polish, phonemes, and humming sounds.

Duration: 27:00

Comments: Quartettino is published separately. White score. Some graphic notation.

215

Mihalovici, Marcel (1898-1985)

Delie, Op. 107 (1978)

Text: Maurice Scève

Publisher: Paris: Radio France

For: Lyric soprano, flute, clarinet in B^b (bass clarinet), piano (celesta), viola, cello, and percussion (2 players).

Percussion instrumentation: vibraphone, marimba, glockenspiel, xylophone, low gong, 3 suspended cymbals, 4 Chinese muyus, woodblock, snare drum, field drum, triangle, and low tam-tam.

Difficulty: Voice: very difficult; Instruments: difficult

Vocal range: b^b - c#

Language: French

Duration: 20:00

216

Milhaud, Darius (1892-1974)

Adieu: Cantata (1964)

Text: Arthur Rimbaud *Extrait d'une saison en enfer*

Publisher: Philadelphia: Elkan-Vogel © 1965

For: Voice (soprano or tenor), flute, viola, and harp.

Difficulty: Voice: moderately difficult; Instruments: moderately difficult

Vocal range: b - a″

Language: English

Duration: 9:00

217

Miller, Edward Jay (b. 1930)

Bashō Songs (1961)

I. Part One (Grave mound, shake too!)
II. Part Two (Wake Up! Wake Up!)

Text: Matsuo Bashō
Publisher: New York: Music for Percussion E-44-11 © 1967
For: Soprano and percussion (3 players).
Percussion instrumentation: (I) bells, maracas, and 4 temple blocks (low to high); (II) vibraphone; (III) xylophone, 4 suspended cymbals (low to high), and gong.
Difficulty: Voice: difficult; Instruments: moderately difficult
Vocal range: b - b″
Language: English

218

Miroglio, Francis (b. 1924)

Magies (© 1963)

Text: Composer
Publisher: Milan: Suvini Zerboni S.6177Z.
For: Soprano, violin, flute, oboe, viola, cello, double bass, alto saxophone, horn, and percussion (one player).
Percussion instrumentation: snare drum, large field drum, cymbal, gong, woodblocks, maracas, whip, tambourine, güiro, Swanee whistle, and glockenspiel.
Difficulty: Voice: difficult; Instruments: difficult
Vocal range: d′ - $d^{b'''}$
Language: French

219

Mohler, Philipp (1908-1982)

Cantata Domestica (© 1963)

I. Preludio
II. Lyrisches Intermezzo
III. Abendlied
IV. Tanzlied

Text: Fritz Brunner
Publisher: Cologne: Hans Gerig H 410 G
For: Voice (soprano or tenor), two violins, and cello.
Difficulty: Voice: moderate; Instruments: moderate
Vocal range: d′ - a″
Language: German
Duration: 16:30

220

Monod, Jacques-Louis (b. 1927)

Cantus contra cantum I (1968, rev. 1980)

I. Introduction (voice tacet)
II. Imbécile Habitant (Paul Éluard)
III. Rue Trésorière (Jean Sénac)
IV. Les Vainquers d'hier Périront (Paul Éluard)
V. Paris Jusqu'à l'aube (Jean Sénac)
VI. Belle et Ressemblante (Paul Éluard)

Publisher: Hillsdale, NY: Boelke-Bomart 1972 B-B18
For: Voice (soprano), flute, oboe, bass clarinet (contrabass clarinet), bassoon, horn, tuba, mandolin, guitar, harp, piano, marimba (b‴ suspended crotale), vibraphone (piccolo), medium and large timpani (bass drum)

(A^{b} gong), violin, and five string double bass.
Difficulty: Voice: difficult; Instruments: moderate
Vocal range: g - c$^{\#'''}$
Language: French
Duration: 9:00
Comments: Read prefatory notes and glossary.

221
Morricone, Ennio (b. 1928)
Da molto lontano (© 1973)
Text: none
Publisher: Paris: Salbert EAS17137
For: Soprano, flute, viola, vibraphone (marimba), harp, and percussion.
Percussion instrumentation: glass chime, wood chime, and marimbula [Afro-Cuban instrument with plucked tongues of metal or wood with a wooden resonator, larger than the mbira (sansa)].
Difficulty: Voice: difficult; Instruments: moderate
Vocal range: a - d$^{b'''}$
Language: phonemes
Comments: The majority of the piece has a very high tessitura. Two (2) other soprano parts serve as an accompaniment in a short section of the piece with same approximate range.

222
Moss, Lawrence (b. 1927)
Unseen Leaves: A Theatrepiece (1975)
I. Goodbye my Fancy
II. Song of Myself
Text: Walt Whitman
Publisher: New York: Carl Fischer
Series: Carl Fischer Facsimile Edition
For: Soprano, oboe, 2 tapes, slide projections, and 3 spotlights.
Difficulty: Voice: very difficult; Instruments: very difficult
Vocal range: b - d'''
Language: English
Duration: 15:00
Comments: A multimedia work; requires 1 conductor, 1 operator of tape decks, 1 operator of slide projectors, and 1 operator of 3 spotlights.

223
Moszumańska-Nazar, Krystyna (b. 1924)
Bel canto (1972)
Text: none
Publisher: Cracow: P W M 7710
For: Soprano, celesta, and percussion (1 player).
Percussion instrumentation: bell, 3 crotales, 2 suspended cymbals, gong, cog rattle, maracas, 4 temple blocks, snare drum, and 2 tom-toms.
Difficulty: Voice: difficult; Instruments: moderately difficult
Vocal range: c$^{\#'}$ - b$^{b''}$
Language: phonemes
Duration: 12:00
Comments: White score; many pitches are to be approximated.

224
Myers, Theldon
Born of the East (© 1986)
I. Look to the Rose
II. Alas! That Spring
III. Into this Universe
IV. The Brave Music
V. Ah, Morn of my Delight

Publisher: Dorn Publications
For: Soprano, alto saxophone, and piano.
Difficulty: Voice: *; Instruments: *
Vocal range: *
Language: English
Duration: *
*Comments: Score not examined.

225
Nelhybel, Vaclav (b. 1919)
Take Time (© 1978)
Text: Paraphrase of anonymous 17th century
Publisher: Dobbs Ferry, NY: General Music
For: Voice (soprano or tenor), flute, and piano.
Difficulty: Voice: moderately difficult; Instruments: moderate
Vocal range: e′ - c‴
Language: English

226
Nielsen, Svend (b. 1937)
Chamber Cantata (1975)
I. Lecture on Poetry
II. There she is!
III. Let's look at her Tonight
Text: Jørgen Leth
Publisher: Copenhagen: Wilhelm Hansen 4323
For: Soprano, flute, vibraphone, crotales, cymbals, guitar, clarinet in B^b, violin, cello, electric organ (or other keyboard instrument), and tape.
Difficulty: Voice: difficult; Instruments: difficult
Vocal range: e′ - b″
Language: Danish (English translation provided for performance)
Duration: 20:00
Comments: Some stage directions; speaking parts for instrumentalists.

227
Nilsson, Bo (b. 1937)
Flöten aus der Einsamkeit (1976)
I. Ich weiss, was da im Park umherirrt = (Jag vet vat som irrar i parken)
II. Rostrot schimmert der Mond = (En roströ mänes skimmer)
Text: Bertil Malmberg
Publisher: Stockholm: Edition Reimers EK47
For: Soprano, piccolo (flute and alto flute), oboe (English horn), bassoon, piano (celesta), harp, violin, viola, cello, and percussion (2 players).
Percussion instrumentation: 2 sizzle cymbals, 2 Chinese tam-tams, and Thailand gongs.
Difficulty: Voice: very difficult; Instruments: difficult
Vocal range: d′ - e‴
Language: Swedish; German translation by Ilmar Laadan.
Duration: 8:30
Comments: Some speaking parts.

228
Nobre, Marlos (b. 1939)
Ukrinmakrinkrin, Op. 17 (1967)
I. Patú Paité
II. Tapipó Xennúnpri
III. Karé Xubêgo
Text: Xucurú Indian poems
Publisher: Washington D.C.: Pan American Union 57-26

For: Soprano, piccolo, oboe, horn, and piano.
Difficulty: Voice: difficult; Instruments: difficult
Vocal range: a - b″
Language: Xucurú Indian dialect. Translations in Portuguese and English provided, but the piece is to be sung in Xucurú.

229
Novák, Jan (b. 1921)
Mimus magicus (1969)
Text: Virgil from *Bucolica* VIII: 64-109
Publisher: Padua: G. Zanibon G. 5183Z
For: Voice (soprano or tenor), clarinet in B^b, and piano.
Difficulty: Voice: difficult; Instruments: difficult
Vocal range: c′ - $c^{b\prime\prime\prime}$
Language: Latin
Duration: 15:00

230
Nystedt, Knut (b. 1915)
The Moment, Op. 52 (1962)
Text: Kathleen Raine
Publisher: New York: Associated AMP-6741-16
For: Soprano, celesta, vibraphone, and percussion (1 or 2 players).
Percussion instrumentation: 3 suspended cymbals, triangle, tamtam, and 2 gongs (medium and small).
Difficulty: Voice: moderately difficult; Instruments: moderate
Vocal range: a - $b^{b\prime\prime}$
Language: English, with Norwegian translation
Duration: 8:00

231
Ogihara, Toshitsugu (b. 1910)
Six Poems of Eiko Sadamatsu (1970)
Text: Eiko Sadamatsu
Publisher: Tokyo: Japan Federation of Composers
For: Soprano, clarinet in B^b, cello, and piano.
Difficulty: Voice: moderately difficult; Instruments: moderately difficult
Vocal range: $c^{\#\prime}$ - b″
Language: Japanese; not transliterated
Comments: All six poems are in Japanese characters.

232
Ohana, Maurice (b. 1914)
Sibylle (1968)
Text: none
Publisher: Paris: Salbert M.C.546
For: Soprano, percussion, and tape.
Percussion instrumentation: 2 pairs crotales, suspended cymbal, suspended Chinese cymbal (played by the singer), crotales, vibraphone, 3 woodblocks, 3 temple blocks, 1 log drum, 1 pair of claves, 2 pairs maracas, 1 güiro, bamboo chimes, tambourine, snare drum, tom-tom, 2 bongos, 2 m'tumbas, 4 Chinese cymbals (2 suspended), and 4 cymbals (2 suspended).
Difficulty: Voice: very difficult; Instruments: difficult
Vocal range: g - c‴
Language: phonemes
Duration: 17:00

233
Olive, Vivienne (b. 1950)
A Thing which fades with no Outward Sign (1985)
Text: Edith Sitwell/Komachi Ono (Ono no Komachi)
Publisher: Darmstadt: Tonos
For: Soprano, bass flute, guitar and percussion.
Percussion instrumentation: 3 woodblocks, 4 temple bells, 4 temple blocks, 4 bongos, 4 tom-toms, 3 triangles, 2 crystales, 2 cymbals, 2 temple gongs, and 2 tam-tams.
Difficulty: Voice: difficult; Instruments: difficult
Vocal range: a - a″
Language: English
Duration: 7:30

234
Oliveira, Willy Corréa de (b. 1938)
Exit (1978)
Text: Haroldo de Campos
Publisher: São Paulo: Editora Novas Metas; 77004
For: Soprano and percussion (several players).
Percussion instrumentation: glockenspiel, vibraphone, marimba, cow's collar, jingles, triangles (5 - low to high), suspended cymbals (4 - low to high), tam-tam (large), 5 temple blocks (low to high), bullroarer, tambourine, 2 bongos, 2 congas, 2 snare drums, 3 tom-toms, 2 bass drums, 5 timpani, rattle, 7 whistles of different pitches, and common primitive flute.
Difficulty: Voice: extremely difficult; Instruments: very difficult
Vocal range: c#′ - b♭″
Language: Portuguese
Comments: Use of quarter tones for singer.

235
Oliveira, Willy Corréa de (b. 1938)
Materiales (1980)
Text: Héctor Olea
Publisher: São Paulo: Editora Novas Metas 77005
For: Soprano and percussion.
Percussion instrumentation: crotales, glockenspiel, xylophone, tubular bells, 4 suspended cymbals (low to high), cymbal submerged in water, 2 Jew's harps (amplified), temple blocks, woodblocks, amplified elastic band, Japanese shell chimes, and 4 timpani.
Difficulty: Voice: very difficult; Instruments: very difficult
Vocal range: c′ - b♭″
Language: Spanish
Comments: Read performance instructions.

236
Oliveira, Willy Corréa de (b. 1938)
Memos (1977)
Text: Augusto de Campos
Publisher: São Paulo: MCA do Brasil Editora Musical: MCA 3019
For: Soprano and percussion (several players).
Percussion instrumentation: xylophone, vibraphones, cow's collar, finger cymbal, jingles, cowbells (2 sets of 7 each, low to high), triangles (set of 4 low to high), suspended cymbals (set of 3 low, medium, high), large tam-tam, temple blocks (set of 5 low to high), claves (set

of 5 low to high), woodblocks (set of 5 low to high), wood chimes, jaw bone, tea kettle, maracas, bull roarer (set of 5), tambourine, bongos (normal set with a high little drum), congas (set of 3 low, medium, high), snare drum, tenor drum, tom-toms (set of 3 low, medium, high), 4 timpani, and bass drum.
Difficulty: Voice: very difficult; Instruments: difficult
Vocal range: $g^{\#\prime}$ - b''
Language: Portuguese
Comments: Use of some graphic notation; aleatoric sections; approximation of pitches by singer.

237

OLKUŚNIK, JOACHIM (B. 1927)

Chamber Musik (1964)

I. Allegretto
II. Scherzando
III. Adagio Svelto

Text: none
Publisher: Warsaw: Edycja Muzyczna
For: Soprano, flute, viola, cello, vibraphone, and piano.
Difficulty: Voice: difficult; Instruments: difficult
Vocal range: c' - c'''
Language: None (singer chooses phonemes)

238

ORBÁN, GYÖRGY (B. 1947)

Szoprán-Klarinét Kettős (1979)
(Duo for Soprano and Clarinet)

I. Találós Kérdés (Conundrum)
II. Ráolvasás Igézetre (Incantation against Witchery)
III. Balladarészlet és Finnugor Madárdaltöredék (Fragment from a Ballad and Finno-Ugrïan Bird-Call Remnants)

Publisher: Budapest: Editio Musica Z.12075
For: Soprano and clarinet in B^b.
Difficulty: Voice: very difficult; Instrument: extremely difficult
Vocal range: $a^{\#}$ - b''
Language: Hungarian or English

239

OSBORNE, NIGEL (B. 1948)

Vienna. Zurich. Constance. (1977)

Text: Dylan Thomas
Publisher: Totowa, NJ: Universal Edition. Sole Agent: European American Music
For: Soprano, cello, 2 clarinets in B^b, violin, and percussion.
Percussion instrumentation: temple blocks, African wood drum, 2 cymbals, gong, tam-tam, and flexatone.
Difficulty: Voice: difficult; Instruments: difficult
Vocal range: a - c'''
Language: English
Comments: Some improvisatory sections; extended speaking part for soprano.

240

PABLO, LUIS DE (B. 1930)

El Manantial (1982)

Text: Jorge Guillén
Publisher: Milan: Suvini Zerboni S 9085Z.
For: Soprano, flute, celesta, harp, violin I, violin II, and percussion.
Percussion instrumentation: crotales, vibraphone, 4 bongos, and marimba.

Difficulty: Voice: difficult; Instruments: difficult
Vocal range: g - g″
Language: Phonemes and Spanish
Duration: 8:00

241
PABLO, LUIS DE (B. 1930)
Glosa, Op. 10 (1961)
Text: Luis de Góngora y Argote
Publisher: Darmstadt: Tonos 7203
For: Soprano, 2 horns, vibraphone, and piano.
Difficulty: Voice: difficult; Instruments: difficult
Vocal range: d′ - $b^{b''}$
Language: Spanish
Duration: 7:00
Comments: White score.

242
PAŁŁASZ, EDWARD (B. 1936)
Fragments to Sappho's Texts (1967)
I. To Aphrodite
II. ...of all the very most has come
III. ...the heart completely
IV. ...night's twilight black eyes get
Text: Sappho Polish version by Janina Brzostowska, English version by Halszka Szoldrska
Publisher: Cracow: P W M 7456
For: Soprano, flute, harp, viola, and percussion (2 players).
Percussion instrumentation: not given.
Difficulty: Voice: difficult; Instruments: difficult
Vocal range: c′ - b″
Language: Polish (English translation provided for performance)
Duration: 9:00
Comments: White score.

243
PASATIERI, THOMAS (B. 1945)
Far from Love (1974)
Text: Emily Dickinson
Publisher: Melville, NY: Belwin-Mills EL 2634
For: Soprano, clarinet in B^b, violin, cello, and piano.
Difficulty: Voice: difficult; Instruments: difficult
Vocal range: b - b″
Language: English
Duration: 22:00

244
PAYNE, ANTHONY (B. 1936)
The World's Winter (1976)
Text: Alfred Lord Tennyson
Publisher: London: Chester/Wilhelm Hansen JWC 55137
For: Soprano, flute (piccolo), oboe, clarinet in B^b (clarinet in E^b and bass clarinet), horn, harp, violin, viola, and cello.
Difficulty: Voice: very difficult; Instruments: difficult
Vocal range: $g^{\#}$ - $b^{b''}$
Language: English
Duration: 16:00

245
PECK, RUSSELL (B. 1945)
Automobile (1965)
I. Straight
II. Mobile
Text: Composer
Publisher: New York: Carl Fischer
For: Soprano, flute, double bass, and percussion.
Percussion instrumentation: vibraphone, glockenspiel, 4 woodblocks, 3 tom-toms, snare drum,

bass drum with foot pedal, suspended cymbals, and tam-tam.
Difficulty: Voice: difficult; Instruments: difficult
Vocal range: a - g#″ (also lowest and highest note possible)
Language: English
Comments: Movement II is aleatoric; follow instructions carefully.

246
Penherski, Zbigniew (b. 1935)
3 Recitativi (1963)
I. Dotknięcie bezimiennych dni (The touch of the nameless days)
II. Muzyka odległego już lata (The music of the far-away summer)
III. Zbłąkane ptaki (Stray birds)
Text: Rabindranath Tagore
Publisher: Warsaw: Wydawnictwo Muzyczne Agencji Autorskiej
For: Soprano, piano, and percussion (5 timpani and cymbal).
Difficulty: Voice: difficult; Instruments: moderate
Vocal range: d#′ - a″ (and highest note possible)
Language: Polish or English
Duration: 6:00

247
Perera, Ronald (b. 1941)
Children of the Sun (1978)
I. The Sun's Travels
II. Rain
III. The Swing
IV. At the Sea-Side
V. Auntie's Skirts
VI. Happy Thought
VII. Summer Sun
Text: Robert Louis Stevenson
Publisher: Boston: E. C. Schirmer E.C.S. 2613
Series: E.C.S. Fascimile Series, No. 167
For: Soprano, horn, and piano.
Difficulty: Voice: moderately difficult; Instruments: moderately difficult
Vocal range: c′ - a″
Language: English
Duration: 16:00
Comments: Use of Sprechstimme.

248
Perkowski, Piotr (1901-1990)
Pieśni Safony (1967) (Poems from Sappho)
I. Nie będę zapomniana (I shall not be forgotten)
II. Dziesięciu szewców (The ten shoe makers)
III. Jak hiacynt...(Like a hyacinth...)
IV. Jest bogiem...(Godlike the man...)
V. Adonis umiera (Dying Adonis)
Text: Sappho
Publisher: Cracow: P W M 7834
For: Soprano, 2 flutes, and 2 clarinets in B♭.
Difficulty: Voice: difficult; Instruments: difficult
Vocal range: g - a♭″
Language: Polish (English translation by Ewa Perkowska provided for performance)

249
Pert, Morris (b. 1947)
Epitaphs, Op. 6 (© 1977)
I. The Earth goeth on the Earth (Melrose Abbey, Scotland)

II. Hymnus circa Exsequias Defuncti (Prudentius)
III. Two Epitaphs from Arbroath Abbey (1882-1847) (Arbroath Abbey, Scotland)
IV. Colours of Rain and Iron (Salvatore Quasimodo Eng. translation by Jack Bevan)

Publisher: London: Josef Weinberger
For: Soprano, piano, and percussion (1 player).
Percussion instrumentation: timpani, vibraphone, glockenspiel, tubular bells, crotales, 2 suspended cymbals (large and medium), 36 inch tam-tam, and wind chimes (brass or glass).
Difficulty: Voice: moderate; Instruments: moderate
Vocal range: d′ - g″
Language: English (1, 3-4) and Latin (2)
Duration: 14:00

250
Pezzati, Romano (b. 1939)
Correspondences (1972)
Text: Charles Baudelaire
Publisher: Milan: Suvini Zerboni S.7683Z.
For: Soprano, flute, clarinet in B^b, trombone or bass clarinet, piano, violin, viola, and double bass.
Difficulty: Voice: very difficult; Instruments: difficult
Vocal range: b - b″
Language: French
Duration: 13:00
Comments: Some graphic notation, pitch approximations, parlando.

251
Pezzati, Romano (b. 1939)
Figure (1975)
Text: none
Publisher: Milan: Suvini Zerboni S.8299Z.
For: Soprano, 2 violins, and viola.
Difficulty: Voice: moderately difficult; Instruments: moderate
Vocal range: d′ - a″
Language: phonemes

252
Pezzati, Romano (b. 1939)
Nel Lontano (1975)
Text: none
Publisher: Milan: Suvini Zerboni S.8157Z.
For: Soprano, violin, viola, cello, and piano.
Difficulty: Voice: moderately difficult; Instruments: moderately difficult
Vocal range: b - b^{b}″
Language: none

253
Phillips, Burrill (1907-1988)
Letters from Italy Hill: Landscape with Figure (1983)
I. Summer-Fall
II. From a Letter to Kathy
III. Winter
IV. For Vera
V. III Spring

Text: Alberta Phillips
Publisher: Berkeley, CA: Fallen Leaf Press
Series: Fallen Leaf Press Publications in Contemporary Music, No. 11
For: Soprano, flute, clarinet in B^b, 2 violins, viola, cello, and piano.

Difficulty: Voice: moderately; Instruments: moderately difficult
Vocal range: e^{b} - $a^{b''}$
Language: English

254
Piechowska, Alina (b. 1937)
Pie'sni Bilitis (1965)
I. Księżyc o niebeskich oczach
II. Ofiara dla bogini
III. Fletnia Pana
IV. Bilitis
Text: Pierre Louÿs (Polish translation by Leopold Staff)
Publisher: Warsaw: Edycja Muzyczna
For: Soprano, flute, piano, harp, and percussion (one player).
Percussion instrumentation: triangle, glockenspiel, vibraphone, suspended cymbals, tenor drum, and timpani.
Difficulty: Voice: very difficult; Instruments: difficult
Vocal range: c′ - $b^{b''}$
Language: French with singable Polish translation.

255
Pinkham, Daniel (b. 1923)
Letters from St. Paul (© 1971)
I. Wherefore seeing we also are... (Hebrews 12:1 and 2)
II. Who shall separate us... (Romans 8:35, 37, 38, 39)
III. Let the word of Christ... (Colossians 3:16)
IV. But of the times and the seasons... (I Thessalonians 5:1-6)
V. Rejoice in the Lord always... (Philippians 4:4-7)
VI. Now it is high time to awake... (Romans 13:11 and 12)
Publisher: Boston: E. C. Schirmer 142
For: High voice (soprano or tenor) and string octet.
Difficulty: Voice: moderately difficult; Instruments: moderately difficult
Vocal range: c′ - $a^{b''}$
Language: English

256
Pinkham, Daniel (b. 1923)
Now the Trumpet summons us Again (© 1964)
Text: John F. Kennedy, from the Inaugural Address.
Publisher: New York: Peters
For: Soprano or tenor, trumpet in B^{b}, 5 violins, viola, cello, double bass, and glockenspiel (or celesta).
Difficulty: Voice: moderately difficult; Instruments: moderately difficult
Vocal range: d′ - a″
Language: English
Comments: Also in versions for large orchestra and high voice with piano.

257
Pinkham, Daniel (b. 1923)
Two Motets (© 1971)
I. Non vos relinquam orphanos (John 14:18 and 28)
II. Te luis ante terminum (Latin hymn attributed to St. Ambrose)
Publisher: Boston: E. C. Schirmer 1997
Series: E.C.S. vocal music, No. 131
For: Soprano or tenor, flute, and guitar.

Difficulty: Voice: moderately difficult; Instruments: moderately difficult
Vocal range: c' - $b^{b''}$
Language: Latin with singable English translation.
Comments: First motet is for voice and flute only.

258
PLOG, ANTHONY (B. 1947)
Four Sierra Scenes (© 1976)
I. Mountains
II. Sunset
III. Temples
IV. Sunrise
Text: John Muir
Publisher: West Hollywood, CA: Brightstar Music Publications BMP66
For: Soprano and brass quintet (2 trumpets in C, horn, trombone, and bass trombone).
Difficulty: Voice: moderate; Instruments: moderate
Vocal range: g' - $g^{\#''}$
Language: English
Duration: 6:30

259
PRADO, ALMEIDA (B. 1943)
Lettre de Jérusalem (1973)
I. A caliga verunt...
II. Ecce lignum Crucis...
III. Sepulcrum Christi viventis...
Text: Job, The Gospels of John, Luke, Matthew, and Latin Hymns.
Publisher: Darmstadt: Tonos 10309
For: Dramatic soprano, piano, percussion, and narrator.
Percussion instrumentation: (I) tam-tam, suspended cymbals, whip, reco-reco, claves, and piano; (II) 4 timpani, 3 tomtoms (small, medium, large), bass drum, and piano; (III) vibraphone, xylophone, tubular bells, and piano.
Difficulty: Voice: difficult; Instruments: difficult
Vocal range: b plus lowest note possible - f''
Language: Latin, narration in French

260
PRESSER, WILLIAM (B. 1916)
Four Herrick Songs (1973)
I. To Daffodils
II. The Hag
III. An Epitaph upon a Child
IV. The Mad Maid's Song
Text: Robert Herrick
Publisher: Tenuto Publications. Sole Agent: Bryn Mawr, PA: Theodore Presser T257
For: Soprano, horn, and piano.
Difficulty: Voice: moderately difficult; Instruments: moderately difficult
Vocal range: b - b''
Language: English
Duration: 8:55

261
PTASZYŃSKA, MARTA (B. 1943)
Un grand sommeil noir (A great dark sleep) (1977)
Text: Paul Verlaine, English translation by Kate Flores
Publisher: Cracow: P.W.M.
For: Soprano, flute, and harp.
Difficulty: Voice: moderately difficult; Instruments: difficult
Vocal range: c' - $g^{b''}$
Language: French (sung) and English (recited in retrograde)

Duration: 8:00
Comments: White score.

262
Pütz, Edward
When We Dead Awaken (1974)
Text: Rudi Holzapfel
Publisher: Darmstadt: Tonos 7267
For: Soprano, flute, electric guitar, electric piano, double bass, and two percussionists.
Percussion instrumentation: cymbals, bongos, 3 tom-toms, vibraphone, snare drums, small cymbal, bass drum with foot pedal, glockenspiel, and triangle.
Difficulty: Voice: difficult; Instrument: difficult
Vocal range: c′ - b″
Language: English
Comments: Improvisatory section for percussion.

263
Read, Thomas (b. 1938)
Naming the Changes (1975) (Songs, Dances, and Interludes)
I. Snow Chant
II. Six Portraits
Text: T. Alan Broughton
Publisher: New York: Peters 66710
For: Soprano, flute, oboe, cello, piano (celesta), and percussion (2 players).
Percussion instrumentation: xylophone, vibraphone, large gong, 2 large woodblocks, bass drum, 4 timpani, and marimba.
Difficulty: Voice: very difficult; Instruments: difficult
Vocal range: b^{b} - c‴
Language: English
Duration: 26:00
Comments: Extensive instrumental interlude.

264
Regner, Hermann (b. 1928)
Drei Lieder (© 1982)
I. Rhodisches Kurrendelied (Wolfgang Schadewaldt)
II. Die Strafe der Götter (Alkman) (Wolfgang Schadewaldt)
III. Haus in Syrakus (Arthur Weigall)
Publisher: Wolfenbüttel: Möseler
For: Soprano, alto recorder, and guitar.
Difficulty: Voice: moderate; Instruments: moderately difficult
Vocal range: c′ - f″
Language: German

265
Reveyron, Joseph (b. 1917)
Le Chant des Noces (Bridal Song) (Hochzeitlied) (© 1966)
Text: Yehuda Halevy, French translation: Composer, English translation: Rachel Vernon, German translation: R.G. Wolfsohn
Publisher: Tel Aviv: Israeli Music Publications I.M.P. 219
For: Soprano or tenor, flute, harpsichord, triangle, and low and high tambourine.
Difficulty: Voice: difficult; Instruments: difficult
Vocal range: $e^{b\prime}$ - a″
Language: French with singable romanized Hebrew, French, and German versions.

266

Rhodes, Phillip (b. 1940)

Autumn Setting (1969)

I. Autumn Fragments
II. Prophecy
III. Remembrance/Reality

Text: Patricia V. Schneider
Publisher: New York: Peters 66472
For: Soprano, 2 violins, cello, and viola.
Difficulty: Voice: very difficult; Instruments: difficult
Vocal range: $f^{\#}$ - e'''
Language: English
Duration: 11:00
Comments: Note extreme range.

267

Riley, Dennis (b. 1943)

Five Songs on Japanese Haiku (1963)

I. Bashō: on the road to Nara
II. Buson: the spring sea
III. Bashō: the entrance of spring
IV. Shiki: letter and spirit
V. Hô-ô: in the meadow

Text: from Harold Stewart's translation of Haiku in *A Net of Fireflies* (C.E. Tuttle)
Publisher: New York: Peters 66137
For: Soprano, clarinet in A, violin, and cello.
Difficulty: Voice: difficult; Instruments: moderately difficult
Vocal range: a - a''
Language: English

268

Ringger, Rolf Urs (b. 1935)

Souvenirs de Capri (1977)

Text: Composer
Publisher: Zurich: Hug Musikverlag G.H.11164
For: Soprano, horn, 2 violins, 2 violas, and 2 cellos.
Difficulty: Voice: moderately difficult; Instruments: moderately difficult
Vocal range: c' - b^{b}''
Language: Italian, English, French (note: not different translations, but the text changes from language to language)
Duration: 17:00

269

Rochberg, George (b. 1918)

Blake Songs (1962)

I. Ah! Sunflower
II. Nurse's Song
III. The Fly
IV. The Sick Rose

Text: William Blake
Publisher: New York: Leeds Music
For: Soprano, flute, clarinet in B^{b} bass clarinet, celesta, harp, violin, viola, and cello.
Difficulty: Voice: difficult; Instruments: difficult
Vocal range: g - b^{b}''
Language: English
Duration: 12:00

270

Rochberg, George (b. 1918)

String Quartet No. 2 (1961)

Text: Rainer Maria Rilke, 9th Duino Elegy, translation by Harry Behn
Publisher: Bryn Mawr, PA: Theodore Presser 114-41063
For: Soprano and string quartet.
Difficulty: Voice: very difficult; Instruments: very difficult
Vocal range: g - c'''
Language: English
Duration: 28:00
Comments: White score.

271
Rojo, Jesús Villa
Apuntes para una realizacion Abierta (1975)
Text: The "LIM"
Publisher: Madrid: Editorial de Música Española Contemporanea
For: Soprano, clarinet in B^b, percussion, and piano.
Percussion instrumentation: gong, large tam-tam, vibraphone, and xylophone.
Difficulty: Voice: moderate; Instruments: moderately difficult.
Vocal Range: Extensive—from quite low to very high. (Actual pitches not notated.)
Language: Phonemes
Comments: Work is notated in symbols of the composer's invention. Vocal tone alterations are required. Piano is played on the inside of the instrument as well as on the keys.

272
Rorem, Ned (b. 1923)
Ariel (1971)
I. Words
II. Poppies in July
III. The Hanging Man
IV. Poppies in October
V. Lady Lazarus
Text: Sylvia Plath
Publisher: New York: Boosey & Hawkes BH.BK. 742
For: Soprano, clarinet in B^b, and piano.
Difficulty: Voice: difficult; Instruments: difficult
Vocal range: e^b (very brief, may be interpolated) - c‴ (held)
Language: English

273
Rorem, Ned (b. 1923)
Last Poems of Wallace Stevens (1972)
I. Not Ideas about the Thing but the Thing Itself
II. The River of Rivers in Connecticut
III. A Child Asleep in its own Life
IV. The Planet on the Table
V. The Dove in Spring
VI. Interlude (voice tacet)
VII. Of Mere Being
VIII. A Clear Day and no Memories
Text: Wallace Stevens
Publisher: New York: Boosey & Hawkes BH.BK.750
For: Voice (soprano or tenor), cello, and piano.
Difficulty: Voice: moderately difficult; Instruments: difficult
Vocal range: b - b″
Language: English
Duration: 24:00
Comments: "Of Mere Being" is unaccompanied.

274
Routh, Francis (b. 1927)
The Death of Iphigenia (1973, rev. 1978)
I. And winds, winds blew...
II. To that which must be he...
III. What came thereafter...
Text: Aeschylus translation by Gilbert Murray
Publisher: London: Redcliffe
For: Soprano, flute (piccolo), oboe, clarinet in B^b, horn, trumpet in C, trombone, piano, harp, vio-

lin, viola, cello, double bass, and percussion (one player).
Percussion instrumentation: bass drum and tom-toms (small, medium, large).
Difficulty: Voice: difficult; Instruments: difficult
Vocal range: b - g#″
Language: English
Duration: 15:00

275
Routh, Francis (b. 1927)
Vocalise, Op. 38 (1979)
Text: none
Publisher: London: Redcliffe
For: Soprano, clarinet in B♭, piano, violin, and cello.
Difficulty: Voice: very difficult; Instruments: difficult
Vocal range: c′ - c‴
Language: none (phonemes of singer's choosing)
Duration: 15:00
Comments: Facsimile of composer's manuscript is somewhat difficult to read.

276
Rovsing Olsen, Paul (1922-1982)
À l'inconnu, Op. 48 (1962)
Text: none
Publisher: Celle: Hermann Moeck E.M.Nr. 5022
For: Voice (soprano), harp, guitar, 5 violins, 3 violas, 2 cellos, and double bass.
Difficulty: Voice: very difficult; Instruments: very difficult
Vocal range: c′ - b″
Language: Phonemes
Duration: 6:40
Comments: Use of quarter tones; white score.

277
Rowland, David (b. 1939)
Roundelay (1979)
I. Introduction (voice tacet)
II. To the execution place...
III. Interlude (voice tacet)
IV. Stars fall to fetch
V. Interlude (voice tacet)
VI. Fair summer droops...
VII. Interlude (voice tacet)
VIII. And then he flew on her...
IX. (no text)
Text: Thomas Nashe
Publisher: Amsterdam: Donemus
For: Soprano, flute, clarinet in B♭, violin, viola, cello, piano, and percussion (one player).
Percussion instrumentation: vibraphone, xylophone, and suspended cymbal.
Difficulty: Voice: very difficult; Instruments: very difficult
Vocal range: c′ - b″
Language: English
Duration: 20:00
Comments: Some Sprechstimme.

278
Rudziński, Zbigniew (b. 1935)
Tutti e solo (1972)
Text: note: the title is the text
Publisher: Warsaw: Wydawnictwo Muzyczne Agencji Autorskiej
For: Soprano, piano, flute, and horn.
Difficulty: Voice: moderate; Instruments: difficult
Vocal range: c#′ - f#″
Language: Italian
Duration: 13:00

279
Ruiter, Wim de (b. 1949)
Four Songs (1983)

I. Introduction (voice tacet)
II. As Imperceptibly as Grief
III. In Winter in My Room
IV. There Are Two Mays
V. Answer July
VI. Coda

Text: Emily Dickinson
Publisher: Amsterdam: Donemus
For: Soprano, flute (piccolo), oboe, clarinet in B^b, bassoon, horn, piano, violin, viola, cello, and double bass.
Difficulty: Voice: very difficult; Instruments: difficult
Vocal range: b - c$^{\#'''}$
Language: English
Duration: 25:00

280

Saeverud, Ketil (Hvoslef) (b. 1939)

Kvartoni (1974)

Text: none
Publisher: Oslo: Norsk Musikforlag. Sole Agent: Wilhelm Hansen
For: Soprano, tenor recorder, guitar, and piano.
Difficulty: Voice: very difficult; Instruments: very difficult
Vocal range: c$'$ - d$'''$
Language: none
Duration: 10:00
Comments: Singer must select phonemes for most of song.

281

Saint-Marcoux, Micheline Coulombe (1938-1985)

Moments (1977)

Text: Composer
Publisher: Montreal: Les Éditions Québec-Musique EQM 112
For: Soprano, treble flute in G, viola, cello, and percussion.
Percussion instrumentation: (played by singer) two different sizzle cymbals, one small triangle, at least four high-pitched crotales or small cymbals, very small metal objects struck with metal rod, and glass chimes.
Difficulty: Voice: very difficult; Instruments: very difficult
Vocal range: g$^{\#}$ - d$^{b'''}$plus highest note possible
Language: French
Duration: 13:30
Comments: Requires certain theatrical effects including transparent masks and lighting instructions. Several vocal effects required. Some graphic notation.

282

Saint-Preux, Brigitte de

Concerto pour une Voix (© 1970)

Text: none
Publisher: Paris: Éditions Musicales Fantasia EMF463
For: Voice (soprano or tenor), violin I, violin II, viola, cello, double bass, harp, and piano.
Difficulty: Voice: moderately difficult; Instruments: moderate
Vocal range: c$'$ - b$^{b''}$
Language: no phonemes incidated

283

Salomon, Karel (1897-1974)

Elegy and Dance (Kinahumahol) (© 1963)

Text: Jeremiah 31
Publisher: Tel Aviv: Israeli Music Publications
For: Soprano (or oboe) and 2 flutes (or 2 violins).

Difficulty: Voice: very difficult; Instruments: moderately difficult
Vocal range: c′ - e^{b}‴
Language: Hebrew (English and German translations provided for performance)

284
Sapiejewski, Jerzy (b. 1945)
Requiem dla Eric Dolphy (© 1967)
Text: repetition of Eric Dolphy
Publisher: Warsaw: Przedstawicielstwo Wydawnictwo Polskich (P.W.P. manuscript series 483)
For: Voice (soprano), violin I, violin II, viola, cello, double bass, piano, and percussion.
Percussion instrumentation: not given except for tubular bells.
Difficulty: Voice: difficult; Instruments: moderately easy
Vocal range: g - d‴
Language: the only words are "Eric Dolphy"

285
Sáry, László (b. 1940)
Quartetto (1968)
Text: Sándor Weöres
Publisher: Budapest: Editio Musica Z.7712
For: Soprano, flute, violin, and Hungarian dulcimer.
Difficulty: Voice: very difficult; Instruments: very difficult
Vocal range: c′ - b″
Language: Hungarian
Comments: Rhythmic and pitch difficulties.

286
Saxton, Robert (b. 1953)
Éloge (1980)
Text: Jules Supervielle, Saint-John Perse
Publisher: London: Chester © 1988 JWC 55556
For: Soprano, flute, oboe, clarinet in B^{b}, horn, piano, and string quartet.
Difficulty: Voice: difficult; Instruments: difficult
Vocal range: d′ - b^{b}″
Language: French
Duration: 13:00

287
Saxton, Robert (b. 1953)
What Does the Song hope for? (1974)
I. Orpheus
II. Our Bias
Text: W. H. Auden
Publisher: London: Chester J.W.C. 55125
For: Soprano, flute, oboe, clarinet in B^{b}, piano, violin, viola, cello, and electronic tape.
Difficulty: Voice: very difficult; Instruments: very difficult
Vocal range: d^{b}′ - b^{b}″
Language: English
Duration: 10:00

288
Schafer, R. Murray (b. 1933)
Enchantress (1971)
Text: from fragments of poems by Sappho
Publisher: Toronto: Berandol Music BER 1739
For: Soprano, exotic flute, and eight cellos.
Difficulty: Voice: difficult; Instruments: difficult
Vocal range: c′ - b^{b}″ (also highest note possible)

Language: Greek
Duration: 12:30
Comments: Use of quarter tones.

289
Schafer, R. Murray (b. 1933)
Five Studies on Texts by Prudentius (© 1965)
I. Adam and Eve
II. Moses has received the Law
III. The City of Bethlehem
IV. The Passion of John
V. The Revelation of Saint John
Text: Prudentius
Publisher: Toronto: BMI Canada V203S
For: Soprano and four flutes (alto flute, piccolo).
Difficulty: Voice: very difficult; Instruments: very difficult
Vocal range: a - $d^{b'''}$
Language: English

290
Schafer, R. Murray (b. 1933)
Hymn to Night: Chamber Version. An aria from Patria IV, Theseus. (1978)
Text: adapted from Novalis
Publisher: Toronto: Universal Edition Canada UE 16524
For: Soprano, flute, clarinet in B^b, trumpet in B^b, trombone, harp, piano (electric organ), violin, cello, double bass, and percussion (2 players).
Percussion instrumentation: suspended cymbal, Japanese tree bell, glockenspiel, triangle, large gong, tam-tam, marimba, crotales, timpani, vibraphone, tubular bells, sandpaper blocks, glass chimes, and maracas.
Difficulty: Voice: very difficult; Instruments: very difficult
Vocal range: b - c‴
Language: German, with English translation
Duration: 16:00
Comments: Voice at one point has a tape delay (see instructions in score).

291
Schäffer, Bogusław (b. 1929)
Bergsoniana (1972)
Text: none
Publisher: Berlin: Ahn & Simrock A&S 486
For: Soprano, flute, piano, horn, double bass (or cello), and electronic tape.
Difficulty: Voice: very difficult; Instruments: difficult
Vocal range: d′ - c‴
Language: phonemes
Duration: 10:48
Comments: Singer is required to perform many vocal effects. Many pitches are approximated.

292
Schat, Peter (b. 1935)
Het Vijfde Seizoen, Op. 23: Cantate (1973)
I. To whom it may concern (Adrian Mitchell)
II. Day (William Blake)
Publisher: Amsterdam: Donemus
For: Soprano, 2 clarinets in B^b, 3 bassoons, trumpet in C, horn, electric guitar, piano, and electric bass.
Difficulty: Voice: very difficult; Instruments: very difficult
Vocal range: e′ - a″
Language: English

Comments: Facsimile of composer's manuscript.

293

SCHIBLER, ARMIN (1920-1986)

String Quartet No. 4, Op. 66 (1960)

Text: Juan Ramón Jiménez; German translation by Klaus Leopold Davi

Publisher: Berlin: Ahn & Simrock A&S 335

For: Soprano or tenor and string quartet.

Difficulty: Voice: moderately difficult; Instruments: difficult

Vocal range: b - b″

Language: German

294

SCHICKELE, PETER (B. 1935)

The Lowest Trees Have Tops: Cantata (1978)

I. Morning Song (voice tacet)
II. The Lowest Trees have Tops (Sir Edward Dyer)
III. Hot Sun, Cool Fire (George Peele)
IV. My True-Love hath my Heart (Sir Philip Sidney)
V. Noon Song (voice tacet)
VI. To Meadows (Robert Herrick)
VII. The Mad Maid's Song (Robert Herrick)
VIII. Evening Song (voice tacet)
IX. To Death (Robert Herrick)

Publisher: Bryn Mawr, PA: Elkan-Vogel 164-00144

For: Soprano, flute, viola, and harp.

Difficulty: Voice: moderate; Instruments: moderate

Vocal range: c′ - f#″

Language: English

Duration: 24:00

295

SCHNITTKE, ALFRED (B. 1934)

Drei Madrigale (© 1981)

I. Sur une Ätoile
II. Entfernung
III. Reflection

Text: Francisco Tanzer's *Stimmen, Tagebuch, Novellen, Gedichte*

Publisher: Hamburg: Hans Sikorski H.S. 844

Series: Exempla nova, 44

For: Soprano, violin, viola, double bass, vibraphone, and harpsichord.

Difficulty: Voice: difficult; Instruments: moderately difficult

Vocal range: g - c#‴

Language: French, German, English

296

SCHUMAN, WILLIAM (1910-1992)

In Sweet Music (based on the melody of his 1944 song "Orpheus and his Lute") (© 1978)

Text: William Shakespeare

Publisher: Bryn Mawr, PA: Merion Music. Sole Agent: Theodore Presser 144-40072

For: Soprano or tenor, viola, flute, harp, alto flute, and piccolo.

Difficulty: Voice: moderately difficult; Instruments: moderately difficult

Vocal range: a - g#″

Language: English and scat syllables

Comments: Partial use of jazz idiom.

297

SCHUMAN, WILLIAM (1910-1992)

The Young Dead Soldiers: Lamentation (1975)

Text: Archibald Macleish

Publisher: Bryn Mawr, PA: Merion Music. Sole Agent: Theodore Presser 446-41026
For: Soprano, horn, 2 oboes, English horn, 2 clarinets in B^b, bass clarinet, 2 bassoons, 4 violas, 4 cellos, and double bass.
Difficulty: Voice: difficult; Instruments: moderately difficult
Vocal range: $c^{\#\prime}$ - b''
Language: English
Duration: 15:00

298
SCHWANTNER, JOSEPH (B. 1943)
Sparrows (1979)
Text: Issa
Publisher: Clifton, NJ: Helicon Music. Sole Agent: Totowa, NJ: European American Music EA 450
For: Soprano, flute (piccolo), clarinet in B^b, violin, viola, cello (strings also play finger cymbals), piano, harp, and percussion (percussion instrumentation not given).
Difficulty: Voice: very difficult; Instruments: very difficult
Vocal range: a - b''
Language: English
Comments: Note scordatura tuning for strings; instrumentalists must also sing at some places. Many rhythmic difficulties for voice and instruments.

299
SCHWANTNER, JOSEPH (B. 1943)
Wild Angels of the open Hills (1977)
1. Wild Angels of the open Hills
2. Angels of the shadowed Ancient Land
3. There
4. Coming of Age
5. The Hawk shapes the Wind

Text: Ursula K. Le Guin
Publisher: New York: Peters 66782
For: Soprano (3 glass crystals, 1 large suspended triangle, tambourine, and wind chimes), flute (alto flute, crotales, wind chimes), and harp (2 glass crystals).
Difficulty: Voice: very difficult; Instruments: difficult
Vocal range: g - c''' (also highest note possible)
Language: English
Duration: 28:00
Comments: Soprano must whistle accurately and play some percussion instruments.

300
SCHWERTSIK, KURT (B. 1935)
Starker Tobak, Op. 47 (1983)
Text: Composer
Publisher: London: Boosey & Hawkes
For: Soprano, flute, oboe, clarinet in B^b, horn, bassoon, violin, and piano.
Difficulty: Voice: difficult; Instruments: difficult
Vocal range: b^b - c'''
Language: German

301
SCIARRINO, SALVATORE (B. 1947)
Aspern-Suite (© 1978)
I. Ouvertura (voice tacet)
II. Aria "Aprite un po'quegli occhi"
III. Canzonetta "Deh vieni non tardar"
IV. Canzone Rituale

V. Passeggiata
VI. Continua la Passeggiata
VII. Aria "Non più andrai"
VIII. Notturno
IX. Intermezzo
X. Finale

Text: Composer, adapted from Lorenzo da Ponte
Publisher: Milan: Ricordi 132996
For: Soprano, flute I (piccolo and alto flute), flute II (alto flute and bass flute), harpsichord, viola (tuned whole tone sharp), cello, and percussion (one player).
Percussion instrumentation: large timpano, cymbal, stainless steel plate (suspended), large plate bell.
Difficulty: Voice: extremely difficult; Instruments: very difficult
Vocal range: $c^{\#\prime}$ - d'''
Language: Italian
Comments: Instrumental and vocal effects required. Texts from Mozart's *Marriage of Figaro.*

302

SCLATER, JAMES S. (B. 1943)

Four Songs on Texts of Emily Dickinson (1972)

I. Softened by Time's Consummate Plush
II. To make a Prairie
III. Here, Where the Daisies fit my Head
IV. Bee! I'm expecting You

Text: Emily Dickinson
Publisher: Clinton, MS: Mt. Salus Music
For: High voice (soprano or tenor) and clarinet in B^b.
Difficulty: Voice: moderate; Instrument: moderately difficult
Vocal range: f′ - g″
Language: English

303

SCULTHORPE, PETER (B. 1929)

The Song of Tailitnama (1974)

Text: from The Song of Tailitnama translated by T.G.H. Strehlow
Publisher: London: Faber Music. Sole Agent: New York: G. Schirmer, © 1985 F 0697.
For: Soprano, 6 cellos, and percussion (2 players).
Percussion instrumentation: tam-tam, water gong, Chinese cymbal, crotalo (high E), Chinese bell tree, pair bongos, pair timbales, Aboriginal music sticks, güiro, wood chimes, and sand block.
Difficulty: Voice: difficult; Instruments: difficult
Vocal range: c′ - b″
Language: Northern Aranda (Australia), with phonetic transcription and English translation.
Duration: 10:00
Comments: Some graphic notation.

304

SEAGARD, JOHN

Epiphany Adoration (© 1975)

Text: Composer
Publisher: Minneapolis: Augsburg 11-0741
For: Medium-high voice (soprano or tenor) and 2 C instruments.
Difficulty: Voice: moderate; Instruments: moderately easy.
Vocal range: c′ - a″
Language: English

305

SEREBRIER, JOSÉ (B. 1938)

Erotica (1968)

Text: none
Publisher: New York: Peer/Southern 2195-7
For: Soprano or trumpet in B^b and woodwind quintet.
Difficulty: Voice: moderately difficult; Instruments: moderately difficult
Vocal range: c′ - b^{b}″
Language: no phonemes indicated
Comments: Singer is off-stage; Some aleatoric elements.

306

Sermilä, Jarmo (b. 1939)

Love Charm Songs (1976)

I. You magic power
II. New moon

Text: Tupi Indians of South America
Publisher: Hameenlinna, Finland: Jasemusiikki Ky. Sole Agent: Stockholm: Editions Reimers
For: Soprano and chamber orchestra.
Instrumentation: flute, oboe, clarinet in B^b, bassoon, horn, 2 violins, viola, cello, double bass, vibraphone, triangle, suspended cymbal, large gong, and 2 timpani.
Difficulty: Voice: moderately difficult; Instruments: moderately difficult
Vocal range: d′ - b″
Language: English
Duration: 14:30

307

Shapey, Ralph (b. 1921)

O Jerúsalem (1975)

I. O Jerúsalem
II. My Name
III. Holy Vity
IV. Shalom Aleicham

Text: Old Testament
Publisher: Bryn Mawr, PA: Theodore Presser 111-4010311
For: Soprano and flute.
Difficulty: Voice: very difficult; Instrument: very difficult
Vocal range: g - d‴
Language: Combination of English and Hebrew words
Duration: 10:40

308

Shifrin, Seymour (1926-1979)

Satires of Circumstance (1969)

I. Waiting Both
II. The Convergence of the Twain
III. What's there to Tell?

Text: Thomas Hardy
Publisher: New York: Peters 66475
For: Soprano, flute, clarinet in B^b, violin, cello, and double bass.
Difficulty: Voice: difficult; Instruments: difficult
Vocal range: g - b^{b}″
Language: English
Duration: 16:30

309

Shostakovich, Dmitri (1906-1975)

Sem' Stikhotvoneniia A Bloka (Seven Poems of Alexander Blok)

I. Pesnia Ofelii (Ophelia's Song) (Lied der Ophelia)
II. Gamaiun, Ptitsa Veshchaia (Gamayn, Bird of Prophecy) (Gamajun, der Prophetenvogel)
III. My Byli Vmeste (That Troubled Night) (Wir waren zusammen)
IV. Gorod Spit (Deep in Sleep) (Die Stadt schläft)

V. Buria (The Storm) (Sturm)
VI. Tainye Znaki (Secret Signs) (Geheimnisvolle Zeichen)
VII. Muzyka (Music) (Musik)

Text: Aleksandr Blok
Publisher: Leipzig: Deutscher Verlag für Musik DVfM-9401
For: Soprano, violin, cello, and piano.
Difficulty: Voice: moderate; Instruments: moderately difficult
Vocal range: $e^{b\prime}$ - $a^{b\prime\prime}$
Language: Russian (German translation by Manfred Koerth provided for performance)
Comments: Also called *Vokal'no - instrumental'naia siuita (Romanzen-Suite.)* Available in two other editions: 1. London: Anglo-Soviet Music Press, 1977, (Sole Agents: New York: Boosey & Hawkes, G. Schirmer). 2. Moscow: Soviet Kompozitor, 1969.

310
Silsbee, Ann (b. 1930)
Scroll (1977)

I. This road
II. The sea darkening
III. Lightning
IV. A storm wind moans
V. In these dark waters

Text: Old Japanese Haiku
Publisher: New York: American Composers Alliance
For: Soprano, flute (alto flute), trumpet in B^b (large Japanese buttongong), violin, double bass, piano (pair of sandblocks), and percussion.
Percussion instrumentation: 3 woodblocks (low to high), 2 log drums (low and high), timpano, glass chimes, sizzle cymbal, ratchet, four tom-toms (small to large), large bass drum, claves, marimba, and vibraphone.
Difficulty: Voice: very difficult; Instruments: very difficult
Vocal range: b^b - $c^{\#\prime\prime\prime}$
Language: English
Duration: 8:00
Comments: Use of quartertones; piano is somewhat "prepared"; some vocal effects.

311
Sinopoli, Giuseppe (b. 1946)
Sunyata: Thema con Varianti (1970)

Text: none
Publisher: Milan: Suvini Zerboni S.7179.Z.
For: Soprano, 2 violins, viola, cello, and double bass.
Difficulty: Voice: difficult; Instruments: difficult
Vocal range: a - $d^{\#\prime\prime\prime}$
Language: phonemes
Duration: 6:00

312
Smit, Leo (b. 1921)
Academic Graffiti (1982)

I. Henry Adams
II. Queen Mary
III. Georg Friedrich Händel
IV. Nietzsche
V. Xantippe
VI. Karl Marx
VII. James Watt
VIII. Søren Kierkegaard
IX. Kant
X. Robert Liston
XI. Mallarmé

Text: W. H. Auden

Publisher: New York: Carl Fischer 05134
For: Histrionic voice (high voice [soprano or tenor]), clarinets in B^b and A, cello, piano, and percussion.
Percussion instrumentation: 2 bongos (high and low), 2 cowbells (high and low), whip, 3 tom-toms (high, medium, low), castanets, 2 woodblocks (high and low), tam-tam (large), xylophone, triangle, suspended cymbal, small handsaw on cardboard, and vibraphone.
Difficulty: Voice: difficult; Instruments: difficult
Vocal range: a - a″
Language: English
Duration: 9:00
Comments: Humorous.

313
Sohal, Naresh (b. 1939)
Kavita II (1972)
Text: John Donne
Publisher: Borough Green, Kent, England: Novello 17 0308 00
For: Soprano, suspended cymbal, flute, and piano.
Difficulty: Voice: very difficult; Instruments: difficult
Vocal range: b - c#‴
Language: English
Duration: 9:00
Comments: Use of quartertones.

314
Soler, Josep (b. 1935)
Ich bin die Seel' im All (1980)
Text: Jalāl ad-Dīn ar Rūmī, Theodor Rückert
Publisher: Frankfurt: Zimmermann ZM2221
For: Soprano, vibraphone, and guitar.
Difficulty: Voice: difficult; Instruments: difficult
Vocal range: b^b - d‴
Language: German

315
Somers, Harry (b. 1925)
Kuyas (1967)
Text: Cree Indian
Publisher: Toronto: Berandol Music
For: Voice: (soprano or tenor), flute, and percussion (2 players).
Percussion instrumentation: sleigh bells, medium pitch tom-tom, tenor drum, and bass drum.
Difficulty: Voice: moderately difficult; Instruments: moderately easy
Vocal range: c′ - c‴
Language: Cree Indian (pronunciation guide provided)
Comments: Excerpt from the opera *Louis Riel* performable as solo vocal chamber music.

316
Sommerfeldt, Øistein (b. 1919)
From William Blake's Poetry, Op. 53 (1979)
I. The Fly
II. The Garden of Love
III. The Little Vagabond
Text: William Blake
Publisher: Oslo: Norsk Musikforlag © 1982 N.M.O. 9361
For: Soprano or tenor, recorder, guitar, and piano.
Difficulty: Voice: moderate; Instruments: moderate

Vocal range: $e^{b\prime}$ - g″
Language: English
Duration: 8:00

317
Speirs, Malcolm
Three Poems of Janet Frame (1970, rev. 1972)
I. In loss the trees bear stings...
II. People are ill, dying...
III. Grief becomes spread...
Text: Janet Frame
Publisher: Dunedin, New Zealand: University of Otago Press
For: High voice (soprano or tenor), flute, oboe, English horn, clarinet in B^b, bass clarinet, bassoon (bassoon in D), horn, trumpet in C, harp, piano, and percussion (2 players).
Percussion instrumentation: marimba, vibraphone, large gong, and suspended cymbal.
Difficulty: Voice: difficult; Instruments: difficult
Vocal range: b - $b^{b\prime\prime}$
Language: English
Duration: 13:00
Comments: Some graphic notation.

318
Stachowski, Marek (b. 1936)
Birds (1976)
I. Prologo (voice tacet)
II. Canzona (Tadeusz Holuj)
III. Serenata (Pawel Hertz)
IV. Intermezzo (Jerzy Harasymowicz)
V. Canzona II (Zbigniew Herbert)
Publisher: Cracow: P W M 8179
For: Soprano, clarinet in B^b, violin, viola, cello, and gong (or tam-tam).
Difficulty: Voice: difficult; Instruments: difficult
Vocal range: c′ - b″
Language: Polish
Duration: 20:00
Comments: White score.

319
Starer, Robert (b. 1924)
To Think of Time (1985)
I. To Think of Time
II. After the Dazzle of Day
III. Yet, Yet, Ye Downcast Hours
IV. Darest Thou Now O Soul
Text: Walt Whitman
Publisher: Saint Louis: MMB Music 86002
For: Soprano and string quartet.
Difficulty: Voice: moderately difficult; Instruments: moderately difficult
Vocal range: $d^{b\prime}$ - g″
Language: English
Duration: 14:00

320
Steffens, Walter (b. 1934)
neue gleichnisse, op. 36 (1968)
I. Neue Gleichnisse (Tadeusz Różewicz)
II. Maske (Manfred Peter Hein)
III. Schmetterling (Nancy Sachs)
Publisher: Wiesbaden: Breitkopf & Härtel 6591
For: Soprano, flute, clarinet in B^b, and viola.
Difficulty: Voice: difficult; Instruments: difficult
Vocal range: c′ - $c^{\#\prime\prime\prime}$
Language: German

321
Stern, Mario (b. 1936)
Pequeño Ostinato (1978)

Text: none
Publisher: Mexico: Liga de Compositores de México
For: Soprano, clarinet in B^b, viola, and cello.
Difficulty: Voice: moderate; Instruments: moderate
Vocal range: d$^{\#\prime}$ - g$^{b\prime\prime}$
Language: Phonemes

322
STOCK, DAVID (B. 1939)
Scat (1970)
Text: none
Publisher: Newton Centre, MA: Margun Music MM-29
For: Soprano, flute, bass clarinet in B^b, violin, and cello.
Difficulty: Voice: extremely difficult; Instruments: difficult
Vocal range: b^b - d$^{b\prime\prime\prime}$
Language: Scat syllables
Duration: 9:00
Comments: Very wide leaps of difficult intervals must be executed at a very fast tempo.

323
STOUT, ALAN (B. 1932)
Canticum Canticorum, Op. 66 (1962)
I. Sicut lilium...
II. Jam enim...
III. Quaesivi quem diligit...
IV. En lectulum Salomonis...
V. Revertere, revertere Sulamitis...
VI. Pone me...
Text: The Song of Solomon
Publisher: New York: Peters
For: Soprano, viola, harp, woodwind quintet, and percussion.
Percussion instrumentation: snare drum, tenor drums, celesta, tamtam, 3 suspended cymbals, tomtoms, tambourine, bongos, and bass drum.
Difficulty: Voice: moderately difficult; Instruments: moderate
Vocal range: a - b$^{b\prime\prime}$
Language: Latin (English translation provided for performance)
Duration: 8:15

324
STRAESSER, JOEP (B. 1934)
All Perishes (1985)
I. All Perishes
II. ...and furiously they fill it...
III. Hither youth...
IV. Of woven flowers...
V. To bear to the gods
VI. Flowery
Text: Alcaeus
Publisher: Amsterdam: Donemus
For: Soprano (2 claves, medium suspended cymbal, small copper bells, high triangle), and flute.
Difficulty: Voice: difficult; Instruments: very difficult
Vocal range: c$'$ - c$'''$ plus highest note possible
Language: English (originally Greek)
Duration: 13:00

325
STRAESSER, JOEP (B. 1934)
Echoes Reversed (1982, rev. 1983)
Text: Old High German cradle song
Publisher: Amsterdam: Donemus
For: Soprano, flute, violin, cello, and piano.
Difficulty: Voice: difficult; Instruments: difficult

Vocal range: c' - a''
Language: Old High German, with English translation.
Duration: 10:11
Comments: Use of microtones, i.e., very low $G^{\sharp}$. Use of some vocal effects.

326

Straesser, Joep (b. 1934)

Nimm dir etwas Schönes (1979)

I. An die Morgensonne
II. Vom Fluss
III. Die Macht der Liebe
IV. Im Tempelkult
V. Die Klage von Merit-Re
VI. Das Haus vom Westland
VII. An die Nacht

Text: Old Egyptian
Publisher: Amsterdam: Donemus
For: Soprano, clarinet in B^{b}, violin, and piano.
Difficulty: Voice: difficult; Instruments: difficult
Vocal range: $a^{\sharp}$ - $b^{b''}$
Language: German
Duration: 20:00

327

Sueyoshi, Yasuo (b. 1937)

Musique pour la voir vocalisée 2° (1965)

Text: none
Publisher: Tokyo: Ongaku no Tomo Sha
For: Soprano, 2 flutes, and percussion (3 players).
Percussion instrumentation: (I) bongos; (II) 2 Chinese cymbals, large suspended cymbal, bongos, and conga; (III) 2 crotales, snare drum, and large tam-tam.
Difficulty: Voice: difficult; Instruments: very difficult
Vocal range: $e^{\sharp\prime}$ - a''
Language: Phonemes of singer's choosing.

328

Suter, Robert (b. 1919)

Heilige Leier, Sprich, sei Meine Stimme (1960)

I. Prolog
II. Invention I
III. Variationen
IV. Invention II
V. Elegie
VI. Invention III

Text: Eckart Peterich
Publisher: Locarno: Heinrichshofens Verlag
For: Soprano, flute, and guitar.
Difficulty: Voice: difficult; Instruments: difficult
Vocal range: a - c'''
Language: German
Duration: 13:45

329

Sydeman, William (b. 1928)

Four Japanese Songs (© 1970)

I. I passed by the beach
II. When I went out
III. In a gust of wind
IV. The mists rise over

Text: Translated from the Japanese by Kenneth Rexroth
Publisher: n.p.: Ione Press. Sole Agent: Boston: E.C. Schirmer E.C.S. 1712
Series: E.C.S. Vocal Music 118
For: Soprano and 2 violins.
Difficulty: Voice: moderately difficult; Instruments: moderately difficult
Vocal range: $e^{\sharp\prime}$ - $a^{\sharp\prime\prime}$
Language: English

330

Sydeman, William (b. 1928)

Jabberwocky (1960)

Text: Lewis Carroll

Publisher: n.p.: Ione Press. Sole Agent: Boston: E. C. Schirmer E.C.S. 2024

Series: E.C.S. Vocal Music 137

For: Soprano (or tenor), flute, and cello.

Difficulty: Voice: moderately difficult; Instruments: difficult

Vocal range: b - b♭″

Language: English

331

Sydeman, William (b. 1928)

Three Songs on Elizabethan Texts (© 1970)

I. A Modest Love (Sir Edward Dyer)
II. Elegy (Chidiock Tichborne)
III. The Fly (William Oldys)

Publisher: n.p.: Ione Press. Sole Agent: Boston: E. C. Schirmer E.C.S. 2022

Series: E.C.S. Vocal Music 135

For: Soprano (or tenor) and flute.

Difficulty: Voice: difficult; Instrument: difficult

Vocal range: c♯′ - a″

Language: English

332

Szajna-Lewandowska, Jadwiga (b. 1912)

12 Wierszy (1973) (12 Verses)

I. Ogród (The Garden)
II. Miłość (Love)
III. Telegram (The Telegram)
IV. Jesień (Autumn)
V. La précieuse (La précieuse)
VI. Tancerka (The Dancer)
VII. Listy (Letters)
VIII. Dni (Days)
IX. Ofelia (Ophelia)
X. Ślepa (The Blind Woman)
XI. Na ciepłej, niebieskiej łące (On a Warm, Blue Meadow)
XII. Różowa magła (Pink Mist)

Text: Maria Pawlikowska-Jasnorzewska

Publisher: Warsaw: Edycja Muzyczna

For: Soprano and string quartet.

Difficulty: Voice: moderately difficult; Instruments: moderately difficult

Vocal range: c′ - b″

Language: Polish

333

Szeligowski, Aleksander (b. 1934)

Cztery Pieśni (1962)

I. Zastukaj palcem, w ścianę
II. Zaświstaj cienko a pobiegnie rzeka
III. Chrząknij znacząco...
IV. Teraz zamknij oczy...

Text: Zbigniew Herbert

Publisher: Warsaw: P W M 5091

For: Soprano, English horn, trombone, xylophone, vibraphone, 4 bongos, suspended cymbal, triangle, tam-tam, celesta, 4 violins, and 4 violas.

Difficulty: Voice: very difficult; Instruments: difficult

Vocal range: b - e♭‴

Language: Polish

Duration: 10:00

Comments: The composer uses high notes in an intelligent manner.

334

Szokolay, Sándor (b. 1931)

A Minden-Titok titka (1980)

I. A Minden-Titok titka... (The Secret's Secret's sunken)
II. A Jégcsap-Szívüember...(The Icicle-Hearted Man)
III. Félhomályban...(In the Half-Dark)
IV. Pénz és Karnevál (Money and Carnival)
V. Haholtan találkozunk (If we meet in Death)

Text: Endre Ady; English translation: László T. András, German translation: K. H. Füssl and H. Wagner
Publisher: Vienna: Universal Edition 16981
For: Soprano, flute, clarinet in B^b, violin, Hungarian dulcimer, harp, and piano.
Difficulty: Voice: difficult; Instruments: difficult
Vocal range: $c^{\#\prime}$ - $b^{b\prime\prime}$
Language: Hungarian with singable German and English translations.

335
Taïra, Yoshihisa

Sonomorphie II (1971)

Text: none
Publisher: Paris: Rideau Rouge R977RC
For: Voice (soprano), oboe, cello, harp, and percussion (1 player).
Percussion instrumentation: marimba, vibraphone, crotales, and small bells (played by singer).
Difficulty: Voice: very difficult; Instruments: difficult
Vocal range: $d^{b\prime}$ - $a^{\prime\prime\prime}$
Language: phonemes
Duration: 13:00
Comments: Extremely high tessitura.

336
Takemitsu, Toru (b. 1930)

Stanza I (1969)

Text: Ludwig von Wittgenstein
Publisher: Vienna: Universal Edition UE 15118
For: Soprano, guitar, harp, piano, celesta, and vibraphone.
Difficulty: Voice: difficult; Instruments: difficult
Vocal range: a - $b^{\prime\prime}$
Language: German 1/2 of song; English 1/2 of song.
Comments: Some use of graphic notation, Sprechstimme, and other vocal effects.

337
Tansman, Alexandre (1897 - 1986)

Huit Stèles de Victor Segalen (1979)

I. Introduction
II. Trois Hymnes Primitifs
  A. Les lacs
  B. L'abîme
  C. Nuées
III. Jade Faux
IV. Interlude pour orchestre (voice tacet)
V. Tempête solide (La Montagne)
VI. Table de Sagesse

Text: Victor Segalen
Publisher: Paris: Max Eschig M.E. 8404
For: Voice (soprano or tenor), flute, oboe, clarinet in B^b, bassoon, horn, violin I, violin II, viola, cello, double bass, and percussion.
Percussion instrumentation: timbales, celesta, vibraphone, xy-

lophone, glockenspiel, triangle, and gong.
Difficulty: Voice: difficult; Instruments: difficult
Vocal range: $e^{b\prime}$ - $b^{b\prime\prime}$
Language: French
Duration: 16:00

338
TAUB, BRUCE (B. 1948)
Fragile Lady (1980)
Text: Edward Gallardo
Publisher: New York: Peters 67042
For: Soprano, double bass, piano, and trap set (ad libitum).
Difficulty: Voice: moderately difficult; Instruments: moderately difficult
Vocal range: $g^{\#}$ - $a^{\#\prime\prime}$
Language: English
Duration: 9:00

339
THOMAS, ANDREW (B. 1939)
Dirge in Woods (1973)
Text: George Meredith
Publisher: Newton Centre, MA: Margun Music MM 52
For: Soprano, harp, and percussion.
Percussion instrumentation: vibraphone, marimba, and glockenspiel.
Difficulty: Voice: difficult; Instruments: very difficult
Vocal range: a - $b^{b\prime\prime}$
Language: English
Duration: 8:00

340
THOMMESSEN, OLAV ANTON (B. 1946)
Et Konsert-Kammer (A Chamber Concert) (1971)
Text: Phonemes
Publisher: Oslo: Norsk Musikforlag. Sole Agent: Wilhelm Hansen 4266
For: Voice (soprano), clarinet in B^b, violin, piccolo (flute), cello, oboe, double bass, bassoon, trumpet in B^b, alto saxophone, tuba, and percussion.
Percussion instrumentation: whip, 5 temple blocks, 2 bongos, 2 tambours, and 1 snare drum.
Difficulty: Voice: difficult; Instruments: difficult
Vocal range: no exact pitches given–pitch approximations and highest note possible
Language: phonemes
Duration: 10:00
Comments: Instrumental groups are to be placed antiphonally to one another. Stereo microphone system required for singer.

341
THOW, JOHN (B. 1949)
Chinese Poems (1975)
I. Prelude
II. The cicada (Yü Shih-Nan)
III. Interlude I (voice tacet)
IV. Question and answer among the mountains (Li Po)
V. Interlude II (voice tacet)
VI. Again in praise of myself (Yang Wan-Li)
Publisher: New York: Pembroke. Sole Agent: Carl Fischer © 1982
Series: Pembroke Fascimile Edition
For: Soprano and flute.
Difficulty: Voice: difficult; Instrument: difficult
Vocal range: b - a″
Language: English
Duration: 12:00

342
Toda, Kunio (b. 1915)
Message (1960)
Text: Raymond Duncan
Publisher: Tokyo: Japan Federation of Composers
For: Soprano, clarinet in A, and harp.
Difficulty: Voice: moderately difficult; Instruments: difficult
Vocal range: b - f#″
Language: English

343
Togni, Camillo (b. 1922)
Rondeaux per Dieci (1963)
I. C'est la prison Dedalus
II. Aucunes foiz je unclus
III. Oncques ne fut tantalus
Text: Charles d'Orléans
Publisher: Milan: Suvini Zerboni S.6158Z.
For: Soprano, guitar, harp, harpsichord, celesta, glockenspiel, bell, timpani, harmonium, and double bass.
Difficulty: Voice: extremely difficult; Instruments: very difficult
Vocal range: b♭ - f#‴
Language: French
Comments: Note extreme vocal range; tessitura is very high.

344
Trimble, Lester (1923-1986)
Four Fragments from the Canterbury Tales (1967)
I. Prologe
II. A Knyght
III. A Yong Squier
IV. The Wyf of Biside Bathe
Text: Geoffrey Chaucer
Publisher: New York: Peters 66068p
For: High voice (soprano or tenor), flute, clarinet in A, and harpsichord or piano.
Difficulty: Voice: moderately difficult; Instruments: moderate
Vocal range: b♭ - a″
Language: middle English (pronunciation guide provided)
Duration: 17:00

345
Trojahn, Manfred (b. 1949)
Hommage au temps perdu (1975)
I. Presto possibile (voice tacet)
II. Moderato molto
Text: none
Publisher: Hamburg: Hans Sikorski H.S.848
For: Soprano, flute, clarinet in B♭, cello, and celesta (piano).
Difficulty: Voice: moderate; Instruments: very difficult
Vocal range: f′ - b♭″
Language: none
Duration: 6:30
Comments: The vocal part is treated as part of the instrumental ensemble.

346
Trojahn, Manfred (b. 1949)
Risse des Himmels (1974)
I. Vorfrühling
II. Wunschmond
III. Kleine Sonne
IV. Spät
Text: Johannes Poethen
Publisher: Hamburg: Hans Sikorski 858
For: Soprano, flute, and guitar.
Difficulty: Voice: difficult; Instruments: difficult
Vocal range: a - b″

Language: German
Comments: Some use of Sprechstimme.

347
Tubb, Monte (b. 1933)
Five Haiku for Soprano and String Quartet
I. Snow whispering down...
II. Into a cold night...
III. Oh, cuckoo
IV. He who climbs
V. Even the soldiers
Text: Anonymous Japanese
Publisher: Ann Arbor, MI: CMP Library Edition, University Microfilms 066-3-02
For: Soprano and string quartet.
Difficulty: Voice: moderate; Instruments: moderately easy
Vocal range: f′ - a″
Language: English
Duration: 9:00

348
Turnage, Mark-Anthony (b. 1960)
Lament for a Hanging Man (1983)
Text: Jeremiah I, Sylvia Plath "The Hanging Man"
Publisher: London: Schott
For: Soprano (syn. drum or snare drum, 2 bass drums with pedal, 2 suspended cymbals), harp, soprano saxophone (lead pipe), bass clarinet I (soprano saxophone II, 2 tom-toms), bass clarinet II (2 tom-toms), and percussion.
Percussion instrumenation: bass drum (soft sticks), bass drum with pedal, suspended cymbal, hi-hat (hard sticks), vibraphone, and 2 bongos (medium and low).
Difficulty: Voice: difficult; Instruments: difficult
Vocal range: b^b - c‴
Language: Hebrew and English
Comments: Some theatrical effects.

349
Twardowski, Romuald (b. 1930)
Cantus Antiqui (1962)
I. Icarus
II. Narcissus
III. Niobe
Text: Ovid
Publisher: Warsaw: Przedstawicielstwo Wydawnictwo Polskich
For: Soprano, harpsichord, piano, and percussion.
Percussion instrumentation: timpani, snare drum, snare drums without snare (soprano, alto, tenor, bass); soprano and alto suspended cymbals, gong, tamtam, and vibraphone.
Difficulty: Voice: difficult; Instruments: difficult
Vocal range: $c^{\#\prime}$ - $a^{b\prime\prime}$
Language: Latin

350
Tyszkowski, Jerzy (b. 1930)
Tre Impresioni Poetiche (1961)
I. Wieczór
II. Z Błyskawic
III. Ścieżka
Text: Julian Przyboś
Publisher: Warsaw: Edycja Muzyczna
For: Soprano, flute, trumpet in B^b, celesta, harp, violin, viola, cello, double bass, and percussion.
Percussion instrumentation: cymbals, tubular bells, tam-tam, timpani, snare drum, and xylophone.

Difficulty: Voice: difficult; Instruments: difficult
Vocal range: a - c‴
Language: Polish (German translation provided for performance)

351
Ung, Chinary (b. 1942)
Tall Wind (1970)
I. Tall Wind
II. Sunset
III. Sonnet
Text: e.e. cummings "Stinging Gold Swarms", "A Wind Has Blown The Rain Away"
Publisher: New York: Peters 6562
For: Soprano, flute, oboe, guitar, and cello.
Difficulty: Voice: difficult; Instruments: difficult
Vocal range: c′ - b^{b}″
Language: English
Duration: 6:00

352
Usher, Julia (b. 1945)
The Causeway (1984)
Text: Charles Dickens's *David Copperfield*, Composer
Publisher: London: Primavera
For: Soprano, trumpet in B^{b}, violin, viola, and cello.
Difficulty: Voice: moderately difficult; Instruments: moderately difficult
Vocal range: a - b″

353
Usher, Julia (b. 1945)
A Chess Piece (1980)
I. Openings
II. A Tempo
III. Endgame
Text: Composer
Publisher: London: Primavera
For: Soprano and three clarinets in B^{b}.
Difficulty: Voice: difficult; Instruments: difficult
Vocal range: a - b^{b}″
Language: English

354
Valls, Manuel (b. 1920)
Canciones Sefarditas (1965)
I. La rosa enflorece.
II. Ven querida, ven amada.
III. Adio, querida.
IV. Durme, durme.
V. Paxaro d'hermozura.
VI. Abrix, mi galanica
VII. Irme quiero, la mi mare.
VIII. Ya viene el cativo
IX. Yo m'enamorí d'un aire.
Text: Sephardic
Publisher: Madrid: Union Musical Española 22029
For: Soprano, flute, and guitar or vihuela.
Difficulty: Voice: moderate; Instruments: moderate
Vocal range: d′ - g″
Language: Ladino

355
Vercken, François
Versets (1973)
Text: none
Publisher: Paris: Editions Françaises de Musique-Technisonor E.F.M. 1704
For: Soprano, flute, clarinet in B^{b}, violin I, violin II, viola, cello, and double bass.
Difficulty: Voice: difficult; Instruments: difficult
Vocal range: c*′ - a″
Language: phonemes

356

Vercoe, Elizabeth (b. 1941)

Herstory II (1979)

I. Lady Murasaki Shikibu
II. Interlude I (voice tacet)
III. Lady Kasa
IV. Lady Otomo No Sakanoe
V. Lady Suo
VI. Lady Horikawa
VII. Lady Ukon
VIII. Lady Otomo No Sakanoe
IX. Interlude II (voice tacet)
X. Lady Akazome
XI. The Mother of the Commander Michitsuna
XII. The Poetess Ono No Komachi
XIII. Lady Shikibu
XIV. Lady Shikibu

Text: Japanese Lyrics
Publisher: Washington, D.C.: Arsis Press 113
For: Soprano, piano, and percussion.
Percussion instrumentation: tone block, finger cymbals, güiro, tambourine, triangle, maraca, castanets, and woodblock.
Difficulty: Voice: difficult; Instruments: difficult
Vocal range: g - c#'''
Language: English
Duration: 20:00
Comments: Use of Sprechstimme, some graphic notation; use of inside of piano.

357

Veretti, Antonio (1900-1978)

Elegie, in friulano (©1965)

I. Ogni sasòn
II. Cuintriciant
III. Piárdisi tal mâr
IV. Cuintriciant
V. Tristizie dissavide
VI. L'è come un fûc...
VII. Ja cia rânde...
VIII. La Bambine muarte
IX. Pás de campagne

Text: Free translation of Franco de Gironcoli
Publisher: Milan: Ricordi 130746
For: Voice (soprano or tenor), violin, guitar, and clarinet in B^b.
Difficulty: Voice: difficult; Instruments: difficult
Vocal range: b^b - b''
Language: Italian (Friuli dialect)

358 DELETED

359

Vinter, Gilbert (b. 1909)

Settings from the Rubáiyát of Omar Khayyam (1968)

I. Awake!
II. I Sometimes Think
III. There Was a Door
IV. The Potter
V. Heart's Desire

Text: Rubáiyát of Omar Khayyam
Publisher: London: Studio Music
For: Soprano, oboe, and piano.
Difficulty: Voice: moderately difficult; Instruments: difficult
Vocal range: b - a''
Language: English
Duration: 12:00

360

Vlad, Roman (b. 1919)

Immer wieder (1965)

Text: Rainer Maria Rilke
Publisher: London: Universal Edition 13750. Sole Agent: Bryn Mawr, PA: Theodore Presser
For: Soprano, English horn, clarinet in B^b, bassoon, viola, cello,

marimbaphone, vibraphone, harp, and piano.
Difficulty: Voice: difficult; Instruments: difficult
Vocal range: b^b - $b^{b''}$
Language: German
Duration: 9:30
Comments: Use of quarter tones.

361
Volkonsky, Andrei Mikhailovich (b. 1933)
Mirror Suite (1960)
I. Symbol
II. The Great Mirror
III. Reflection
IV. Rays
V. Echo
VI. Syntony
VII. Eyes
VIII. Beginning
IX. Lullaby for the Mirror which Fell Asleep
Text: Federico García Lorca/Translated from the Spanish by V. Burich
Publisher: Moscow: Sovyetski Kompozitor C1405K
For: Soprano, flute, violin, guitar, small organ, and percussion.
Percussion instrumentation: triangle, temple block, wood drum, snare drum, cymbals, and gong.
Difficulty: Voice: very difficult; Instruments: difficult
Vocal range: c′ - $b^{b''}$
Language: Russian

362
Walaciński, Adam (b. 1928)
Liryka sprzed zaśnięcia (1963) (A Lyric Before Falling Asleep)
Text: Miron Bialoszewski
Publisher: Warsaw: P W M 5644
For: Soprano, flute, and two pianos.
Difficulty: Voice: moderately difficult; Instruments: moderately difficult
Vocal range: c′ - g″
Language: Polish
Duration: 9:00
Comments: White score; some graphic notation.

363
Walker, George (b. 1922)
Poem (© 1987)
Text: T. S. Eliot
Publisher: Saint Louis: MMB Music
For: Soprano, clarinet in B^b, flute, piano (harpsichord), harp, violin, cello, percussion, and spoken bass voice.
Percussion instrumentation: xylophone, vibraphone, timpani, snare drum, triangle, roto-toms, tubular bells, tom-toms, gong, glockenspiel, maracas, tambourine, suspended cymbal with wire brush, glass chimes, temple blocks, claves, woodblock, cowbells, and timbales.
Difficulty: Voice: difficult; Instruments: difficult
Vocal range: c′ - b″
Language: English

364
Warren, Elinor Remick (1906-1991)
Sonnets (1965)
Text: Edna St. Vincent Millay (Sonnets 7, 11, 35, 50)
Publisher: New York: Carl Fischer
For: Soprano and string quartet.

Difficulty: Voice: moderately difficult; Instruments: moderately difficult
Vocal range: c′ - a♭″
Language: English

365
Waxman, Donald (b. 1925)
Lovesongs (© 1989)
I. Lovesong (Rainer Maria Rilke, translated by M.D. Herder Norton)
II. The Mad Maid's Song (Robert Herrick)
III. Nocturne (Anonymous French)
IV. A Bygone Occasion (Thomas Hardy)
Publisher: New York: Galaxy Music 1.3078, 1 390
Series: Contemporary Artsong Series
For: Soprano, violin, and piano.
Difficulty: Voice: moderately difficult; Instruments: moderately difficult
Vocal range: b - a♭″
Language: English

366
Weis, Flemming (1898-1981)
Japanske Fågelrop (1975)
I. Morgenskymning (Tsuraynki)
II. Samma Väntan (Tomonori)
III. Om Hösten (Saigyo)
Text: Lars Englund
Publisher: Copenhagen: Samfundet til Udgivelse af Dansk Musik © 1980
Series: 3. serie, nr. 300
For: Soprano, viola, and guitar.
Difficulty: Voice: difficult; Instruments: moderately difficult
Vocal range: d′ - c‴
Language: Danish
Duration: 11:00
Comments: c‴ at end of piece is to be hummed.

367
Welin, Karl-Erik (b. 1934)
Renovationes (1960)
Text: none
Publisher: Darmstadt: Tonos 7204
For: Soprano, flute, violin, mandolin, celesta, and percussion.
Percussion instrumenation: four suspended cymbals (low to high) and large tam-tam.
Difficulty: Voice: difficult; Instruments: difficult
Vocal range: f′ - c‴
Language: Phonemes (indicated by composer)
Duration: 6:00

368
Wellesz, Egon (1885-1974)
Four Songs of Return, Op. 85 (1961)
I. Where suddenly the wanderer comes...
II. Separate the shrivell'd moon...
III. The stubble was pale...
IV. Befriend us fortune...
Text: Elizabeth Mackenzie
Publisher: Locarno: Heinrichshofens Verlag L1106
For: Soprano, flute, clarinet in B♭, harp, piano, and string quartet.
Difficulty: Voice: difficult; Instruments: difficult
Vocal range: c′ - b♭″
Language: English
Duration: 19:00

369
Wernick, Richard (b. 1934)
Oracle II (1985)
Text: by Menahem Mendel of Kotzk (English translation by Chaim Potok)
Publisher: Bryn Mawr, PA: Theodore Presser 111-40107
For: Soprano, oboe, and piano.
Difficulty: Voice: very difficult; Instruments: difficult
Vocal range: g - a″
Language: English and Hebrew
Duration: 12:00

370
Wernick, Richard (b. 1934)
A Poison Tree (1979)
Text: William Blake
Publisher: Bryn Mawr, PA: Theodore Presser 416-41112
For: Soprano, flute, clarinet in A, violin, cello, and piano.
Difficulty: Voice: moderately difficult; Instruments: difficult
Vocal range: b^{b} - g″
Language: English
Duration: 12:00

371
Wilkins, Margaret Lucy (b. 1939)
Struwwelpeter, Op. 21 (1972)
I. Struwwelpeter
II. Cruel Frederick
III. Harriet and the Matches
IV. Augustus
V. The Inky Boys
VI. Flying Robert
Text: Heinrich Hoffmann
Publisher: Huddersfield, West Yorkshire, England: Satanic Mills Press
For: Soprano, three clarinets in B^{b} (bass clarinet, alto saxophone, male voice with megaphone, clarinet in E^{b}), piano (piano II [out of tune]) and percussion (one player).
Percussion instrumentation: bass drum, side drum (with snare), whip, matches and cigarette, xylophone, vibraphone, maracas, suspended cymbal, small pedal timpano, and flexatone.
Difficulty: Voice: moderately difficult; Instruments: moderately difficult
Vocal range: b^{b} - b^{b}″
Language: English
Duration: 14:00
Comments: Multi-media presentation with slides.

372
Williams, Graham (b. 1940)
Japanese Fragments (1973)
I. Spring (Matsuo Bashō)
II. To the Sun's Path (Matsuo Bashō)
III. Summer Grasses (Matsuo Bashō)
IV. The Beginning of Autumn (Matsuo Bashō)
V. The Winds of Autumn (Matsuo Bashō)
VI. Winter Blast (Mukai Kyori)
Publisher: London: Chester
For: Soprano, viola, and guitar.
Difficulty: Voice: difficult; Instruments: moderately difficult
Vocal range: c′ - b″
Language: English
Comments: White score.

373
Wimberger, Gerhard (b. 1923)
Singsang (1970)

Text: none
Publisher: Mainz: Schott 6502
For: Voice (soprano or tenor), electric organ, electric guitar, electric bass, and percussion (normal trap set).
Difficulty: Voice: difficult; Instruments: difficult
Vocal range: c′ - a″
Language: Scat syllables
Duration: 10:00
Comments: Improvisatory elements; spatial as well as metrical time.

374
WYNER, YEHUDI (B. 1929)
Memorial Music I (1971) (Man comes from Dust) (from the prayer "Ki K'shimcho")
Memorial Music II (1973) (Lord, Let me Know my End) (Psalm 39, Isaiah 40)
Publisher: New York: Associated AMP-7440
For: Soprano and 3 flutes (I in C, II with B extension, and III alto).
Difficulty: Voice: moderately difficult; Instruments: moderately difficult
Vocal range: a - b♭″
Language: English

375
XENAKIS, IANNIS (B. 1922)
Akanthos (1977)
Text: none
Publisher: Paris: Salabert
For: Soprano, flute (piccolo, alto flute), clarinet in B♭ (bass clarinet), piano, violin I, violin II, viola, cello, and double bass.
Difficulty: Voice: very difficult; Instruments: very difficult
Vocal range: f - d‴
Language: Phonemes
Duration: 11:00
Comments: Note extreme range.

376
YUN, ISANG (B. 1917)
Teile dich, Nacht (1980)
Text: Nelly Sachs
Publisher: Berlin: Bote & Bock B&B 22 900 (1433)
For: Soprano, flute, oboe, clarinet in B♭, bassoon, horn, harp or piano, violin I, violin II, viola, cello, double bass, and percussion.
Percussion instrumentation: xylophone, bass drum, tam-tam, 5 tom-toms, 5 temple bells, glockenspiel, and 3 cymbals.
Difficulty: Voice: very difficult; Instruments: very difficult
Vocal range: a - c♯‴
Language: German
Duration: 12:00
Comments: Use of Sprechstimme.

377
ZIMMERMANN, UDO (B. 1943)
Hymne an die Sonne (1977)
Text: Heinrich von Kleist
Publisher: Leipzig: Deutscher Verlag für Musik DVfM 9405
For: Soprano, alto flute, and harpsichord.
Difficulty: Voice: moderately difficult; Instruments: difficult
Vocal range: c′ - b″
Language: German

Mezzo Soprano

378
AMY, GILBERT (B. 1936)
Après d'un Désastre Obscur (1976)
Text: none
Publisher: Vienna: Universal Edition 16858
For: Mezzo soprano (whip, 2 gongs), flute (piccolo), clarinet in B^b, bass clarinet, horn, piano (small bell), harp, violin, cello, and 2 woodblocks.
Difficulty: Voice: difficult; Instruments: difficult.
Vocal range: f - $f^{\#''}$
Language: phonemes
Comments: Use of piano harmonics.

379
ANDRIESSEN, JURRIAAN (B. 1925)
Polderpastiches (1977)
I. Zomeronweer
II. Herfstpolder
III. Wintergezicht
IV. Voorjaarsonrust
Text: Daniel de Lange
Publisher: Amsterdam: Donemus
For: Voice (mezzo soprano), clarinet in B^b, and cello.
Difficulty: Voice: moderate; Instruments: difficult
Vocal range: d' - f''
Language: Dutch
Comments: Also published for baritone, oboe, and guitar.

380
ANTONIOU, THEODORE (B. 1935)
Epilog nach Homer (1963)
Text: Homer "The Odyssey"
Publisher: Kassel: Bärenreiter BA4379
For: Mezzo soprano, speaker, oboe, horn, guitar, piano, double bass, and percussion.
Percussion instrumentation: bass drum, gong, vibraphone, snare drum, triangle, woodblocks (other wood instruments), bongos, side drum (other skin instruments), metal blocks, and cymbals (other metal instruments).
Difficulty: Voice: difficult; Instruments: difficult
Vocal range: $f^{\#}$ - f''
Language: Ancient Greek (narrator however speaks in translation of whatever country in which the work is performed).

381
ANTUNES, JORGE DE FREITAS (B. 1942)
Trio en la Pis (1973)
Text: none
Publisher: Paris: Salabert
For: Voice (mezzo soprano), cello, and piano.
Difficulty: Voice: moderately difficult; Instruments: moderate
Vocal range: a^b - $a^{b''}$
Language: phonemes
Duration: 10:01
Comments: The piece is somewhat aleatoric. The musicians are required to perform abnormally on the cello and piano, and singer sings for a time with pencil in her mouth.

382
APERGHIS, GEORGES (B. 1945)
La Tragique Histoire du Nécromancien Hiéronimo et de son Miroir

Overture
I. Recitativo
II. Jene crains plus

Text: Horatio et Bellimperia
Publisher: Paris: Amphion A.279
For: Mezzo soprano (bass drum, cog rattle, sheet metal to thunder, lions roar, hunting horn, snare drum, and antique cymbals); narrator (whip, wind machine, hunting horn, snare drum, and small bells); lute or guitar (cello bow and 1 bongo); cello (hunting horn, hi-hat, and 1 tom-tom); and electronic tape.
Difficulty: Voice: extremely difficult; Instruments: very difficult
Vocal range: f# - d‴(also highest pitch possible, d⁗is indicated)
Language: French
Comments: The four soloists must play other instruments. Note extreme range.

383
Armer, Elinor (b. 1939)

Lockerbones/Airbones (1983)

I. The Anger
II. The Child on the Shore
III. Footnote
IV. Hard Words
V. For Katya

Text: Ursula K. Le Guin
Publisher: Berkeley: Fallen Leaf Press
Series: Fallen Leaf Press Publications in Contemporary Music, 2
For: Mezzo soprano, flute, violin, piano, and percussion.
Percussion instrumentation: 4 timbales, 2 bongos, vibraphones, two brake drums, three gongs, two suspended cymbals, and breakable wood lath (1").
Difficulty: Voice: difficult; Instruments: difficult
Vocal range: f# - f#″
Language: English
Comments: Use of unusual meter.

384
Artemov, Viacheslav Petrovich (b. 1940)

Severnye pesni (1966)

Publisher: Moscow: Moskva Muzyka
For: Mezzo soprano, piano, and percussion.
Percussion instrumentation: triangle, crotales, Sonagli [pellet bell], suspended cymbal, hi-hat, tam-tam, woodblocks, tambourine, and timpani.
Difficulty: Voice: moderately difficult; Instruments: moderately difficult
Vocal range: a - f#″
Language: Russian

385
Ashkenazy, Benjamin (b. 1940)

Kinderkreuzzug 1939 (1981)

Text: Bertolt Brecht
Publisher: Amsterdam: Donemus
For: Mezzo soprano, cello, piano, and percussion (1 player).
Percussion instrumentation: side drum, bass drum, tam-tam, triangle, 5 cymbals (S.Ms.A.T.B.), 5 temple blocks, 3 cowbells (small, medium, low), vibraphone, and marimbaphone.
Difficulty: Voice: difficult; Instruments: moderately difficult
Vocal range: a - f#″

Language: German
Duration: 35:00
Comments: Use of unusual meter. Some Sprechstimme. Spoken section for singer.

386
Avni, Tzvi (b. 1927)
Collage (1967)
Text: Yehuda Amichai
Publisher: Tel Aviv: Israel Music Institute I.M.I.140
For: Mezzo soprano, flute, percussion, and electronic tape.
Percussion instrumentation: vibraphone, triangle, woodblock, tambourine, suspended cymbal, and tam-tam.
Difficulty: Voice: moderate; Instruments: moderate
Vocal range: $e^{b\prime}$ - g''
Language: Hebrew (English translation by Gila Abrahamson provided for performance)
Duration: 8:00
Comments: Use of quarter tones in voice and flute.

387
Baird, Tadeusz (1928-1981)
Five Songs (1968)
I. Rozstanie jest ptakiem...
II. Podziel się ze mną...
III. Boże mój...
IV. Rozcinam pomarńczę bólu
V. Zawsze, kiedy chcę żyć krzyczę
Text: Halina Poświatowska
Publisher: Copenhagen: Wilhelm Hansen 4146
For: Mezzo soprano, flute (alto flute), 2 clarinets in B^b (bass clarinet), alto saxophone, horn, trumpet in C, trombone, harp, 3 cellos, double bass, and percussion (4 players).
Percussion instrumentation: vibraphone, xylophone, 3 suspended cymbals (small, medium and large), 4 fixed cymbals, 4 tom-toms, 2 bongos, small drum, 3 temple blocks, whip, güiro, tambourine, tam-tam, suspended gong, and bass drum.
Difficulty: Voice: difficult; Instruments: moderately difficult
Vocal range: a - a''
Language: Polish (German translation by Maria Kurecka provided for performance)
Duration: 12:30
Comments: There are some rhythm changes in German version to accommodate the text. The score includes a piano reduction.

388 DELETED

389
Bank, Jacques (b. 1943)
Brommerlied (1983)
Text: Composer
Publisher: Amsterdam: Donemus
For: Mezzo soprano or tenor, accordion, and percussion.
Percussion instrumentation: snare drum, large tam-tam, bass drum, 3 cymbals, and marimba.
Difficulty: Voice: very difficult; Instruments: difficult
Vocal range: a - a'''
Language: Dutch (singable English translation provided)
Duration: 16:00

390
Bank, Jacques (b. 1943)
Mesmerised (1977)

I. April 27 - 1871
II. May 5 - 1868
III. August 16 - 1873
IV. July 13 - 1874
V. May 11 - 1868
VI. April 8 - 1873

Text: Gerard Manley Hopkins
Publisher: Amsterdam: Donemus
For: Mezzo soprano or tenor, 3 trumpets in B^b, piano and percussion (3 players).
Percussion instrumentation: (I) xylophone, 3 tuned bongos, timpano, and 4 temple blocks; (II) bell, 3 tuned bongos, and 4 temple blocks; (III) 2 tuned bongos, bass drum, 4 temple blocks, anvil, 6 cowbells, triangle, snare drum, tam-tam, 2 cymbals, marimba, 4 woodblocks, rattle (large), güiro, 3 cymbals, 4 maracas, 2 tambourines, triangle, flexatone, and wood chimes.
Difficulty: Voice: moderately difficult; Instruments: moderately difficult
Vocal range: c′ - a″
Language: English

391
BARNETT, DAVID (1907-1985)
Five Songs to Poems of Ralph Hodgson (© 1984)
I. The Mystery
II. A Song
III. The Moor
IV. The Gipsy Girl
V. After

Text: Ralph Hodgson
Publisher: Weston, CT: Ledgbrook Associates
For: Mezzo soprano, flute, French horn, and piano.
Difficulty: Voice: moderately difficult; Instruments: moderate
Vocal range: b - g#″
Language: English

392
BARRETT, RICHARD
Coïgitum (1985)
Text: Phonemes
Publisher: London: United Music Publishers
For: Mezzo soprano, alto flute, oboe damore, piano, and percussion.
Percussion instrumentation: bongos, 2 timbales, 4 roto-toms, 2 large floor toms or congas, 1 pedal bass drum, large single-headed bass drum, 4 temple blocks, mokubyo, and smallest tambourine possible.
Difficulty: Voice: extremely difficult; Instruments: extremely difficult
Vocal range: g - c‴
Language: IPA symbols
Duration: 15:00
Comments: Use of quartertones. Use of vocal effects including senza vibrato, vocal tremolo, extended trills, etc. From *After Matta* based on paintings by Roberto Matta.

393
BARTOLOZZI, BRUNO (1911-1980)
Tres Recuerdos Del Cielo (1968)
I. Prólogo
II. Premier Recuerdo
III. Secundo Recuerdo
IV. Tercer Recuerdo

Text: Rafael Alberti
Publisher: Milan: Suvini Zerboni S.6751Z.

For: Voice (mezzo soprano or baritone), flute, English horn, clarinet in B^b, bassoon, guitar, viola, cello, double bass, and timpano.
Difficulty: Voice: moderately difficult; Instruments: moderately difficult
Vocal range: g - $f^{\#''}$
Language: Spanish
Duration: 12:00

394
Benson, Warren (b. 1924)
Five Lyrics of Louise Bogan (1978)
I. My Voice not Being Proud
II. The Alchemist
III. Juan's Song
IV. Fifteenth Farewell II
V. Knowledge
Text: Louise Bogan
Publisher: Bryn Mawr, PA: Theodore Presser #411-41086 © 1984
For: Mezzo soprano and flute.
Difficulty: Voice: difficult; Instruments: difficult
Vocal range: $f^{\#}$ - $a^{b''}$
Language: English
Duration: 20:00

395
Berger, Jean (b. 1909)
Six Rondeaux (© 1968)
I. Le premier jour du mois de mai
II. Gardez le trait de la fenêtre
III. Fuyez le trait de doux regard
IV. Hiver, vous n'êtes qu'un vilain
V. C'est fait, il n'en faut plus parler
VI. Puis, çà, puis là
Text: Charles d'Orléans
Publisher: Denver: John Sheppard Music Press 3003
For: Voice (mezzo soprano) and viola.
Difficulty: Voice: moderately difficult; Instrument: moderate
Vocal range: g - f''
Language: French

396
Berio, Luciano (b. 1925)
Circles (1960)
I. Stinging
II. Riverly is a Flower
III. N(o)W
Text: e. e. cummings
Publisher: Vienna: Universal Edition UE 13231 Mi
For: Female voice (mezzo soprano), harp, and percussion (2 players).
Percussion instrumentation: 3 woodblocks, 5 cowbells, vibraphone, Mexican bean [dried bean pod which rattles], lujon [bass metallophone], 4 Chinese gongs, log drum, 6 suspended chimes, tambourine, marimbaphone, 6 glass chimes, snare drum, 6 bongos, güiro, 2 congas, 6 tom-toms, wood chimes, foot pedal bass drum, 2 small timpani, sand block, 5 temple blocks, 6 triangles, tablas [small drum of northern India], maracas, hi-hat, celesta, xylophone, 6 suspended cymbals, glockenspiel, and 4 tam-tams.
Difficulty: Voice: difficult; Instruments: difficult
Vocal range: f - a''
Language: English
Comments: White score; use of some graphic notation.

397
Berio, Luciano (b. 1925)
O King (1968)
Text: Composer
Publisher: Vienna: Universal Edition 13781 Mi
For: Mezzo soprano, flute, clarinet in B^b, violin, cello, and piano.
Difficulty: Voice: moderately difficult; Instruments: moderate
Vocal range: $d^{b\prime}$ - g''
Language: English

398
Binkerd, Gordon (b. 1916)
Portrait Intérieur (1972)
I. Le sublime est un départ
II. Ce ne sont pas des souvenirs
III. Comment encore reconnaître
IV. Tel cheval qui boit à la fontaine
Text: Rainer Maria Rilke
Publisher: New York: Boosey & Hawkes BH.BK.737
For: Mezzo soprano, violin, and cello.
Difficulty: Voice: moderately difficult; Instruments: difficult
Vocal range: a^b - a''
Language: French

399
Binkerd, Gordon (b. 1916)
Three Songs (© 1971)
I. Never the Nightingale (Adelaide Crapsey)
II. How Lillies Came White (Robert Herrick)
III. Upon Parting (Robert Herrick)
Publisher: New York: Boosey & Hawkes BH.BK.700
For: Mezzo soprano and string quartet.
Difficulty: Voice: difficult; Instruments: moderate
Vocal range: g (d) - $b^{b\prime\prime}$
Language: English

400
Bischof, Rainer
In Memoriam memoriae, Op. 9 (© 1982)
I. Kommer mein Freund (Marceline...Desbordes-Valmore)
II. Lass deine Hand... (Stefan Zweig)
III. Wer je gelebt in Liebes... (Theodor Storm)
IV. Ein Traum... (Johann Gottfried Herder)
Publisher: Vienna: Doblinger 08827
For: Mezzo soprano, speaker, celesta, vibraphone, bass clarinet, and cello.
Difficulty: Voice: moderately difficult; Instruments: moderately difficult
Vocal range: b^b - $f^{\#\prime\prime}$
Language: German

401
Blumenfeld, Harold (b. 1923)
Le carnet d'un damné (Notebook of the Damned) (1987)
I. Adieu
II. L'éternité
Text: Arthur Rimbaud
Publisher: Saint Louis: MMB Music
For: Mezzo soprano, oboe, clarinet in B^b, viola, cello, bass, piano, and percussion (one player).
Percussion instrumentation: glockenspiel, vibraphone, marimba, tubular chimes [on and offstage

(d′ and $g^{\#\prime}$)], three gongs [on and offstage ($f^{\#}$ onstage, d and $g^{\#}$ offstage)], large tam-tam, snare drum, 5 roto-toms, 3 sizzle cymbals (small, medium, large), woodblocks, temple blocks, maracas, and bamboo chimes.

Difficulty: Voice: difficult; Instruments: difficult

Vocal range: a^{b} - $a^{b\prime\prime}$

Language: French

402

Bon, Willem Frederik (1940-1983)

"Dag" (1979)

I. Melopee
II. Marc groet's morgens de dingen
III. Berceuse voor volwassenen
IV. Zeer kleine speeldoos

Text: Paul van Ostaijen

Publisher: Amsterdam: Donemus

For: Mezzo soprano and percussion.

Percussion instrumentation: vibraphone, xylorimba, marimba, 3 bongos, 3 tom-toms, tambourine, 3 triangles (small, medium, large), large cymbals, (medium), tam-tam (large), and woodblock.

Difficulty: Voice: moderate; Instruments: moderately difficult

Vocal range: f - g″

Language: Dutch

Comments: The score is somewhat difficult to read.

403

Bon, Willem Frederik (1940 - 1983)

Silence (1978)

Text: Edgar Allan Poe

Publisher: Amsterdam: Donemus

For: Mezzo soprano, woodwind quintet, and piano.

Difficulty: Voice: difficult; Instruments: very difficult

Vocal range: g - $g^{\#\prime\prime}$

Language: English

Duration: 10:00

404

Brown, Newel Kay (b. 1932)

Déjeuner sur l'Herb (1982)

I. The little thought-flowers...
II. When the sun goes slant...
III. (voice tacet)
IV. Little gardener, fill your vases...
V. When the sun goes slant.(2)...
VI. Put the flowers in your mouth...
VII. When the sun goes slant.(3)...
VIII. The little thought-flowers.(2)...
IX. In the chilling rooms of memory...
X. They say, "Spring was the time of endless night"...
XI. They say, "There was no need to ask for more"...

Text: Richard B. Sale

Publisher: New York: Seesaw

For: Mezzo soprano, flute, alto saxophone, and piano.

Difficulty: Voice: moderately difficult; Instruments: moderately difficult

Vocal range: d′ - a″

Language: English

405

Bruzdowicz, Joanna (b. 1943)

Rysunki Z Przystani (1967)
(Sketches from the Harbour)

I. Źwit (El alba)
II. Wieczór (La tarde)
III. Nokturn (Nocturno)

IV. Elegia
V. Piosenka (Cantarcillo)
VI. Latarnia morska (El faro)
VII. Modlitwa (Oración)
Text: José Gorostiza
Publisher: Warsaw: P.W.M.
For: Mezzo soprano, flute, piano, and percussion (3 players).
Percussion instrumentation: claves, castanets, güiro, cabaça [maraca-like gourd], 2 congas, triangle, and vibraphone.
Difficulty: Voice: difficult; Instruments: difficult
Vocal range: g# - a″
Language: Polish and Spanish
Duration: 6:00

406
Canino, Bruno (b. 1935)
Cantata No. 2 (1966)
Text: Anonymous Latin, Joseph Weinheber (German portion)
Publisher: Milan: Ricordi 131014
For: Mezzo soprano, flute, viola, harp, harmonium, and percussion.
Percussion instrumentation: marimba, woodblock, castanet, 2 African tambourines, slit drum, vibraphone, and other membrane and metal instruments.
Difficulty: Voice: very difficult; Instruments: very difficult
Vocal range: f - a^{b}″
Language: Latin, German
Comments: Score is difficult to read.

407
Carr, Edwin (b. 1926)
An Edith Sitwell Song Cycle (1965)
I. Prelude (oboe solo)
II. O yet Forgive
III. O Dionysus of the Tree (piano and voice)
IV. The Queen Bee Sighed (oboe and voice)
V. Mandoline
Text: Edith Sitwell
Publisher: Milan: Ricordi LD556
For: Mezzo soprano, oboe, and piano.
Difficulty: Voice: moderate; Instruments: moderate
Vocal range: g - g#″
Language: English
Duration: 10:30

408
Chaikovsky, Boris (b. 1925)
The Last Spring (© 1984)
I. Radostnoye Nastroeniye
II. Ovizhyenie Vesni
III. Sodntse Vzoshdo
IV. Zeleniiluch
V. Stenyab'
VI. Osen'
VII. Kto Mne Otvetip
Text: Nikolai Zabolotsky
Publisher: Moscow: Muzyka
For: Mezzo soprano, flute, clarinet, and piano.
Difficulty: Voice: moderate; Instruments: moderate
Vocal range: a - f″
Language: Russian

409
Chatman, Stephen (b. 1950)
Dandy Man (1974)
Text: Jurgen Dankleff
Publisher: Toronto: Berandol BER 1759
For: Female voice (mezzo soprano), large suspended cymbal with 2 wire brushes, and flute.

Difficulty: Voice: difficult; Instrument: difficult
Vocal range: c′ - f″
Language: mixture of English and German
Duration: 8:00
Comments: Singer must smoke cigarettes; flute player must be male; theatrical effects; pitch approximations; white score.

410
Colgrass, Michael (b. 1932)
New People (1969)
I. Baby's eyes...
II. Psst!
III. Bègă Bomba
IV. Earth is the Theatre
V. Skyscrapers are the Trees
VI. Starling
VII. Goodnight Day
Text: Composer
Publisher: New York: MCA 17538-044
For: Mezzo soprano, viola, and piano.
Difficulty: Voice: difficult; Instruments: difficult
Vocal range: f - g″
Language: English

411
Constant, Franz (b. 1910)
Triade, Op. 30 (1967)
I. Poème des bruits (Georges Linze)
II. Rythme (Camille Biver)
III. La grande brosse (Norwegian)
Publisher: Brussels: Ce Be De M
For: Voice (mezzo soprano), piano, alto saxophone, and percussion.
Percussion instrumentation: cymbals, small drum, tom-tom, bass drum, woodblocks, triangle, gong, and gong aigu [high].
Difficulty: Voice: difficult; Instruments: difficult
Vocal range: g^b - a″
Language: French
Duration: 11:00

412
Crosse, Gordon (b. 1937)
World Within, Op. 40 (1976)
I. Prologue
II. Nocturne I
III. Diaries and Song
IV. Nocturne II
V. Nocturne III
VI. Diaries and Song II
VII. Nocturne IV
VIII. Epilogue
Text: Emily Brontë
Publisher: New York: Oxford University Press
For: Mezzo soprano, actress, flute (piccolo, alto flute, crotale in A), clarinet in B^b (bass clarinet, metronome), horn, trumpet in C, violin (metronome), viola, cello (crotale in B^b), harp, piano (wind chimes, tam-tam, metronome), and percussion.
Percussion instrumentation: lyra, glockenspiel, bell (out of tune school bell), crotale (b″), triangle, suspended cymbal, small timpano and 4 tom-toms (all at given pitch), tam-tam (shared with piano), clock chime [e′ (out of tune)], and stretched wire in box.
Difficulty: Voice: very difficult; Instruments: very difficult

Vocal range: g* - g″
Language: English
Duration: 35:00
Comments: Some graphic notation; not a piece of musical theatre, but the work is dramatic.

413
Dallapiccola, Luigi (1904-1975)
Sicut umbra (1970)
I. Introduzione (voice tacet)
II. El olvido
III. El recuerdo
IV. Epitafio ideal de un marinero
Text: Juan Ramón Jimenez (*Piedra y cielo*)
Publisher: Milan: Suvini Zerboni: S.7077Z.
For: Mezzo soprano and 4 groups of instruments.
I. piccolo, flute, and alto flute
II. sopranino clarinet in E^b, clarinet, and bass clarinet
III. violin, viola, and cello
IV. harp, celesta, and vibraphone
Difficulty: Voice: difficult; Instruments: difficult
Vocal range: f* - f″
Language: Spanish
Duration: 10:00

414
Davies, Peter Maxwell (b. 1934)
The Blind Fiddler (1975)
I. Introduction
II. He was with the Saint...
III. Interlude
IV. The word was imprisoned...
V. Few must vanish...
VI. (not in score - score apparently misnumbered)
VII. Interlude
VIII. Heaven & Hell...
IX. Interlude
X. Seven crofts...
XI. Interlude
XII. Between the thief and hoard...
XIII. Interlude
XIV. Therefore he no more troubled...
Text: George MacKay Brown
Publisher: London: Boosey & Hawkes © 1978 B&H 20538
For: Mezzo soprano, crotales (B♮), violin, harpsichord, bass clarinet, cello, guitar, flute, and various percussion instruments.
Percussion instrumentation: marimba, 2 woodblocks (large and very small), small Chinese cymbal, 2 temple blocks (large and small), spoons, maracas, tabor, castanet machine, 2 suspended cymbals (large and small), bell tree, bones, crotales, tom-toms, 2 timpani, large Japanese temple gong placed on pedal timpano, and very large nipple gong.
Difficulty: Voice: very difficult; Instruments: very difficult
Vocal range: g - b″
Language: English

415
Davies, Peter Maxwell (b. 1934)
Fiddlers at the Wedding (1974)
I. Fiddlers at the Wedding
II. Interlude (voice tacet)
III. Ikey's Day
IV. Interlude (voice tacet)
V. Roads
VI. Interlude (voice tacet)
VII. Peat Cutting
Text: George MacKay Brown (*Fishermen with Ploughs*)

Publisher: London: Boosey & Hawkes 20488
For: Mezzo soprano, alto flute, mandolin, guitar, and percussion (one player).
Percussion instrumentation: 5 glass brandy bowls (B^b, A, A^b, F, E^b) placed on medium pedal timpano, bongo (very small), marimba, crotales, Chinese cymbal, deep nipple gong, bell tree, small woodblock, glass wind chimes, and sandpaper block.
Difficulty: Voice: difficult; Instruments: moderately difficult
Vocal range: e - a″
Language: English
Duration: 19:00

416

Davies, Peter Maxwell (b. 1934)
From Stone to Thorn (1971)
Text: George MacKay Brown
Publisher: London: Boosey & Hawkes 20484
For: Mezzo soprano, clarinet in A or Basset clarinet in A, guitar, 2-manual harpsichord, and percussion (one player).
Percussion instrumentation: glockenspiel, coiled spring (ideally a large grandfather clock spring), 3 temple blocks (very small, small, large), 2 woodblocks (very small, small), bell tree, 3 cymbals (small, large, very large), wind chimes, tam-tam, small bass drum (with double-headed beater), and flexatone.
Difficulty: Voice: extremely difficult; Instruments: very difficult
Vocal range: $d^{\#}$ - $b^{b\prime\prime}$
Language: English
Duration: 20:00

417

Davies, Peter Maxwell (b. 1934)
Miss Donnithorne's Maggot (1974)
I. Prelude
II. Miss Donnithorne's Maggott
III. Recitative
IV. Her Dump
V. Nocturne (voice tacet)
VI. Her Rant
VII. Recitative
VIII. Her Reel
Text: Randolph Snow
Publisher: London: Boosey & Hawkes B&H 20337
For: Mezzo soprano, flute (piccolo and alto flute), clarinet in A, cello, piano (balloon), 4 metronomes set in motion by the players, and percussion.
Percussion instrumentation: small and large suspended cymbals, large bass drum, large temple block, 4 woodblocks (very small, small, medium, large), tam-tam, football rattle, snare drum, bell tree, bass drum, and cymbal with foot pedal, sandpaper, glass chimes, police whistle, bosun's whistle, chamois leather rubbed on glass, balloon to pop, thundersheet, glockenspiel, and marimba.
Difficulty: Voice: extremely difficult; Instruments: very difficult
Vocal range: e^b - $c^{\#\prime\prime\prime}$
Language: English
Duration: 32:00

418

Davies, Peter Maxwell (b. 1934)
My Lady Lothian's Lilt (1975)

Text: None
Publisher: London: Boosey & Hawkes B & H 20571
For: Mezzo soprano, alto flute, bass clarinet, viola, cello, and percussion.
Percussion instrumentation: glockenspiel and marimba.
Difficulty: Voice: moderate; Instruments: moderately difficult
Vocal range: c - a″
Language: none - singer vocalizes on "ah"
Duration: 6:03

419
DAVIES, PETER MAXWELL (B. 1934)
Tenebrae super Gesualdo (1972)
Text: from the Tenebrae
Publisher: London: Chester J.W.C. 55183
For: Mezzo soprano, alto flute, bass clarinet, harpsichord (celesta, chamber organ or harmonium), marimba (glockenspiel), guitar, violin (viola), and cello.
Difficulty: Voice: moderate; Instruments: difficult
Vocal range: e - e″
Language: Latin
Duration: 20:00
Comments: Voice plays minor role; no voice part in fourth movement. Some sections in somewhat free time but controlled by the conductor.

420
DENCH, CHRIS
Shunga (© 1986)
I. Iroha
II. Anata no/Ikahoro no
III. Komoncho
IV. Suma no ama no
V. Kuro Kami no
Text: Kobo Daishi
Publisher: London: United Music Publishers
For: Mezzo soprano (claves, jingles, chime bar), flute (piccolo, alto flute, bass flute), oboe (oboe damore), piano, and percussion.
Percussion instrumentation: 3 bowed cymbals (low, medium, high), large roto-tom, vibraphone, small triangle, large bass drum, smaller foot pedal bass drum, 2 cowbells, chime bar, 3 temple blocks, and crotale (A^b).
Difficulty: Voice: difficult; Instruments: difficult
Vocal range: b - g″
Language: Japanese
Duration: 18:00

421
DÖHL, FRIEDHELM (B. 1936)
Szene über einen kleinen Tod (1975)
Text: Composer
Publisher: Wiesbaden: Breitkopf und Härtel BG 1188
For: Mezzo soprano, flute (alto flute, bass flute), cello, cymbals, and tape.
Difficulty: Voice: very difficult; Instruments: very difficult
Vocal range: f - b″ plus highest note possible
Language: German
Comments: Read performance notes carefully; use of some graphic notation; some aleatoric sections; pitch approximations in voice part.

422
DRUCKMAN, JACOB (B. 1928)
Animus 2 (1968)
Text: none
Publisher: New York: MCA
For: Mezzo soprano, tape, and percussion (2 players).
Percussion instrumentation: maracas, bongos, 2 pair timbales, conga, 4 tom-toms, large bass drum, bass drum with pedal, small cymbal, large cymbal, large sizzle cymbal, hi-hat, small gong, large gong, large tam-tam, 3 coil springs (2 with sizzles–small metal rings hung on coils), 3 temple blocks, 3 cowbells, 2 woodblocks, 2 West Indies steel drums, 1 pair claves, 1 brass wind chime (Japanese tubular), 1 bamboo wind chime, flexatone, 4 triangles, sleigh bells (Somali), bell tree, tambourine frame, marimba, vibraphone, celesta, tubular chimes, and tuned antique cymbals.
Difficulty: Voice: very difficult; Instruments: difficult
Vocal range: f# - a″
Language: International Phonetic Alphabet
Duration: 18:48
Comments: Some graphic notation; white score.

423
DRUCKMAN, JACOB (B. 1928)
Dark upon the Harp: Psalms (© 1967)
I. Be not far from me... (Psalm 22: 12-17, 20)
II. The wicked are estranged from the womb...(Psalm 57: 4-9)
III. Praised is the Lord... (Psalm 18: 4-9)
IV. Thou didst turn for me... (Psalm 30:12,13)
V. Behold how good it is... (Psalm 133)
VI. The lines are fallen unto me... (Psalm 16:6-8)
Publisher: Bryn Mawr, PA: Theodore Presser
For: Mezzo soprano, two trumpets in B^b, horn, trombone, tuba, and percussion (2 players).
Percussion Instrumentation: (I) vibraphone, triangle, timbales, small suspended cymbal, tom-tom. (II) side drum, small tom-tom, large floor tom-tom, bass drum with pedal, 2 temple blocks, large suspended cymbal, maracas, and glockenspiel.
Difficulty: Voice: very difficult; Instruments: very difficult
Vocal range: g - a″
Language: English
Duration: 18:00

424
DURKÓ, ZSOLT (B. 1934)
Dartmouth Concerto (1966)
I. Invocation (voice tacet)
II. Recitative (voice tacet)
III. Song
IV. Double
Text: John Masefield (*The Lemings*)
Publisher: Budapest: Editio Musica © 1970 Z.10.092
For: Mezzo soprano, flute, clarinet in B^b, bass clarinet, bassoon, horn, trumpet in C, 2 trom-

bones, harp, prepared piano (harmonium), violin, viola, cello, and percussion (2 players).
Percussion instrumentation: timpani, bass drum, snare drum without snare, tambourine, castanet, Chinese gong, and suspended cymbal.
Difficulty: Voice: difficult; Instruments: moderate
Vocal range: d′ - a″
Language: English
Duration: 4:00

425
DUSAPIN, PASCAL
Igitur (1977)
Text: Lucretius
Publisher: Munich: Edition Modern M 2031
For: Female voice (mezzo soprano), 3 horns, 2 trumpets in B^b, 2 trombones, and 6 cellos.
Difficulty: Voice: difficult; Instruments: difficult
Vocal range: g$^\#$ - g″
Language: Latin
Comments: Use of quartertones.

426
FARBERMAN, HAROLD (B. 1929)
New York Times, Aug. 30, 1964 (1964)
I. The Blue Whale
II. Politics
III. Science
IV. Civil Rights
Text: from same
Publisher: Hastings-on-Hudson, NY: General Music Publishing
For: Mezzo soprano, piano, and percussion.
Percussion instrumentation: tom-tom, lujon [bass metallophone], xylophone, triangle, suspended cymbal, cowbell, 2 woodblocks, tambourine, and vibraphone.
Difficulty: Voice: moderately difficult; Instruments: moderate
Vocal range: g$^\#$ - g″
Language: English
Duration: 9:35

427
FERRARI, GIORGIO (B. 1925)
Al Fratelli Cervi (1964)
Text: Salvatore Quasimodo
Publisher: Milan: Casa Musicale Sonzogno di Piero Ostali
For: Mezzo soprano or baritone, flute, oboe, clarinet in B^b, horn, trumpet in C, trombone, harp, violin, viola, cello, and percussion.
Percussion instrumentation: 4 tom-toms and suspended cymbal.
Difficulty: Voice: difficult; Instruments: moderately difficult
Vocal range: b^b - f″
Language: Italian

428
FORTNER, JACK (B. 1935)
S pr ING no. 6 (1966)
I. first robin the ;
II. in just
III. because it's
IV. Now i lay (with everywhere around)
Text: e. e. cummings
Publisher: Paris: Jobert J.J.753
For: Female voice (mezzo soprano), flute, alto saxophone, bassoon, viola, cello, double bass, vibraphone, harp, and piano.

Difficulty: Voice: difficult; Instruments: difficult
Vocal range: g - g″
Language: English
Duration: 9:00
Comments: Use of Sprechstimme; spoken sections.

429
FURSTENAU, WOLFRAM
Sechs Porträts aus einer grossen Stadt (1960)
I. Teenager
II. Alte Bogenlampe
III. Zwölf Uhr mittags
IV. Auf dem Hinterhof
V. Der alte Mann
VI. Ferienreise
Text: Composer
Publisher: Regensburg, Germany: Gustav Bosse Verlag 103
For: Voice (mezzo soprano or baritone), flute, oboe, clarinet in B^b, violin I, violin II, violin III, cello, and double bass.
Difficulty: Voice: moderate; Instruments: moderate
Vocal range: g - f″
Language: German

430
GABER, HARLEY (B. 1943)
Voce II (1965)
I. Macinarngala (Issa)
II. Oto (Buson)
III. Akai Botan (Buson)
IV. Seshi (Bashō)
V. Naru ano Michi Nite (Bashō)
VI. Bashô no Michi (Bashō)
VII. Yoru no Inazuma (Bashō)
Publisher: Cincinnati: Apogee Press, © 1967 ESE-1311-1
Series: Apogee Series I, Young American Composers
For: Female voice (mezzo soprano), alto flute, and percussion (one player).
Percussion instrumentation: vibraphone, mallets, and wind chimes.
Difficulty: Voice: very difficult; Instruments: moderate
Vocal range: g - g#″
Language: Japanese, romanized
Comments: White score

431
GABURO, KENNETH (1926-1993)
Two (1971)
Text: Virginia Hommel
Publisher: Bryn Mawr, PA: Theodore Presser 111-40073 (New Music Edition)
For: Mezzo soprano, alto flute, and double bass.
Difficulty: Voice: moderately difficult; Instruments: moderately difficult
Vocal range: f# - a″
Language: English
Comments: Voice is required to change timbre and quality; white score; some rhythmic difficulties.

432
GOTTLIEB, JACK (B. 1930)
Downtown Blues for Uptown Halls (1977)
I. Big Little Girl
II. Impulsive, Neon Night
Text: Composer
Publisher: New York: G. Schirmer ME 1070

For: Female voice (mezzo soprano), clarinet in B^b, and piano.
Difficulty: Voice: moderately difficult; Instruments: moderately difficult
Vocal range: a - $a^{b''}$
Language: English

433

Harris, Donald (b. 1931)

For the Night to Wear (1978)

Text: Hortense Flexner
Publisher: Bryn Mawr, PA: Theodore Presser 411-41083
For: Mezzo soprano, flute (alto flute), clarinet in B^b (alto clarinet), bass clarinet, violin (viola I), viola II, cello, and piano.
Difficulty: Voice: difficult; Instruments: difficult.
Vocal range: $g^{\#}$ - $b^{b''}$
Language: English
Duration: 8:00

434

Heider, Werner (b. 1930)

Picasso - Musik (1966)

I. Ophélie
II. Mirakel das der Torero
III. Locusche der Stunde
IV. Junges Mädchen "Kss" schöner Schreiner
V. Ins geheim schweige
VI. Le cygne sur le lac
VII. Bau reiss aus verrenk und schlag Tot

Text: Composer
Publisher: New York: Peters 8281
For: Mezzo soprano, clarinet in B^b, violin, and piano.
Difficulty: Voice: extremely difficult; Instruments: very difficult
Vocal range: a^b - $a^{b''}$
Language: German (French translation provided for performance)
Comments: Many rhythmic difficulties as well as potential pitch problems.

435

Heiss, John (b. 1938)

Songs of Nature: A Cycle of Five Songs on Texts of Nineteeth-Century American Poets (1975)

I. From "Thanatopsis" (William Cullen Bryant)
II. The Yellow Violet (William Cullen Bryant)
III. The Sound of the Sea (Henry W. Longfellow)
IV. Men Say (Henry David Thoreau)
V. From "If I Shouldn't Be Alive" and "How Happy is the Little Stone" (Emily Dickinson)

Publisher: New York: Boosey & Hawkes VAB0190
For: Mezzo soprano, flute, clarinet in B^b, violin, cello, and piano.
Difficulty: Voice: moderately difficult; Instruments: moderately difficult
Vocal range: g - $f^{\#''}$
Language: English
Duration: 14:00
Comments: Number III to be performed in a "very musical speech".

436

Hoyland, Victor

Jeux-thème (1972)

Text: Composer
Publisher: London: Universal Edition UE 16054 L

For: Mezzo soprano, flute I, flute II (alto flute), clarinet I in B^b, clarinet II in B^b (bass clarinet), trumpet I in B^b, trumpet II in B^b, trombone, bass trombone, vibraphone (glockenspiel), harp, marimba, Hammond or Lowry organ, celesta, piano, cello I, cello II, cello III, cello IV, double bass I, double bass II, and percussion.

Percussion instrumentation: (I) bongos, 3 tom-toms, 2 congas, 1 snare drum, 1 tenor drum, 1 bass drum, 2 tambourines, 1 glass chime, 3 triangles (high, medium, low), and 1 suspended cymbal. (II) 1 bongos, 3 tom-toms, 2 congas, 1 snare drum, 1 tenor drum, 1 bass drum, 2 tambourines, 1 wood chime, 3 triangles (high, medium, low), and 1 suspended cymbal (III) 1 tom-tom, 3 triangles (high, medium, low), 1 pair of crotales, 3 suspended cymbals (high, medium, low), 3 gongs (high, medium, low), 1 tam-tam, 1 maraca, 1 wood chime, and 1 pair of cymbals. (IV) 1 pair of congas, 3 triangles (high, medium, low), 1 pair of crotales, 3 suspended cymbals (high, medium, low), 3 gongs (high, medium, low), 1 tam-tam (very large), 1 sizzle cymbal, and 1 glass chime.

Difficulty: Voice: very difficult; Instruments: extremely difficult

Vocal range: a - f″

Language: French

Duration: 10:00

Comments: Read performance notes carefully; some use of new notation; aleatoric sections; some use of spatial time; some speaking for singer.

437

Jeney, Zoltán (b. 1943)

12 Songs (© 1985)

I. May I feel... (e. e. cummings)
II. Hahahahahahahahahaha!... (Dezsö Tandori)
III. un(bee)mo (e. e. cummings)
IV. in Just (e. e. cummings)
V. o (round) moon... (e. e. cummings)
IV. n
OthI
N
g can (e.e. cummings)
VII. Silent, Silent Night (William Blake)
VIII. Hold (Sándor Weöres)
IX. Me up at does (e. e. cummings)
X. Annie died the other day (e. e. cummings)
XI. tw (e. e. cummings)
XII. Ein Zeichen sind wir... (Friedrich Hölderlin)

Publisher: Budapest: Editio Musica Z.13 069

For: Female voice (mezzo soprano), violin, and piano.

Difficulty: Voice: difficult; Instruments: difficult

Vocal range: g* - a″

Language: English, German

Duration: 27:00

438

Jenkins, Joseph Willcox (b. 1928)

Three Carols from the Quiet Wars (1964)

I. Preface
II. Carol of a Bride

III. Carol of a Father
IV. Carol of a Nun
V. Epilogue

Text: Samuel Hazo
Publisher: Ann Arbor: University Microfilms (MENC Contemporary Music Project)
For: Mezzo soprano, string quartet, and piano.
Difficulty: Voice: difficult; Instruments: difficult
Vocal range: a* - g″
Language: English
Duration: 20:00

439

Johnston, Ben (b. 1926)

A Sea Dirge: Full fathom five thy father lies (1962)

Text: William Shakespeare (*The Tempest*)
Publisher: Baltimore: Smith Publications © 1974
For: Mezzo soprano, flute, violin, and oboe.
Difficulty: Voice: moderately difficult; Instruments: moderately difficult
Vocal range: d*′ plus - g″ plus (*see comments)
Language: English
Comments: Music is meant to be performed in just intonation. *Read instruction sheet carefully.

440

Kadosa, Pál (1903-1983)

Népdal-Kantáta ,Op. 30 (© 1966)

I. Istenem, Istenem
II. Csiná losi erdön
III. Jánoshidi vágártéren

Publisher: Budapest: Zenemükiadó Vállalat Z.3663
For: Voice (mezzo soprano or baritone), clarinet in B^b, violin, and cello.
Difficulty: Voice: moderate; Instruments: moderate
Vocal range: g - f″
Language: Hungarian (German translation provided for performance)

441

Katzer, Georg (b. 1935)

Bobrowski - Lieder (1972)

I. Dorfmusik
II. September
III. Der Wanderer

Text: Johannes Bobrowski
Publisher: Leipzig: Edition Peters 5667
For: Mezzo soprano, piccolo (alto flute), and piano.
Difficulty: Voice: difficult; Instruments: moderate
Vocal range: c′ - g″
Language: German

442

Katzer, Georg (b. 1935)

Lieder nach Leising: Sechs Lieder und ein Gedicht (1983)

I. Über Mittag
II. Vom Minimum
III. Orion
IV. Shakespeare, fünfter Akt
V. Feuer und Flamme
VI. Gegenlicht (poem, no music)
VIII. Der Sieg

Text: Richard Leising
Publisher: Leipzig: VEB Deutscher Verlag für Musik © 1985 DVFM 9407
For: Voice (mezzo soprano), flute (alto flute, piccolo, large tri-

angle), clarinet in B^b (claves), cello, piano (2 small chains), and percussion.
Percussion instrumentation: glockenspiel, xylorimba, bells, 3 tom-toms, 2 bongos, snare drum, 3 cymbals, suspended cymbal, woodblocks, bass drum, birdcall, tambourine, ratchet, flexatone, cucumber, whistle (short, high pitch flute), claves, triangle, bamboo reed, cowbell, castanets, sleighbells, maracas, and Japanese rattle.
Difficulty: Voice: difficult; Instruments: difficult
Vocal range: g - f#″
Language: German
Comments: Some Sprechstimme.

443
Kelemen, Milko (b. 1924)
Epitaph (1961)
Text: Grigor Vitez
Publisher: Frankfort: Henry Litolff's Verlag/New York: Peters 5817
For: Mezzo soprano, viola, vibraphone, and percussion (3 players).
Percussion instrumentation: snare drum, cymbal, tam-tam, nipple gong, tubular chimes, bongos (high, medium, low), tambourine, triangle, güiro, maracas, claves, and woodblock.
Difficulty: Voice: difficult; Instruments: moderately difficult
Vocal range: a - a″
Language: Serbo-Croatian (German translation by the composer provided for performance).
Duration: 5:00

444
Kocsár, Miklos (b. 1933)
Kassák-Dalok (© 1980)
I. Alkonyi szél (Twilight wind)
II. Monoton (Monotonous)
III. Ó csend (O silence)
IV. Széltölcsér (Wind Cornet)
V. Hétköznapi csoda (Everyday Miracle)
Text: Composer
Publisher: Budapest: Editio Musica Z.8746
For: Mezzo soprano, flute, and Hungarian cimbalom [large Hungarian gypsy dulcimer].
Difficulty: Voice: moderately difficult; Instruments: difficult
Vocal range: c′ - f#″
Language: Hungarian

445
Košťál, Arnošt
Vandrovali Hudci (1975)
Text: Ladislav Svatoš
Publisher: Prague: Panton P1981
For: Mezzo soprano, clarinet in B^b, viola, and piano.
Difficulty: Voice: moderately difficult; Instruments: moderately difficult
Vocal range: a - f″
Language: Czechoslovakian (with singable German translation)
Duration: 10:00

446
Krol, Bernhard (b. 1920)
Die Nachtigall Op. 77 (© 1985)
I. Prolog
II. Der Kaiser auf dem Thron...
III. Der Hofstadt sucht...
IV. Der Hofstadt, angeführt vom Küchenmädchen...

V. Bewegungslos lauchen...
VI. Die Nachtigall singt vor dem Kaiser...
VII. Der Kaiser becommt eine kunstliche Nachtigall...
VIII. Die Nachtigall fliegt davon
IX. Der Kaiser schilt die Nachtigall...
X. Der kranke Kaiser
XI. Der Tod mit Krone
XII. Die Nachtigall besiegt den Tod

Text: based on tales by Hans Christian Anderson
Publisher: Hamburg: J. Schuberth J.S. 118
For: Mezzo soprano, flute, and piano.
Difficulty: Voice: difficult; Instruments: difficult
Vocal range: b - g″
Language: German

447

KURTÁG, GYÖRGY (B. 1926)

Scenes from a Novel, Op. 19 (1985)

I. Pridi (Come)
II. Otvstrechi (From Meeting to Parting)
III. Mol'ba (Supplication)
IV. Pozvod'Mne (Allow Me)
V. Schitadochka (Counting Out Rhyme)
VI. Son (Dream)
VII. Rondo (Rondo)
VIII. Nagota (Nakedness)
IX. Vad'sdya Sharmanki (Hurdy Gurdy Waltz)
X. Skazka (Tale)
XI. Snova (Again)
XII. Beskonechn'iiryad Voskre senii (Sundays)
XIII. Vizit (Visit)
XIV. Bi'd' (True Story)
XV. Zpidog (Epilogue)

Text: Rimma Dalos
Publisher: Budapest: Editio Musica Z 12.661
For: Voice (mezzo soprano), violin, double bass, and cimbalom (large Hungarian gypsy dulcimer).
Difficulty: Voice: very difficult; Instruments: difficult
Vocal range: g♯ - b♭″
Language: Russian; Hungarian, English, and German translations provided.
Comments: Use of quartertones.

448

LANZA, ALCIDES (B. 1929)

Penetrations VI (1972-II) (1972)

Text: Composer
Publisher: New York: Boosey & Hawkes
For: Voice (mezzo soprano), trombone, synthesizer, organ, piano, double bass, electric bass, 2 electronic tapes, percussion, and colored lights.
Percussion instrumentation: finger cymbal, temple blocks, 3 suspended cymbals, 3 tam-tams, and bass drum.
Difficulty: Voice: difficult; Instruments: difficult
Vocal range: f - b′
Language: English
Duration: 17:00
Comments: Graphic notation; read performance notes. Requires singer to scream; theatrical effects required.

449

Lechner, Konrad (b. 1911)

Drei Gedichte (1968, rev. 1978)

I. April
II. Zikade
III. Schläferung

Text: Hans Magnus Enzensberger
Publisher: Celle, Germany: Moeck Verlag 5219
For: Voice (mezzo soprano) and flute.
Difficulty: Voice: very difficult; Instruments: difficult
Vocal range: g^{*} - a''
Language: German

450

Leedy, Douglas (b. 1938)

Symphoniae Sacrae (1976)

I. The Forty-Sixth Psalm (Psalm 46)
II. Lamentatio Super Babylonis (Apocalypsis 18)
III. Abendmahlslied (Johann Crüger)

Publisher: Oceanside, Oregon: Harmonie Universelle
For: Mezzo soprano, 6 or 7 string bass viola da gamba and harpsichord.
Difficulty: Voice: difficult; Instruments: difficult
Vocal range: g - g''
Language: I. English II. Latin III. German
Duration: 25:00

451

Lerdahl, Fred (b. 1943)

Eros: Variations (1975)

Text: Ezra Pound
Publisher: Hillsdale, NY: Mobart Music
For: Mezzo soprano, alto flute, viola, electric guitar, electric bass guitar, harp, electric piano, and percussion (2 players).
Percussion instrumentation: (I) congos [Haitian drumset], and bongos; (II) congos, bongos, low drums with "jingle attachment", and tam-tam.
Difficulty: Voice: extremely difficult; Instruments: very difficult (viola, alto flute)
Vocal range: f - $b^{b''}$
Language: English
Duration: 23:00

452

Luff, Enid (b. 1935)

Sŵn Dŵr (The Sound of Water) (1981)

I. O Litus vita mihi dulcius (Petronius Arbiter)
II. Domestic Economy (Anna Wickham)
III. Der Abschied (Friedrich Hölderlin)
IV. Sŵn Dŵr (Euros Bowen)

Publisher: London: Primavera
For: Mezzo contralto (mezzo soprano), piano, and flute.
Difficulty: Voice: difficult; Instruments: difficult
Vocal range: b - $f^{*''}$
Language: I. Latin, II. English, III. German, IV. Welsh with English translation.

453

Madey, Bogusław (b. 1932)

Transfiguracje (1965)

Text: none
Publisher: Warsaw: P.W.M. PWM-6661

For: Mezzo soprano, flute, oboe, English horn, clarinet in B^b (bass clarinet), bassoon, piano, double bass, and percussion (2 players).

Percussion instrumentation: (I) vibraphone, marimba, 3 tom-toms, 2 snare drums (soprano & alto), 2 triangles (soprano & alto), 2 cymbals (soprano & alto), medium gong, 3 near Eastern timpano, woodblocks, and slapstick; (II) 2 timpani, tambourine, bass drum, 2 triangles (tenor, bass), 3 suspended cymbals (alto, tenor, bass), tam-tam, 3 temple blocks, claves, and castanets.

Difficulty: Voice: very difficult; Instruments: difficult

Vocal range: g# - d‴

Language: phonemes and humming

Comments: Note extreme range.

454

Malipiero, Riccardo (b. 1914)

Monologo (1968)

Text: Giacomo Leopardi *Liberamente Scelti*

Publisher: Milan: Suvini Zerboni S. 6874 Z.

For: Voice (mezzo soprano), 4 violin I, 4 violin II, 2 violas, 2 cellos, and double bass.

Difficulty: Voice: moderately difficult; Instruments: difficult

Vocal range: b - f#″

Language: Italian

Duration: 14:00

455

Malipiero, Riccardo (b. 1914)

Preludio, Adagio e Finale (1963)

I. Mar de Aire (Miguel Gallardo Drago)
II. Es war einmal (Giacomo Noventa)
III. Mattina (Giuseppe Ungaretti)

Publisher: Milan: Suvini Zerboni S.6137Z.

For: Voice (mezzo soprano), piano, and percussion.

Percussion instrumentation: marimba, vibraphone, xylophone, 3 suspended cymbals, 3 bongos, 3 tom-toms, 3 cocos [cococello] (large, medium, small), large tam-tam, snare drum, tambourine, drum and cymbals, tubular chimes, and crotalo.

Difficulty: Voice: difficult; Instruments: difficult

Vocal range: f - a″

Language: I. Italian II. German III. Italian

456

Matsudaira, Yoritsunè (b. 1907)

Katsura (© 1967)

I. Katsura 1
II. Katsura 2
III. Kamashiro
IV. Shinsenkyo
V. Gepparo
VI. Shokintei
VII. Ama-no-Hashidate 1
VIII. Ama-no-Hashidate 2

Text: Composer

Publisher: Tokyo: Ongaku no Tomo Sha

For: Voice (mezzo soprano), flute, harpsichord, harp, guitar, piano, and percussion.

Percussion instrumentation: whip and bongo.

Difficulty: Voice: very difficult; Instruments: difficult
Vocal range: b^b - a″
Language: Japanese

457
Mestres-Quadreny, Josep Maria (b. 1929)
Musica per a Anna (1967)
Text: none
Publisher: Celle, Germany: Moeck Verlag 5066
For: Mezzo soprano and string quartet.
Difficulty: Voice: very difficult; Instruments: difficult
Vocal range: g^b - a″
Language: phonemes
Duration: 10:00

458
Milburn, Ellsworth (b. 1938)
Spiritus Mundi (1974)
I. Pluto
II. Venus
III. Mars
Text: C. Everett Cooper
Publisher: Saint Louis: MMB Music
For: Mezzo soprano (crotales in D# and E and suspended cymbal); violin (triangle and suspended cymbal); cello (crotales in A and B^b and small tam-tam); piano (small or medium bass drum, timpani, mallets for playing inside piano, glass wind chimes, block of wood to prop the pedal); conductor (triangle, suspended cymbal, two large tom-toms), and percussion (2 players).
Percussion instrumentation: (I) large pedal timpano (D-A), snare drum, bongos, suspended cymbals, maracas, and tubular chimes; (II) snare drum, 2 medium tom-toms, large bass drum, large tam-tam (shared with percussion I), metal wind chimes, and vibraphone.
Difficulty: Voice: difficult; Instruments: difficult
Vocal range: b^b - g″ plus highest and lowest notes possible
Language: English and Latin
Comments: Instrumentalists must sing brief section; some graphic notation.

459
Mitrea-Celarianu, Mihai (b. 1935)
Le Chant des Étoiles (1967, rev. 1969)
Text: Ancient poetry of the Algonquin Indians
Publisher: Paris: Salabert
For: Mezzo soprano or soprano, piccolo, flute, alto flute, oboe, English horn, clarinet in B^b, bass clarinet, bassoon, horn, trumpet in B^b, trombone, violin, viola, cello, double bass, electric guitar, piano, and percussion (3 players).
Percussion instrumentation: Tubular bells, vibraphone, marimba, 3 cowbells (low, medium and high), 2 woodblocks, snare drum, 3 tom-toms (low, medium and high), jingles, maracas, cymbal with foot pedal, and deep tam-tam.
Difficulty: Voice: difficult; Instruments: difficult
Vocal range: b - a^{b}″
Language: Romanian with singable French translation

Duration: minimum of 5:10; maximum of 7:46.

460
Molineux, Allen (b. 1950)
Crystals (© 1975)
I. Head against window
II. He took me out
III. Crystalizing you indoors
IV. Blackness is distressing
Text: Kathleen Geminder
Publisher: Huntington, NY: HaMaR Percussion Publications ES9
For: Mezzo soprano (maracas) and percussion (3 players).
Percussion instrumentation: (I) triangle, vibraphone, temple blocks, suspended cymbals, wind chimes, bongos, woodblocks, and tambourine; (II) tubular bells, xylophone, antique cymbals, suspended cymbals, triangle, and timpani; (III) marimba, suspended cymbals, bass drum, triangle, snare drum, tom-toms, and glockenspiel.
Difficulty: Voice: moderately difficult; Instruments: moderate
Vocal range: a^b - a″
Language: English

461
Nielsen, Svend (b. 1937)
Romancer (1974)
I. Sommerstaevnemøde (Frank Jaeger)
II. Skoumøde (Frank Jaeger)
III. Vandring i vinterskov (Frank Jaeger)
IV. Lille højsang (Thorkild Bjørnvig)
Publisher: Copenhagen: Wilhelm Hansen 4334
For: Mezzo soprano, 2 flutes (piccolo), vibraphone (glockenspiel), 2 cellos, and double bass.
Difficulty: Voice: difficult; Instruments: difficult
Vocal range: g - g″
Language: Danish
Duration: 20:00

462
Nobre, Marlos (b. 1939)
O canto multiplicado, Op. 38 (1972)
I. Sobre teu corpo...
II. Vergonha, vergonha...
III. Lágrimas De noturno orvalho...
Text: Carlos Drummond de Andrade
Publisher: Darmstadt: Tonos 10208
For: Voice (mezzo soprano) and strings (one or more per part).
Difficulty: Voice: difficult; Instruments: difficult
Vocal range: g - a″
Language: Portuguese

463
Pablo, Luis de (b. 1930)
Ein Wort (© 1965)
I. Prelude (voice tacet)
II. Version I^1 - I^8
III. Interlude I (voice tacet)
IV. Version II^1 - II^8
V. Interlude II (voice tacet)
VI. Version III^1 - III^8
VII. Interlude III (voice tacet)
VIII. Version IV^1 - IV^8
IX. Postlude
Text: Gottfried Benn
Publisher: Darmstadt: Tonos 7205
For: Voice (mezzo soprano), clarinet in B^b, violin, and piano.

Difficulty: Voice: difficult; Instruments: difficult
Vocal range: g - $a^{b''}$
Language: German
Duration: will vary
Comments: The singer can perform the versions in any order but the prelude, interludes, and the postlude must be performed in the designated order. Some Sprechstimme and some speaking.

464

Pablo, Luis de (b. 1930)

Pocket Zarzuela (1978)

I. Obertura (voice tacet)
II. Segunda vision de marzo
III. Coral-Anochecia-Mortaja
IV. Marcha-Edicto-Comentario (voice tacet)
V. Goyesca

Text: José Miguel Ullán
Publisher: Milan: Suvini Zerboni S.8528 Z.
For: Mezzo soprano, piccolo (flute and bass flute), clarinet in B^b, violin, cello, and piano.
Difficulty: Voice: very difficult; Instruments: difficult
Vocal range: g - b″
Language: Spanish
Duration: 14:00
Comments: White score.

465

Perera, Ronald (b. 1941)

Three Poems of Günter Grass (1974)

I. Gleisdreieck
II. Klappstühle
III. Schlaflos

Text: Günter Grass
Publisher: Boston: E. C. Schirmer 2478
For: Mezzo soprano, flute (piccolo, alto flute), clarinet in B^b (alto saxophone, bass clarinet), piano, violin, viola, cello, and stereo tape.
Difficulty: Voice: difficult; Instruments: difficult
Vocal range: g - b″
Language: German
Duration: 22:00
Comments: Use of microtones.

466

Pope, Conrad (b. 1951)

At That Hour (1977)

Text: James Joyce
Publisher: Hillsdale, NY: Mobart Music
For: Mezzo soprano, flute, clarinet in B^b, violin, viola, cello, and piano.
Difficulty: Voice: moderately difficult; Instruments: difficult
Vocal range: $g^{\#}$ - f″
Language: English
Duration: 11:00

467

Powers, Anthony

The Winter Festivals (1985)

I. Nos Galan gaeaf
II. La Toussaint
III. Dydd Gwyl eneidau
IV. St. Cecilia in Sagittarius
V. Half-Tongue Day
VI. Saturnalia
VII. At Solstice
VIII. Interlude: Nativity
IX. Y Plygaint/Carol
X. Benedicamus Domino

Text: Nigel Wells (*The Winter Festivals*)
Publisher: Oxford: Oxford University Press ISBN 0 19 358297X
For: Mezzo soprano, flute (alto flute and piccolo), oboe (English horn), clarinet in B^b (bass clarinet), bassoon (contrabassoon), horn, harp, viola, cello, and double bass.
Difficulty: Voice: very difficult; Instruments: difficult
Vocal range: g - b″
Language: English
Duration: 28:00

468

Prigozhin, Lûîtsian Abramovich (b. 1926)

Solntse i Kamni (1975)

I. Requiem
II. Dies Irae
III. Libera eas
IV. Sanctus
V. Agnus Dei

Text: Stikhi M. Alechkovich
Publisher: Saint Petersburg: Izdatel'stvo "Sovetskii Kompozitor"
For: Mezzo soprano, flute, string quartet, and piano.
Difficulty: Voice: difficult; Instruments: moderately difficult
Vocal range: e - g#″
Language: Latin and Russian

469

Pütz, Edward

Requiem im Park (1980)

I. Verwestes hab ich lange schon...
II. Schauen beliebt nur den sanftrunden Dolden...
III. Zwischen den Wimpern der Lärche hängt...
IV. Am See die Zigeunerin streift...
V. Rosig am Wölbbruchgrau...
VI. Winterlang mit blinden Blicken...

Text: Ursula Claude
Publisher: Darmstadt: Tonos 7266
For: Mezzo soprano, oboe, clarinet in B^b, horn, bassoon, cello, piano, and bongos.
Difficulty: Voice: difficult; Instruments: difficult
Vocal range: b - g″
Language: German
Duration: 17:30

470

Ran, Shulamit (b. 1949)

O the Chimneys (1969)

I. A dead child speaks
II. Already embraced by the arm of heavenly solace
III. Fleeing
IV. Someone comes
V. Hell is naked

Text: Nancy Sachs
Publisher: New York: Carl Fischer
For: Mezzo soprano, flute, clarinet in B^b (bass clarinet), cello, piano, tape, and percussion.
Percussion instrumentation: cymbals, timpani, vibraphone, 6 drums, bass drum, gong, and chimes.
Difficulty: Voice: very difficult; Instruments: difficult
Vocal range: g - a″
Language: German
Comments: The last movement has a partly aleatoric section.

471
Rands, Bernard (b. 1934)
Ballad I (1970)
Text: Derived from Gilbert Sorrentino's "Pentagram"
Publisher: London: Universal Edition UE 15414L
For: Mezzo soprano, flute (alto flute), trombone, double bass, piano, and percussion.
Percussion instrumentation: glass chimes, hi-hat, cymbals, vibraphone, tam-tam, woodblocks, temple blocks, bongos, snare drum, and tom-tom.
Difficulty: Voice: very difficult; Instruments: difficult
Vocal range: a^{b} - a″
Language: English
Duration: 14:00
Comments: Most sounds are not really pitched; singer must perform a number of vocal effects; in some places instrumentalists must play and "sing" sounds at the same time.

472
Riley, Dennis (b. 1943)
Cantata I, Op. 8 (1966)
I. Those that go Searching for Love...
II. If there were not an utter and absolute dark of silence...
Text: D. H. Lawrence
Publisher: New York: Peters
For: Mezzo soprano, tenor saxophone, vibraphone, cello, and piano.
Difficulty: Voice: difficult; Instruments: difficult
Vocal range: a - a″
Language: English

473
Rorem, Ned (b. 1923)
Serenade on five English Poems (1975)
I. Hold bade Thy Hours (Ecologues)
II. Th' expense of Spirit in a Waste of Shame
III. Flower in the Crannied Wall
IV. Peace
V. Never Weather-Beaten Sail
Text: John Fletcher, William Shakespeare, Alfred Lord Tennyson, Gerard Manley Hopkins, and Thomas Campion.
Publisher: New York: Boosey & Hawkes BH.BK.790
For: Voice (mezzo soprano), violin, viola, and piano.
Difficulty: Voice: moderate; Instruments: moderate
Vocal range: b - $a^{b\prime\prime}$
Language: English
Duration: 18:00
Comments: To be performed as one continuous movement.

474
Sachse, Hans Wolfgang (b. 1899)
Kinder der Republik (© 1973)
Text: Max Zimmering
Publisher: Berlin: Verlag Neue Musik Bestell - NM1020, 20(378)
For: Mezzo soprano or baritone and string quartet.
Difficulty: Voice: moderate; Instruments: moderate
Vocal range: b - e″
Language: German

475
Sargon, Simon (b. 1938)
Patterns in Blue (1974)

I. Cabaret Song (James Agee)
II. Snatch of Sliphorn Jazz (Carl Sandburg)
III. Lonesome Boy Blues (Kenneth Patchen)

Publisher: New York: Boosey & Hawkes BH.BK.769
For: Mezzo soprano, piano, and clarinet in B^b.
Difficulty: Voice: moderately easy; Instruments: moderately easy
Vocal range: a - e″
Language: English
Duration: 6:00

476
SCHAFER, R. MURRAY (B. 1933)
Requiems for the Party-girl; Ariadne's Arias from "Patria II" (1966)
Text: Composer
Publisher: Don Mills, Ontario: BMI Canada, Toronto: Clark & Cruickshank © 1969
For: Mezzo soprano, flute (piccolo), clarinet in B^b (bass clarinet in B^b), horn, piano, harp, violin, viola, cello, and percussion (1 player).
Percussion instrumentation: tam-tam, large suspended cymbal, marimba, triangle, small tom-tom, snare drum, tambourine, temple blocks, side drum, log drum, bass drum, tubular chimes, güiro, woodblock, and glockenspiel.
Difficulty: Voice: very difficult; Instruments: difficult
Vocal range: g - c‴
Language: English
Duration: 17:00
Comments: The piece calls for many vocal effects including a scream, a whisper, and alteration of tone color.

477
SCHERCHEN-HSIAO, TONA (B. 1938)
Wai (1967)
Text: Composer
Publisher: Zurich: Universal Edition UE 14799Z
For: Mezzo soprano, string quartet, and percussion (played by singer).
Percussion instrumentation: low tam-tam, 1 timpano, small portable drum, güiro, large fan, long metal necklace, and Chinese blocks.
Difficulty: Voice: difficult; Instruments: very difficult
Vocal range: g - f″ (plus higher pitch approximations)
Language: Stylized declamation based on Chinese.
Comments: White score; some graphic notation; performers must read "instructions for performance"; singer has many pitch approximations; movement III contains a "Version I" and "Version II" before a coda to end the piece. The voice must display rapidly changing moods and emotions throughout much of the piece.

478
SETER, MORDECAI (B. 1916)
Autumn: Songs Without Words (1970)
Text: none
Publisher: Tel Aviv: Israel Music Institute IMI 183

For: Mezzo soprano, clarinet in A, and harp or piano.
Difficulty: Voice: difficult; Instruments: moderately difficult
Vocal range: a* - f*″
Language: phonemes
Duration: 11:00

479

Świerzyński, Adam (b. 1914)

Liryki Morskie, (Sea Lyrics) (1972)

I. W Rybackim Porcie
II. Zapach Morza
III. Pomorze

Text: Franciszek Fenikowski
Publisher: Warsaw: Edycja Muzyczna Agencja Autorska
For: Mezzo soprano, string quartet, and piano.
Difficulty: Voice: moderately difficult; Instruments: moderately difficult
Vocal range: g - f″
Language: Polish

480

Thoresen, Lasse (b. 1949)

Hagen (1976)

I. Introduction (voice tacet)
II. Emnet (the subject)
III. Kommentar (I) (Commentary) (voice tacet)
IV. Kommentar (II) (Commentary)

Text: 'Abdu' l-Bahá
Publisher: Oslo: Norsk Musikferlag/Wilhelm Hansen N.M.O. 9357A
For: Mezzo soprano, violin, cello, piano, and percussion (2 players).
Percussion instrumentation: (I) marimba, 2 triangles of different size, and crotales; (II) vibraphone and tam-tam.
Difficulty: Voice: difficult; Instruments: very difficult
Vocal range: a - f*′
Language: Either English or Norwegian and phonemes
Duration: 29:00

481

Ung, Chinary (b. 1942)

Mohori (1974)

Text: phonemes
Publisher: New York: Peters
For: Mezzo soprano, flute, oboe, classical guitar, cello, harp, piano, and percussion (2 players).
Percussion instrumentation: antique cymbals, glass wind chimes, metal wind chimes, anvils, cowbells, woodblocks, temple blocks, tambourine, 4 suspended cymbals (small to large), congas, timbales, 3 snare drums, 2 tom-toms, marimba, claves, bamboo wind chimes, bongos, 2 tam-tams (large & small), Javanese gong, 2 bass drums (12" x 18" and 14" x 24"), and vibraphone.
Difficulty: Voice: very difficult; Instruments: difficult
Vocal range: e - a″
Language: phonemes, IPA symbols
Duration: 12:45
Comments: Note extreme range; several vocal tremolos are indicated.

482

Veyvoda, Gerald (b. 1948)

Through the Looking Glass (1971)

I. Imagining L.S.D.

II. L.S.D. Big Sur
III. After-Dream
Text: Lawrence Ferlinghetti
Publisher: New York: SeeSaw
For: Mezzo soprano, flute, oboe, clarinet in B^b, horn, bassoon, and two channels of pre-recorded electronic sounds.
Difficulty: Voice: difficult; Instruments: difficult
Vocal range: b^b - $b^{b''}$
Language: English
Comments: Speaking part on approximate pitches.

483
Virgin, Douglas J.
Show Me Your Tuigar (© 1976)
Text: none
Publisher: Toronto: Berandol Music BER 1705
Series: Canadian Composers Facsimilie Series
For: Voice (mezzo soprano), soprano recorder, alto recorder, tenor recorder, bass recorder, oboe, guitar, and double bass.
Difficulty: Voice: difficult; Instruments: difficult
Vocal range: $f^\#$ - g''
Language: phonemes
Comments: The voice is treated as a member of the instrumental ensemble.

484
Wernick, Richard (b. 1934)
A Prayer for Jerusalem (1971) (rev.1975)
Text: Portions of Psalm 122
Publisher: Bryn Mawr, PA: Presser 110-40083
For: Mezzo soprano and percussion (1 player).
Percussion instrumentation: vibraphone, glockenspiel, crotales, finger cymbals, and chimes (played by singer).
Difficulty: Voice: very difficult; Instruments: difficult
Vocal range: e - a''
Language: Hebrew (romanized)
Comments: Use of metric modulation.

485
Wetzler, Robert (b. 1932)
God, Hurrah (© 1970)
I. Lord, remember us...
II. Lord, surround us...
III. Lord, we are glad...
IV. Lord, praise be to you...
V. Doxology...
Text: Herbert Brokering
Publisher: Minneapolis: Art Masters Studios V-13
For: Mezzo soprano, English horn (or viola or clarinet in B^b), cello, and piano.
Difficulty: Voice: moderately difficult; Instruments: moderately difficult
Vocal range: a - $f^{\#''}$
Language: English

486
Wilkins, Margaret Lucy (b. 1939)
Ave Maria, Op. 27 (1974)
I. Refrain I
II. The Temptation
III. Refrain II
IV. Eve's Lullaby
V. Refrain III
VI. Eve's Son Slain
VII. Refrain IV
VIII. Adam Lay y-bounden

IX. Refrain V
X. Mary with Child
XI. Refrain VI
XII. Marys Lullaby
XIII. Refrain VII
XIV. Mary Suffers with Her Son
XV. Refrain VIII

Text: Chester Mystery Plays and anonymous English lyrics from the 14th-15th centuries.
Publisher: Huddersfield, West Yorkshire, Great Britain: Satanic Mills Press
For: Mezzo soprano (wood chimes, appill tree, cross); flute (tubular bell [c″]); clarinet in B^b (bass clarinet and crotales (c′ - g′ chromatically); violin, viola, cello, harp, piano (celesta), and percussion (one player).
Percussion instrumentation: 2 woodblocks (high and low), chromatic crotales, glockenspiel, 3 tubular bells (c′, e^{b}′, c″), and tam-tam.
Difficulty: Voice: difficult; Instruments: difficult
Vocal range: e - g^{b}″
Language: Old English
Duration: 30:00

487

Wilkins, Margaret Lucy (b. 1939)
Witch Music: Eight Witches' Cures Op. 17 (1971)

I. Cure for Toothache
II. Prayer to Cure a Scald
III. Cure for Rabis
IV. Curse on James VI
V. Another Cure for Rabis
VI. Cure for Staunching Blood
VII. Cure for Dislocated Bones
VIII. To Cure One Bewitched

Text: Composer
Publisher: Huddersfield, West Yorkshire, Great Britain: Satanic Mills Press
For: Mezzo soprano (2 triangles, 2 finger cymbals), clarinet in A, trumpet in B^b (bell), and double bass.
Difficulty: Voice: moderately difficult; Instruments: moderately difficult
Vocal range: b^b - g″
Language: English
Duration: 10:20

Alto

488

Baervoets, Raymond (1930-1989)

Erosions (1) (1965)

Text: Géo Soetens

Publisher: Brussels: Ce Be De M D/1967/0565/21

For: Alto, flute, alto saxophone, trumpet in B^b, cello, harp, celesta, vibraphone, and percussion (2 players).

Percussion instrumentation: 3 bongos, 3 cymbals, 3 woodblocks, 3 tom-toms, 2 maracas, bells, 3 tam-tams, 2 claves, and glockenspiel.

Difficulty: Voice: very difficult; Instruments: very difficult

Vocal range: f$^\#$ - f$^{\#''}$

Language: French

Duration: 11:20

Comments: Score is very difficult to read.

489

Booren, Jo van der (b. 1953)

Diotima an Hyperion, Op. 50 (1984)

Text: Friedrich Hölderlin

Publisher: Amsterdam: Donemus

For: Alto, flute, viola, and harp.

Difficulty: Voice: difficult; Instruments: difficult

Vocal range: g - f″

Language: German

Duration: 10:00

508

Bose, Hans-Jürgen von (b. 1953)

Fünf Kinderreime (© 1985)

I. Die Ammenuhr
II. Kuckuck hat sich totgefallen
III. Abzählreim
IV. Das bucklicht Männleim
V. Es was einmal ein Wald

Text: Nursery rhymes

Publisher: Mainz: Ars Viva Verlag AV121

For: Contralto, 5 recorders (1 player) (sopranino, soprano, alto, tenor, bass); clarinet in B^b (clarinet in E^b, bass clarinet); trumpet in D (trumpet in C), viola, and double bass.

Difficulty: Voice: very difficult; Instruments: difficult

Vocal range: f - b″ plus highest and lowest note possible

Language: German

Comments: Some graphic notation; some Sprechstimme.

490

Crumb, George (b. 1929)

Night of the Four Moons (1969)

I. La luna está muerta, muerta... (The moon is dead, dead...)
II. Cuando sale la luna... (When the moon rises...)
III. Otro Adán oscuro está soñando (Another obscure Adam dreams)
IV. ¡Huye luna, luna, luna!... (Run away moon, moon, moon!...)

Text: fragments from Federico García Lorca

Publisher: New York: Peters: 66462

For: Alto, alto flute (piccolo), banjo, electric cello, and percussion (1 player).

Percussion instrumentation: bongo drums, Chinese temple gong, Tibetan prayer stones, alto African thumb piano, large tam-tam, crotales, suspended cymbal, tambourine, pair of Japanese kabuki blocks, vibraphone; (the following instruments are to be played by the singer): finger cymbals, small tam-tam, castanets, and glockenspiel; (played by all performers: a single detached crotale A′ or A″).

Difficulty: Voice: very difficult; Instruments: very difficult

Vocal range: g - f″

Language: Spanish

Duration: 16:00

Comments: Vocal part employs: Sprechstimme, unvoiced singing (pure wind sound) in which pitches must be perceptible; whispering, speaking, shouting.

491

Garant, Serge (1929-1986)

Phrases I (1969)

Text: Composer

Publisher: Don Mills, Ontario: BMI Canada

For: Alto, piano (celesta), and percussion.

Percussion instrumentation: brass chimes, rattle, claves, and maracas (all played by singer); 1 large suspended cymbal (played by pianist); tubular chimes, bells, xylophone, marimba, vibraphone, 3 suspended cymbals, 3 gongs, 1 tam-tam, snare drum, 2 or 3 tom-toms, bongos, timbales, whip, log drum, woodblocks, Chinese blocks, temple blocks, sand blocks, basque drum, 3 or 4 cowbells, Chinese bell-tree, bamboo chimes, glass chimes, antique cymbals, and 1 double bass bow.

Difficulty: Voice: moderately difficult; Instruments: moderately difficult

Vocal range: f# - f#″

Language: French

Duration: 26:00

Comments: Aleatoric; voice required to change timbre.

492

Haubiel, Charles (1892-1978)

A Threnody for Love (1966)

Text: Frederika Blankner

Publisher: Los Angeles: The Composer's Press

For: Alto, flute, clarinet in B♭, violin, cello, and piano.

Difficulty: Voice: moderate; Instruments: moderate

Vocal range: g - e″

Language: English

493

Holliger, Heinz (b. 1939)

Glühende Rätsel (1964)

I. Diese Nacht
II. Einsamkeit lautlos samtener Acker
III. Im verhexten Wald
IV. Ausgeweidet die Zeit
V. Meine geliebten Toten

Text: Nelly Sachs

Publisher: Mainz: Schott E.S. 5001

For: Alto, flute, viola, bass clarinet (contrabass clarinet), harp, cimbalom [Hungarian dulcimer], and percussion (5 players).

Percussion instrumentation: 2 maracas, 3 temple blocks, 4 bongos, 3 tom-toms, 1 tambourine, 1 tenor drum, bass drum, 2 snare drums, 2 triangles (high &

low), 4 crash cymbals, 3 tam-tams (small, medium & large), 3 gongs, 13 plate bells, tubular bells, 7 crotales, glockenspiel, marimba, and celesta.
Difficulty: Voice: very difficult; Instruments: very difficult
Vocal range: f - $a^{b''}$
Language: German
Duration: 15:00
Comments: Score is difficult to read.

494
Holmboe, Vagn (b. 1909)
Quintet: Zeit, Op. 94 (© 1974)
I. Zu was musste sich der Mann
II. Ich erlebe den Raum voller Duft
III. Immerzu warte ich auf ein grosses Fest
Text: Renata Pandula
Publisher: Copenhagen: Wilhelm Hansen 29246
For: Alto and string quartet.
Difficulty: Voice: moderately difficult; Instruments: moderately difficult
Vocal range: g - f″
Language: German
Duration: 15:00

495
Hunfeld, Xander (b. 1949)
Wedergeboorte (1984)
I. Wedergeboorte
II. Liefde
III. Het Seizoen
Text: Van Luceberte
Publisher: Amsterdam: Donemus
For: Contralto, alto flute, acoustic guitar, electric guitar, and viola.
Difficulty: Voice: difficult; Instruments: difficult
Vocal range: g - $a^{b''}$
Language: Dutch
Duration: 8:30

496
Johansen, Svend Aaquist
Wiegenlied (1974)
Text: Bertolt Brecht
Publisher: Copenhagen: Samfundet til Udgivelse af Dansk Musik
Series: Series 3, No. 272
For: Alto, flute, violin, and cello.
Difficulty: Voice: moderate; Instruments: moderate
Vocal range: f# - g″
Language: German
Comments: Some speaking sections.

497
Krauze, Zygmunt (b. 1938)
Pantuny malajskie (Malay Pantuns) (1961)
I. Dario mana...
II. Koilauadau mur...
III. Pisang masboiwabawa
Text: from Malaya
Publisher: Warsaw: P.W.M. PWM-6588
For: Alto (or mezzo soprano) and 3 flutes.
Difficulty: Voice: moderate; Instruments: moderate
Vocal range: g - e″
Language: Malayan
Duration: 7:00
Comments: A Polish and English translation by Robert Stiller is included only for interpretation purposes.

498
Lomon, Ruth (b. 1930)
Five Songs after Poems by William Blake (© 1980)

I. The Sunflower
II. The Fly
III. The Sick Rose
IV. The Clod and the Pebble
V. Injunction

Text: William Blake: Songs of Experience; Satiric Verses and Epigrams
Publisher: Washington D.C.: Arsis Press 103
For: Contralto and viola.
Difficulty: Voice: difficult; Instruments: difficult
Vocal range: f* - e″
Language: English
Duration: 6:00

499

Mimaroglu, Ilhan K. (b. 1926)

String Quartet No. 4 (Like Theres No Tomorrow): with voice obligato (1978)

I. (Voice tacet)
II. The Wall Your Wall...
III. (Voice tacet)
IV. We both know my love...
V. (Voice tacet)
VI. You sell the sight
VII. (Voice tacet)
VIII. Night and snow...
IX. (Voice tacet)
X. These men, Dino...
XI. (Voice tacet)
XII. To sleep now...
XIII. (Voice tacet)
XIV. Your eyes...
XV. (Voice tacet)
XVI. One day the reaches...
XVII. (Voice tacet)
XVIII. The most beautiful sea...

Text: Nâzim Hikmet
Publisher: Port Chester, NY: Cherry Lane Music 9410
Series: Contemporary Classics
For: Voice (contralto) and string quartet.
Difficulty: Voice: moderately difficult; Instruments: difficult
Vocal range: g^{b} - f*″
Language: English
Duration: 32:00

500

Pärt, Arvo (b. 1935)

Es sang vor langen Jahren (1984)

Text: Clemens V. Brentano
Publisher: Vienna: Universal Edition 18421
For: Contralto (or countertenor), violin, and viola.
Difficulty: Voice: moderate; Instruments: moderate
Vocal range: g - c″
Language: German
Duration: 4:00

501

Pope, Conrad (b. 1951)

Rain (1976)

Text: James Joyce: Chamber Music 32
Publisher: Hillsdale, NY: Mobart Music
For: Alto, violin, cello, clarinet in B^{b}, and piano.
Difficulty: Voice: moderately difficult; Instruments: difficult
Vocal range: g - f″
Language: English

502

Pousseur, Henri (b. 1929)

Échos II, de Votre Faust (1969)

I. La ligne des toits (voice tacet)
II. Couleur de l'air A
III. Insinuations

IV. Grande loterie du labyrinthe des fantômes
V. Les herbes des yeux (voice tacet)
VI. Couleur de l'air B
VII. Le tremble et le rossignol (voice tacet)

Text: Gérard de Nerval, Johann Wolfgang von Goethe, Francesco Petrarca, Luis de Gongora y Argote, Christopher Marlowe
Publisher: Vienna: Universal UE 15104
For: Voice (alto), flute, cello, and piano.
Difficulty: Voice: very difficult; Instruments: very difficult
Vocal range: f# - f″
Language: German, French, Spanish, English, and Italian.
Duration: 20:00
Comments: The poems are in the original languages.

503
Prytz, Holger (b. 1928)
Quartetto, Op. 8 (© 1971)
Text: Savetri Devi: Arkadisk Fabel
Publisher: Copenhagen: Samfundet til Udgivelse af Dansk Musik
Series: Series 3, No. 272
For: Alto, clarinet in A, cello, and piano.
Difficulty: Voice: difficult; Instruments: difficult
Vocal range: a - g″
Language: Danish (Italian and English translations by the composer provided for performance).

504
Raxach, Enrique (b. 1932)
Paraphrase (1969)
Text: Composer
Publisher: London; New York: Peters 7137
For: Alto, alto flute (flute), bass clarinet (clarinet in B♭), bassoon, horn, trumpet in C, harp, violin, viola, cello, and percussion (2 players).
Percussion instrumentation: (I) marimba, vibraphone, suspended Chinese cymbal, large suspended cymbal, snare drum, 4 tom-toms, and bamboo wood chimes; (II) tubular bells, hihat, suspended cymbal, tamtam, 2 bongos, 2 congas, and whip.
Difficulty: Voice: very difficult; Instruments: very difficult
Vocal range: f - f#″
Language: phonemes and French
Duration: 14:30

505
Reutter, Hermann (1900-1985)
Prediger Salomo 12, 1-9
Text: Ecclesiastes 12:1-9
Publisher: Mainz; New York: Schott 6423
For: Deep voice (alto), flute, and piano (or organ)
Difficulty: Voice: moderately difficult; Instruments: moderately difficult
Vocal range: g - f♭″
Language: German
Duration: 19:15

506
Samuel, Gerhard (b. 1924)
The Relativity of Icarus (1970, rev. 1971)
Text: Jack Larson

Publisher: Melville, NY: Belwin-Mills EL 2567
For: Alto or young bass-baritone, flute, oboe, clarinet in B^b, violin, viola, cello, piano, and percussion (1 player).
Percussion instrumentation: crotales or glockenspiel, vibraphone, small traingle, tam-tam, suspended cymbal, Bak [Korean multiboard whip] or whip, tenor drum, and very high metal wind chimes.
Difficulty: Voice: moderately difficult; Instruments: moderately difficult
Vocal range: A - a$^{b\prime}$
Language: English
Comments: The composer recommends a microphone for spoken and whispered passages. The vocal part is in bass clef, but the composer prefers a contralto to a bass.

507
Słowiński, Władysław (b. 1930)
Makowskie Bajki (© 1975)
Text: Jerzy Ficowski
I. Dziad i baba
II. Promień słónca
III. Szewc
IV. Kobziarze
V. Dzieci przed klatką z kanarkiem
VI. Grupa dzieci
Publisher: Cracow: P.W.M. PWM-7741
For: Alto, oboe, clarinet in B^b, and bassoon.
Difficulty: Voice: moderate; Instruments: moderate
Vocal range: g - e″
Language: Polish

508 Von Bose, Hans-Jürgen moved to Bose, Hans-Jürgen von

509
Wilkinson, Marc (b. 1929)
Voices (© 1960)
Text: Samuel Beckett: Waiting for Godot
Publisher: London: Universal Edition UE 12912
For: Contralto, flute, clarinet in E^b, bass clarinet, and cello.
Difficulty: Voice: difficult; Instruments: difficult
Vocal range: f - f$^{\#\prime\prime}$
Language: English or German
Duration: 10:00
Comments: Piece is pointillistic; much of the voice part is spoken; piece may have been composed before 1960.

510
Wimberger, Gerhard (b. 1923)
Four Songs (© 1971)
I. Song of Yourself (Hans-Jürgen Heise)
II. Die Verlassene (Heinz Piontek)
III. Middle class blues (Hans Magnus Enzensberger)
IV. Mein Famili (Ror Wolf)
Publisher: Kassel: Bärenreiter 6062a
For: Voice (alto or baritone), piano, double bass, and trap set with bongos.
Difficulty: Voice: moderately difficult; Instruments: moderately difficult

Vocal range: a - e″
Language: German
Duration: 15:00

511

Wood, Hugh (b. 1932)

Four Logue Songs, Op. 2 (1961, rev. 1963)

I. The Image of love...
II. Bargain My love...
III. In the beloveds face...
IV. Love, do not believe...

Text: Christopher Logue: Wand and Quadrant
Publisher: London: Chester Music J.W.C. 55491
For: Contralto, clarinet in B^b, violin, and cello.
Difficulty: Voice: moderately difficult; Instruments: moderately difficult
Vocal range: g - g″
Language: English

512

Zender, Hans (b. 1936)

Drei Rondels nach Mallarmé (1961)

I. Rein du réveil...
II. (no text, no title)
III. Si tu veux nous nous aimerons...

Text: Stéphane Mallarmé
Publisher: Berlin: Bote & Bock B&B 21929 (1013)
For: Alto, flute, and viola.
Difficulty: Voice: moderately difficult; Instruments: moderately difficult
Vocal range: a^b - f″
Language: French

Tenor

513
Baker, David N. (b. 1931)
Through this Vale of Tears: In Memoriam: Martin Luther King, Jr. (1988)
I. Thou dost lay me in the Dust of Death (Psalm 22)
II. If there be Sorrow (Mari Evans)
III. My God, Why hast Thou Forsaken Me (Psalm 22)
IV. Parades to Hell (Solomon Edwards)
V. Deliver My Soul (Psalm 22)
VI. Sometimes I Feel like a Motherless Child (Traditional)
VII. Now that he is safely Dead (Carl Hines)
Publisher: Saint Louis: Norruth Music
For: Tenor, string quartet, and piano.
Difficulty: Voice: difficult; Instruments: difficult
Vocal range: B - c″

514
Bauld, Alison (b. 1944)
Egg (1973)
Text: Composer
Publisher: Borough Green, Kent, England: Novello
For: Tenor, flute, cello, vibraphone, and drum.
Difficulty: Voice: moderate; Instruments: moderate
Vocal range: c - c*″ (not sung but laughed)
Language: English
Duration: 9:00
Comments: Duration of measures indicated in spatial time (seconds).

515
Bavicchi, John (b. 1922)
Fragments from "Vega" (1982)
Text: Michael Taylor
Publisher: BKJ Publications
For: Tenor (or soprano), trombone, and percussion.
Percussion instrumentation: small suspended cymbal, medium suspended cymbal, large suspended cymbal, large gong, large tam-tam, shallow snare drum, deep snare drum, high tenor drum, low tenor drum, amd bass drum.
Difficulty: Voice: difficult; Instruments: very difficult
Vocal range: c - a′
Language: English
Comments: Trombonist must sing and play simultaneously; use of quarter tones.

516
Bedford, David (b. 1937)
The tentacles of the dark nebula (1969)
Text: Arthur C. Clarke: "Transcience"
Publisher: London: Universal Edition UE 15342
For: Tenor, 3 violins, 2 violas, 2 cellos, and double bass.
Difficulty: Voice: difficult; Instruments: difficult
Vocal range: c - $b^{b\prime}$
Language: English
Duration: 14:30

517
Bedford, David (b. 1937)
When I Heard the Learn'd Astronomer (1972)
Text: Walt Whitman: "Leaves of Grass" and Camille Flammarion: "La Pluralité des modes habités"
Publisher: London: Universal Edition UE 15508L
For: Tenor, 2 flutes, 2 oboes, 2 clarinets in B^b, 2 bassoons, 3 horns, trombone, bass trombone, and tuba.
Difficulty: Voice: very difficult; Instruments: very difficult
Vocal range: d - b′
Language: English
Duration: 15:00
Comments: Use of spatial as well as metrical time.

518
Birtwistle, Harrison (b. 1934)
Prologue (1971)
Text: Aeschylus: Agamemnon
Publisher: London: Universal Edition UE 15491L
For: Tenor, bassoon, horn, 2 trumpets in B^b, trombone, violin, and double bass.
Difficulty: Voice: difficult; Instruments: moderately difficult
Vocal range: c - $a^{b\prime}$
Language: English
Duration: 8:00

519
Blake, David (b. 1936)
From the Mattress Grave
Introduction
I. Doktrin
II. Warnung
III. Der Asra
IV. Weltauf
V. Ein Weib
VI. Solidtät
VII. Lumpentum
VIII. from Die Heimkehr
IX. Lotosblume I
X. Lotosblume II
XI. "Wer ein Herz hat"
XII. An die Jungen
Text: Heinrich Heine, English translation by Peter Palmer
Publisher: Borough Green, Kent, England: Novello 89 0103 01
For: High voice (tenor), flute (piccolo), oboe, clarinet in B^b (clarinet in A), bass clarinet (clarinet in B^b), bassoon, horn, violin I, violin II, viola, cello, and double bass.
Difficulty: Voice: difficult; Instruments: moderately difficult
Vocal range: A - c″
Language: German (singable English translation by Peter Palmer provided)
Duration: 30:00
Comments: Some Sprechstimme.

520
Boatwright, Howard (b. 1918)
Prologue, Narrative and Lament (1987)
I. Prologue
II. Narrative
III. Lament
Text: Walt Whitman
Publisher: Fayetteville, NY: Walnut Grove Press 117
For: Tenor and string quartet.
Difficulty: Voice: difficult; Instruments: moderately difficult
Vocal range: d - a′
Language: English

521
Bois, Rob du (b. 1934)
Diotima (1984)
Text: Friedrich Hölderlin
Publisher: Amsterdam: Donemus
For: Voice (tenor), clarinet in B^b, viola, and piano.
Difficulty: Voice: difficult; Instruments: difficult
Vocal range: d - a′
Language: German
Duration: 9:30
Comments: The instrumental version of this piece is called "Hyperion."

522
Borris, Siegfried (1906-1987)
Three Poems by Rupert Brooke, Op. 123 (© 1976)
I. Sonnet
II. The Wayfarer
III. Springtime
Text: Rupert Brooke
Publisher: Wilhelmshaven: Sirius-Edition/Heinrichshofen's Verlag 8309
For: Tenor, flute, oboe, clarinet in B^b, and horn.
Difficulty: Voice: difficult; Instrument: difficult
Vocal range: b - a′
Language: English
Comments: Possibly written before 1960.

523
Bose, Hans-Jürgen Von (b. 1953)
Three Songs (1978)
I. Love's Farwell (Michael Drayton)
II. Dirge (Sir Philip Sidney)
III. Hey Nonny No! (Anonymous)
Publisher: Mainz: Ars Viva Verlag A859V
For: Tenor, flute (piccolo and alto flute), oboe (English horn), clarinet in B^b (clarinet in E^b), bass clarinet, bassoon, bass trombone, 5 timpani (1 pair cymbals, snare drum, old newspaper, wrapping paper, harp, harpsichord, Hammond organ), 2 violins, 2 cellos, 1 double bass, and percussion (2 players).
Percussion instrumentation: 5 slide whistles, snare drum, bass drum, antique cymbal, 2 cowbells, 2 crash cymbals, 4 suspended cymbals, small tam-tam, flexatone, glockenspiel, tubular bells, plate bells, 2 friction drums, 2 foil to rattle, 4 sand blocks, sand box, plastic cup, old newspaper, wrapping paper, and balloon.
Difficulty: Voice: extremely difficult; Instruments: very difficult
Vocal range: c - c#″
Language: English

053
Burgon, Geoffrey (b. 1941)
At the Round Earth's Imagined Corners (1971)
Text: John Donne
Publisher: London: Chester 55493
For: Soprano (or tenor), trumpet in B^b, and organ.
Difficulty: Voice: moderate; Instruments: moderate
Vocal range: e - g′
Language: English

524
Bush, Geoffrey (b. 1920)
A Lover's Progress (1961)
I. Hope
II. Resolution
III. Doubt
IV. Jealousy
V. Grief
VI. Despair
Text: Anonymous ca. 1600
Publisher: Borough Green, Kent, England: Novello 19419
For: Tenor, oboe, clarinet in B^b, and bassoon.
Difficulty: Voice: moderately difficult; Instruments: moderate
Vocal range: c^b - $b^{b\prime}$
Language: English

525
Carter, Elliott (b. 1908)
In Sleep, in Thunder (1981)
I. Dolphins
II. Across the Yard: La Ignota
III. Harriet
IV. Dies irae
V. Careless Night
VI. In Genesis
Text: Robert Lowell
Publisher: New York: Boosey & Hawkes HPS 979
For: Tenor, flute (alto flute, piccolo), oboe (English horn), clarinet in B^b (bass clarinet), bassoon, horn (metal and cardboard mutes), trumpet in C (straight metal mutes, straight cardboard mutes, tight cup mutes), trombone (bass trombone), piano, violin I, violin II, viola, cello, double bass, and percussion.
Percussion instrumentation: vibraphone, marimba, woodblock, medium cowbell, güiro, bottle, high maracas, small sizzle cymbal, medium suspended cymbal, side drum with releasable snares, tenor or field drum with releaseable snares, bass drum (2 stiff metal brushes), and tam-tam.
Difficulty: Voice: very difficult; Instruments: very difficult
Vocal range: c - b′
Language: English
Duration: 21:00
Comments: Use of metric modulation.

526
Cowie, Edward (b. 1943)
The Moon, Sea, and Stars (1973)
I. It is a beautious ev'ning
II. As I looked up
III. And I remember well
Text: William Wordsworth
Publisher: London: J. & W. Chester/ Wilhelm Hansen JWC 8901
For: Tenor or high voice, 14 solo strings (4 violin I, 4 violin II, 2 violas, 2 cellos, 2 double basses), horn, and percussion.
Percussion instrumentation: celesta, glockenspiel, large tam-tam, 4 pedal timpani, vibraphone, large triangle, large mounted cymbal (played with cello or bass bow), and tubular bells.
Difficulty: Voice: very difficult; Instruments: difficult
Vocal range: e - $g^{\#\prime\prime}$
Language: English
Duration: 20:00
Comments: Very high tessitura.

527

Cumming, Richard (b. 1928)

As Dew In April (1960)

Text: Anonymous 14th century English

Publisher: New York: Boosey & Hawkes S.2648

For: High voice (tenor), oboe (or violin or clarinet in B^b), and piano.

Difficulty: Voice: moderately easy; Instruments: moderately easy

Vocal range: d# - a'

Language: English

528

Davis, Sharon (b. 1937)

The Prodigal Planet (© 1987)

Text: Walt Whitman

Publisher: Los Angeles: Western International Music AV256

For: Tenor, bass trombone, and piano.

Difficulty: Voice: moderately difficult; Instruments: moderately difficult

Vocal range: c - a'

Language: English

529

Devčić, Natko (b. 1914)

Konzert für Kammerensemble (1969)

Text: none

Publisher: Zagreb: Udruženje Kompozitora Hevatske

For: Tenor, ondes martenot, marimba, vibraphone, 4 violins, 4 violas, and percussion (2 players).

Percussion instrumentation: maracas, 4 wood drums, 5 temple blocks, triangle, 5 cowbells, 3 suspended cymbals, tam-tam, 1 small tambourine, 1 large tambourine, and 5 tom-toms.

Difficulty: Voice: difficult; Instruments: difficult

Vocal range: c# - a#'

Language: phonemes

Duration: 15:30

530

Dillon, James (b. 1950)

Who Do You Love (1981)

Text: Phonemes

Publisher: London: Peters P-7245

For: Tenor (mezzo soprano or soprano), flute (piccolo and bass flute), bass clarinet, violin (viola), cello, and percussion.

Percussion instrumentation: 2 suspended cymbals, 1 hi-hat, snare drum, 3 timbales, and bass drum with footpedal.

Difficulty: Voice: extremely difficult; Instruments: extremely difficult

Vocal range: g# - e^b sung either as written or for tenor, one octave below and after rehearsal number 17 in falsetto.

Language: IPA symbols

Duration: 10:00

Comments: Use of quartertones; vocal effects.

531

Druckman, Jacob (b. 1928)

Animus IV (1977)

Text: Nicolaus Lenau

Publisher: New York: Boosey & Hawkes

For: Tenor, violin, piano (electric piano with "wa" pedal and elec-

tric organ), trombone, percussion (2 players), and tape.
Percussion instrumentation: vibraphone or sizzle cymbal, cymbal, metal wind chimes, tom-toms, bass drum, tam-tam and marimba or large cymbal, triangle, 5 temple blocks, and gong or small tam-tam.
Difficulty: Voice: very difficult; Instruments: very difficult
Vocal range: $A^{\#}$ - b'
Language: German and French
Comments: "Die drei Zigeuner" by Franz Liszt (1811-1886) is sung at the same time as portions of the Druckman; also a French song appears on the tape.

532
Fortner, Wolfgang (1907-1987)
Farewell (© 1981)
Text: Pablo Neruda
Publisher: Mainz; New York: Schott ED6883
For: Tenor, 2 flutes, cello, and piano.
Difficulty: Voice: moderately difficult; Instruments: moderately difficult
Vocal range: A - g'
Language: Spanish or German (translation by Erich Arendt)
Duration: 9:30
Comments: Also available with piano reduction ED6884.

533
Fowler, Marje (b. 1917)
Deux Ballades Sombres de François Villon (1967)
I. Ballade des Pendus
II. Ballade des Dames du Temps jodis
III. Envoi
Text: François Villon
Publisher: Redondo Beach, CA: Composer's Autograph Publications
For: Tenor, viola, and piano.
Difficulty: Voice: difficult; Instruments: moderately difficult
Vocal range: B^{b} - $b^{b'}$
Language: French (English translation by Algernon Charles Swinburne provided for performance).

534
Füssl, Karl Heinz (1924-1992)
Cantiunculae Amoris (1976)
I. Iam super oceanum... (Ovid)
II. Aestus erat... (Ovid)
III. Lecto compositus... (Petronius Arbiter)
Publisher: Vienna: Universal Edition UE16831
For: Tenor and string quartet.
Difficulty: Voice: very difficult; Instruments: difficult
Vocal range: c - $b^{b'}$
Language: Latin
Duration: 12:00

535
Füssl, Karl Heinz (1924-1992)
Dialogue in praise of the owl and the cuckoo (1961)
I. Winter
II. Spring
Text: William Shakespeare
Publisher: Vienna: Universal Edition UE 15180

For: Tenor, flute, clarinet in B♭, trombone, harp, guitar, violin, and double bass.
Difficulty: Voice: moderately difficult; Instruments: moderately difficult - difficult
Vocal range: d - b♭′
Language: English
Duration: 16:00

536

Gideon, Miriam (b. 1906)

The Resounding Lyre (© 1983)

I. Mutterbildnis (Frederic Ewen)
II. Wähebûf und Nichtenvint (Süezkint von Trimperg)
III. Halleluja (Heinrich Heine)

Publisher: Hillsdale, New York: Mobart Music; Sole agent: Jerona Music
For: High voice (tenor), flute, oboe, bassoon, violin, viola, and cello.
Difficulty: Voice: difficult; Instruments: difficult
Vocal range: e - a′
Language: German with English translation

537

Holliger, Heinz (b. 1939)

Erde und Himmel (1961)

I. Erde und Himmel
II. Zwischenspiel (voice tacet)
III. Rondo
IV. 2 Zwischenspiel (voice tacet)
V. Die letzte Stunde

Text: Alexander Xaver Gwerder
Publisher: Mainz: Schott 5031
For: Tenor, flute, violin, viola, cello, and harp.
Difficulty: Voice: very difficult; Instruments: difficult
Vocal range: G* - c″
Language: German

538

Isaacson, Michael (b. 1946)

Kol Sason (A Sound of Joy) (1971)

I. Processional (voice tacet)
II. Opening Welcome
III. Birchat Erusin
IV. Sheva B'rachot
V. Benediction
VI. Recessional (voice tacet)

Text: Assembled by composer from Hebrew textual sources not indicated. Readings from Genesis and by Yehuda Halevy.
Publisher: New York: Transcontinental Music TCL695
For: Tenor cantor, organ, soprano recorder or flute, and percussion.
Percussion instrumentation: small hand drum, triangle, finger cymbals, and tambourine.
Difficulty: Voice: moderately difficult; Instruments: moderately difficult
Vocal range: d - f′
Language: Hebrew (interpolated readings in English)
Comments: A wedding service with interpolated readings.

539

Kagel, Mauricio (b. 1931)

Tango Alemán (1978)

Text: None
Publisher: Frankfurt: Peters 8412/ Henry Litoff's Verlag 31127
For: Voice (dramatic tenor or baritone), violin, bandoneon, and piano.

Difficulty: Voice: difficult; Instruments: moderately difficult
Vocal range: c - $e^{b\prime}$
Language: "an incomprehensible, imaginary language"
Duration: 9:30
Comments: Singer must also whistle.

540
KELEMEN, MILKO (B. 1924)
O Primavera
I. Prolog
II. O primavera...
III. Epilog
Text: Anonymous Italian poets
Publisher: Frankfurt: Peters 8041/ Henry Litoff's Verlag
For: Tenor, 7 violins, 3 violas, 2 cellos, and double bass (note: violin 7 also plays glockenspiel and jaycall).
Difficulty: Voice: difficult; Instruments: difficult
Vocal range: d - c″
Language: Italian
Duration: 9:00
Comments: Voice part employs Sprechstimme, rhythmic speech.

541
KELLY, BRYAN (B. 1934)
The Shield of Achilles (1967)
Text: W. H. Auden
Publisher: London: Novello
For: Tenor, 2 violin I, 2 violin II, 2 violas, 2 cellos, 2 double basses, timpani, and percussion (3 players).
Percussion instrumentation: congas, suspended cymbal, side drum, gong, castanets, and small suspended cymbal.
Difficulty: Voice: difficult; Instruments: moderate
Vocal range: d - a′
Language: English
Comments: High tessitura.

542
KEULEN, GEERT VAN
Op een paar uren (1964)
Text: Hans Lodeizen
Publisher: Amsterdam: Donemus
For: Tenor, flute, bass clarinet, violin, viola, and harp.
Difficulty: Voice: moderately difficult; Instruments: moderately difficult
Vocal range: e^{b} - g′
Language: Dutch

543
KÓSA, GYÖRGY (1897-1984)
Karinthy Kantáta (© 1981)
I. Egyedül
II. Gyalázat
III. Ó álom...
IV. Ez ő
V. Ma délután...
Text: Napló Jegyzetek
Publisher: Budapest: Editio Musica Z.8598
For: Tenor, violin, viola, and cello.
Difficulty: Voice: moderately difficult; Instruments: moderate
Vocal range: c - b′
Language: Hungarian or German

544
LAPORTE, ANDRÉ (B. 1931)
Le Morte Chitarre (1969)
Text: Salvatore Quasimodo
Publisher: Darmstadt: Tonos
For: Tenor, flute, and 14 solo strings

String instrumentation: 4 first violins, 4 second violins, 3 violas, 2 cellos, and 1 double bass.
Difficulty: Voice: very difficult; Instruments: difficult
Vocal range: d - b′ ($d^{b''}$ optional)
Language: Italian

545

LAVENDA, RICHARD

The Weary Man Whispers (1985)

Text: Steve Kepetar
Publisher: Saint Louis: Norruth Music
For: Tenor, alto saxophone (sleigh–bells), trombone (four triangles, maracas), piano (glass wind chimes), and percussion (1 player).
Percussion instrumentation: marimba, vibraphone, glockenspiel, tam-tam, tambourine, large suspended cymbal (with sizzle attachment), woodblock, five roto-toms. Conductor also plays mark tree.
Difficulty: Voice: very difficult; Instruments: difficult
Vocal range: B - b′
Language: English
Duration: 18:00
Comments: Instrumentalists required to play some percussion instruments.

546

LEFANU, NICOLA (B. 1947)

Rondeaux (1972)

Text: French Medieval Poetry
Publisher: Borough Green, Kent, England: Novello 17 0299 08
For: Tenor and horn.
Difficulty: Voice: difficult; Instrument: difficult
Vocal range: c - a′
Language: French
Duration: 9:00
Comments: Use of quarter tones; rhythmic difficulties.

547

LEWKOVITCH, BERNHARD (B. 1927)

Songs of Solomon (1985)

Text: Song of Solomon
Publisher: Copenhagen: Wilhelm Hansen 29849, Distributed by MMB Music
For: Tenor, clarinet in B^{b}, horn, and bass trombone.
Difficulty: Voice: moderately difficult; Instruments: moderately difficult
Vocal range: f - $f^{\#'}$
Language: Latin with Danish and English translations.

548

LUTOSŁAWSKI, WITOLD (B. 1913)

Paroles Tissées (Woven words): Quatre tapisseries pour la chatelaine de Vergi (1965)

Text: Jean-François Chabrun
Publisher: London: Chester Music 28.750 Chester 4121
For: Tenor, 10 solo violins, 3 solo violas, 3 solo cellos, 1 double bass, piano, harp, and percussion.
Percussion instrumentation (1 player): 3 tom-toms, snare drum. bass drum, suspended cymbal, large tam-tam, 3 bells (d′, $e^{b'}$, e′), and xylophone.
Difficulty: Voice: difficult; Instruments: difficult

Vocal range: d - $b^{b\prime}$
Language: French
Duration: 16:00
Comments: Contains several ad libitum sections; all rhythmic values in such sections are approximate.

549

Lutyens, Elisabeth (1906-1983)

And suddenly it's evening, Op. 66 (1966)

I. On the Willow Boughs (Alle fronte dei salici)
II. In the Just Human Time (Nelgiusto tempo umano)
III. Almost a Madrigal (Quasi un Madrigale)
IV. And Suddenly it's Evening (Ed è subito sera)

Text: Salvatore Quasimodo: "Ed è Subito Sera"
Publisher: Schott: London 6858
For: Tenor, 2 trumpets in B^{b}, 2 trombones, double bass, harp, celesta, violin, horn, cello, and percussion.
Percussion instrumentation: large tam-tam, 4 small tam-tams, large cymbal, 4 suspended cymbals (different pitches), claves, maracas, triangle, tambourine, bass drum, tenor drum, 4 woodblocks (different pitches), and 4 tom-toms (different pitches).
Difficulty: Voice: difficult; Instruments: difficult
Vocal range: c - $b^{b\prime}$
Language: Italian, English translation by Jack Bevan.
Duration: 24:00
Comments: Arranged, in 3 groups of players: I. tenor e coro d'istrumenti; II. Ritornello I; III. Ritornello II

550

Piccolo, Anthony (b. 1946)

Found in Machaut's Chamber Op. 3 (1968)

Text: Kenneth Patchen
Publisher: Redondo Beach, CA: Composer's Autograph Publications
For: Tenor, flute, guitar, and cello.
Difficulty: Voice: difficult; Instruments: difficult
Vocal range: B^{b} - $a^{b\prime}$
Language: English

551

Rawsthorne, Alan (1905-1971)

Tankas of the Four Seasons (1965)

Text: Carles Riba
Publisher: London: Oxford University Press 1.9.64
For: Tenor, oboe, clarinet in B^{b}, bassoon, violin, and cello.
Difficulty: Voice: moderately difficult; Instruments: moderate
Vocal range: c - $a^{b\prime}$
Language: English, translation by J.L. Gili
Duration: 8:15

552

Reimann, Aribert (b. 1936)

Epitaph (1965)

I. Prelude (voice tacet)
II. Song
III. Autumn: A Dirge
IV. Interlude (voice tacet)
V. The Past
VI. A Lament
VII. Epilogue (voice tacet)

Text: Percy Bysshe Shelley

Publisher: Mainz: Ars Viva Verlag
For: Tenor, flute, English horn, celesta, harp, viola, cello, and double bass.
Difficulty: Voice: very difficult; Instruments: difficult
Vocal range: A - c″
Language: English
Duration: 16:00

553

RUBBRA, EDMUND (1901-1986)

Cantata Pastorale, Op. 92 (© 1962)

Text: Plato
Publisher: London: Alfred Langnick 3980
For: High voice (tenor), treble recorder (or flute), harpsichord or piano, and cello.
Difficulty: Voice: moderate; Instruments: moderate
Vocal range: d♯ - a′
Language: English, translation by Walter Leaf

554

SACCO, P. PETER (B. 1928)

Three Psalms (1966)

I. How long wilt Thou forget me, O Lord (Psalm 13)
II. The Sorrows of Death (Psalm 18)
III. Keep not Thou Silence, O God (Psalm 83)

Publisher: Los Angeles: Western International Music OP-110
For: Tenor (or soprano) and brass quintet.
Instrumentation: 2 trumpets in B♭, horn, trombone, and tuba.
Difficulty: Voice: difficult; Instruments: moderately difficult
Vocal range: c - c″
Language: English

555

TATE, PHYLLIS (1911 - 1987)

Apparitions (1968)

Evocation (voice tacet)
I. The Wife of Usher's Well
II. The Suffolk Miracle
III. The Unquiet Grave
IV. Unfortunate Miss Bailey
Envoi (voice tacet)

Text: traditional English or Scottish
Publisher: London: Oxford University Press
For: Tenor, harmonica, string quartet, and piano.
Difficulty: Voice: difficult; Instruments: moderately difficult
Vocal range: c - b♭′
Language: English
Duration: 20:00

556

TESTI, FLAVIO (B. 1923)

Cantata prima, Op. 22 (1971)

Text: William Shakespeare
Publisher: Milan: Ricordi 131966
For: Tenor, flute, oboe, harp, harpsichord, viola, cello, and double bass.
Difficulty: Voice: difficult; Instruments: difficult
Vocal range: B - g′
Language: English
Duration: 10:00

557

TESTI, FLAVIO (B. 1923)

Cantata Seconda, Op. 24 (Devouring Time) (1972)

Text: William Shakespeare
Publisher: Milan: Ricordi 132057

For: Tenor, violin, clarinet in B^b, trumpet in C, trombone, and piano.
Difficulty: Voice: very difficult; Instruments: very difficult
Vocal range: c - g′
Language: English
Duration: 9:00

558
Warren, B.
Dieu vous gard' (1975)
Text: Pierre de Ronsard
Publisher: Boston; London: Wiscasset Music Publishing
For: Tenor, violin I, violin II, viola, cello, and double bass.
Difficulty: Voice: moderate; Instruments: moderate
Language: French

559
Weisgall, Hugo (b. 1912)
End of Summer (1974)
I. After Lunch (Pai Chü-i)
II. Quasi Fantasia (oboe)
III. Hearing Someone Sing a Poem by Yuan Chen (Pai Chü-i)
IV. Presto (oboe, strings)
V. De Senectute (George Boas)
Publisher: Bryn Mawr, PA: Theodore Presser 114-40203
For: Tenor, oboe, and string trio (violin, viola, and cello).
Difficulty: Voice: very difficult; Instruments: difficult
Vocal range: d - c″ (falsetto)
Language: English (translation by composer)

560
Wilson, Donald M. (b. 1937)
Five Haiku (1962)
I. Bell tones (Matsuo Bashō)
II. Evening Shadows (Taniguchi Buson)
Interlude I (voice tacet)
III. The Sudden Chillness (Taniguchi Buson)
Interlude II (voice tacet)
IV. Morning Haze (Taniguchi Buson)
V. A Cove at the "Lake of the Views" (Matsuo Bashō)
Publisher: New York: Galaxy Music/Highgate Press
For: Tenor, English horn, guitar, and string quartet.
Difficulty: Voice: moderately difficult; Instruments: difficult
Vocal range: c^b - b′
Language: English, translation by Harold G. Henderson
Duration: 8:00

561
Wright, Maurice (b. 1949)
Cantata (1975)
I. To music to becalm his fever (Robert Herrick)
II. To Lucia playing on her flute (Samuel Pordage)
III. The Commendation of Music (William Strode)
IV. Wit Predominant (Thomas Rymer)
V. To music to becalm his fever (continued) (Robert Herrick)
Publisher: Hillsdale, NY: Mobart Music M305

For: Tenor, tape, and percussion.
Percussion instrumentation: 4 timpani, antique cymbal, 6 tuned drums, 5 temple blocks, vibraphone, marimba, and large tam-tam.
Difficulty: Voice: difficult; Instruments: difficult
Vocal range: A - c″ (falsetto)
Language: English
Duration: 17:00

562

Zender, Hans (b. 1936)

Muji No Kyo (1975)

Text: Medieval Japanese
Publisher: Berlin: Bote & Bock
For: Voice (tenor or soprano), flute, violin (or cello), and piano (electric organ).
Difficulty: Voice: difficult; Instruments: difficult
Vocal range: d - g′
Language: Japanese
Duration: 18:00
Comments: White score and use of graphic notation; use of designated register.

Baritone and Bass

563
Adler, Samuel (b. 1928)
The Passionate Sword (1974)
Text: Jean Star Untermeyer, Louis Untermeyer
Publisher: New York: Carl Fischer
For: Baritone, flute, clarinet in B^b, violin, cello, and percussion.
Percussion instrumentation: crotales, vibraphone, 2 tom-toms, suspended cymbal, and bass drum.
Difficulty: Voice: difficult; Instruments: moderately difficult
Vocal range: g - g$^{\#\prime}$
Language: English

564
Amram, David (b. 1930)
Three Songs for America (1969)
I. The courage of life (John F. Kennedy: Profiles in Courage)
II. Americans, you may give (Martin Luther King, Jr.: Strength to Love)
III. History has placed us all (Robert F. Kennedy: Public speeches)
Publisher: New York: Peters © 1974 66469
For: Bass, flute, English horn, clarinet in B^b, horn, bassoon, violin I, violin II, viola, cello, and double bass.
Difficulty: Voice: moderately difficult; Instruments: moderately difficult
Vocal range: E - e′
Language: English
Duration: 8:30

565
Andriessen, Jurriaan (b. 1925)
Thy black is fairest (1977)
I. How oft when thou, my music...
II. Thou art as tyrannous...
III. The little love-god lying...
Text: William Shakespeare
Publisher: Amsterdam: Donemus
For: Baritone, piano, and string quartet.
Difficulty: Voice: difficult; Instruments: moderately difficult
Vocal range: A - g′
Language: English
Duration: 13:30

566
Antoniou, Theodore (b. 1938)
Chorochronos II (© 1973)
Publisher: Kassel: Bärenreiter BA6285
For: Baritone, speaker, and chamber orchestra.
Percussion instrumentation: *
Difficulty: Voice: *; Instruments: *
Vocal range: *
Language: Hebrew, English, Greek, German, Hindi, and Chinese.
Duration: 16:00 - 17:00
Comments: *Score not examined. German and English translations provided.

567
Antoniou, Theodore (b. 1938)
Chorochronos III (1975)
Text: Composer
Publisher: Kassel: Bärenreiter 6170
For: Voice (baritone), piano, percussion, tape, and audience

Percussion instrumentation: (played by singer): suspended cymbal, 4 glasses (c , b″, a*″, f*″), a bow, and timpani mallets; (played by pianist): vibraphone, suspended cymbal, triangle, and a bow.
Difficulty: Voice: difficult; Instruments: difficult
Vocal range: A - b′ (falsetto)
Language: several (English, German, and another unknown to the writer, possibly Greek)
Duration: 14:10
Comments: Many unusal effects; note participation of audience.

568

ANTONIOU, THEODORE (B. 1938)

Moirologhia for Jani Christou

Publisher: Kassel: Bärenreiter © 1975
For: Baritone, piano, and any combination of flute, clarinet in B^b, guitar, 2 percussion instruments, and double bass.
Difficulty: Voice: *; Instruments: *
Vocal range: *
Language: Greek (romanized) with English translation.
Duration: *
Comments: *Score not examined.

569

ARZUMANOV, VALERIR GRANDOVICH

Iz drevnearmi͡anskogo ėposa (1971)

I. Pozhdeni Vaagna
II. O Tsare Artashese
III. Vospominaniya Artashesa

Text: Perevody V. Sryusva
Publisher: Moscow: Izdatelistvo Sovetskii Kompozitor S 279 K
For: Baritone, oboe, bassoon, trumpet in C, and trombone.
Difficulty: Voice: moderately difficult; Instruments: moderate
Vocal range: B - g′
Language: Russian

570

BAIRD, TADEUSZ (1928-1981)

Cztery Sonety miłosne
Four Love Sonnets (1969)

I. Sonnet 23 - Spójrz, co tu ciche serće Wypisala
II. Sonnet 91 - Drwię, mając ciebie, z calej ludzkiej pychy...
III. Sonnet 56 - Słodka miłości
IV. Sonnet 97 - Jakże podobna zimie jest rozłąka

Text: William Shakespeare: Sonnets 23, 91, 56, and 97.
Publisher: Warsaw: P.W.M. PMW-7169
For: Baritone, 6 violin I, 5 violin II, 4 violas, 3 cellos, double bass, and harpsichord.
Difficulty: Voice: moderate; Instruments: moderate
Vocal range: B - $d^{b\prime}$
Language: Polish (translated by Maciej Słomczyński)
Duration: 11:30

571

BANK, JACQUES (B. 1943)

Finale (1984)

I. Spring
II. Summer
III. Autumn
IV. Winter

Text: Composer
Publisher: Amsterdam: Donemus
For: Baritone, alto saxophone (bass clarinet), and marimba (vibraphone).

Difficulty: Voice: very difficult; Instruments: very difficult
Vocal range: G - $a^{\#\prime}$
Language: Dutch (singable English translation provided)
Duration: 30:00

572
Bassett, Leslie (b. 1923)
Time and Beyond (1973)
I. Days (Ralph Waldo Emerson: Days)
II. Day After Day (Rabindranath Tagore: Gitanjali)
III. from "Psalm Four" (Mark Van Doren: Psalm Four)
Publisher: New York: Peters 66574
For: Baritone, clarinet in B^b, cello, and piano.
Difficulty: Voice: difficult; Instruments: difficult
Vocal range: G - f′
Language: English
Duration: 9:00

573
Birtwistle, Harrison (b. 1934)
Epilogue: "Full Fathom Five" (1972)
Text: William Shakespeare
Publisher: London: Universal Edition UE 16056L
For: Baritone, horn, 4 trombones, and 6 tam-tams.
Difficulty: Voice: moderate; Instruments: moderately easy
Vocal range: $F^{\#}$ - d′
Language: English
Duration: 7:00

574
Bliss, Sir Arthur (1891-1975)
A Knot of Riddles (1963)
I. Fish in River
II. Swallows
III. Oyster
IV. Weathercock
V. A Bookworm
VI. A Cross of Wood
VII. Sun and Moon
Text: Translated from the Old English of the Exeter Book by Kevin Crossley-Holland
Publisher: London: Novello
For: Baritone, flute, oboe, clarinet in B^b, bassoon, harp, violin I, violin II, viola, cello, and double bass.
Difficulty: Voice: moderate; Instruments: moderate
Vocal range: A^b - f′
Language: English

575
Blumenfeld, Harold (b. 1923)
Voyage (1977)
I. Above the fresh ruffles of the surf...
II. And yet this great wink of eternity...
III. Infinite consanguinity it bears...
IV. Meticulous, past midnight in clear rime...
V. Where icy and bright dungeons lift...
Text: after Hart Crane
Publisher: Saint Louis: MMB Music
For: Baritone (high maracas), guitar, viola, and percussion (two players).
Percussion instrumention: Left percussion–celeste, 4 tubular chimes, 4 cymbals, nipple gong or plate bell, large tam-tam, large shekere, maracas, 3 woodblocks, 3 temple blocks, tenor

drum, and 4 pedal timpani. Right percussion–vibraphone, 14 crotales, steel drum: ping pan, 4 tubular chimes, 3 cymbals, nipple gong or plate bell 2, medium-large tam-tam, marimba, maracas, sand block, 3 woodblocks, 3 temple blocks, 5-prong slit drum, snare drum, 3 double-headed tom-toms, 2 congas, and 2 bongos.

Difficulty: Voice: extremely difficult; Instruments: very difficult

Vocal range: G# - a♭′

Language: English

Duration: Parts I and II - 20:00

Comments: Use of quarter tones, microtones. Performance notes are extensive.

576

Bozay, Attila (b. 1939)

Két Tájkép: Two Landscapes, Op. 20 (1971)

I. Taj

II. A hóhullásban

Text: András Fodor

Publisher: Budapest: Editio Musica Z.8588

For: Baritone, flute, and zither.

Difficulty: Voice: very difficult; Instruments: difficult

Vocal range: A - f#′

Language: Hungarian

Duration: 8:00

577

Capdenat, Philippe (b. 1934)

Rituel pour cenci (1974)

I. L'église: choral-prélude

II. L'orgie: toccata

III. L'inceste: aria

IV. Le supplice: marche funèbre

Text: Composer

Publisher: Paris: Amphion A343

For: Bass, horn, 2 trumpets in B♭, 2 trombones, tuba, organ, synthesizer, and percussion (2 players).

Percussion instrumentation: 2 woodblocks, 2 temple blocks, 2 cowbells with leather hangings, 3 suspended cymbals, 2 snare drums, 2 tumbas [Afro-Cuban drum], 3 tom-toms, 3 tubular bells, 9 cow bells, 3 chromatic timpani, gong, cymbal, bass drum, metal plate, and tam-tam.

Difficulty: Voice: very difficult; Instruments: difficult

Vocal range: C# - f#′ (normal); a′ (falsetto)

Language: French

578

Calafato, Salvatore

Guerra a la Guerra por la Guerra (1967)

Text: Rafael Alberti

Publisher: Milan: Suvini Zerboni S.6893Z.

For: Baritone, flute I, flute II, piano, viola, cello, and percussion.

Percussion instrumentation: Small and large temple blocks, snare drum, large tabor, small and large suspended cymbals, and medium tam-tam.

Difficulty: Voice: difficult; Instrument: difficult

Vocal range: F - g′

Language: Spanish

Duration: 7:00

Comments: White score.

579
Christiansen, Henning (b. 1932)
3 Beckett - sange, Op. 14 (1963)
I. Je voudrais que mon amour meur
II. Dieppe
III. Elles viennent
Text: Samuel Beckett
Publisher: Copenhagen: Dan Fog Musikforlag © 1967
Series: Samfundet til udgivelse af Dansk Musik Pub. 3, Number 190.
For: Baritone, celesta, violin, harp, vibraphone, and percussion.
Percussion instrumentation: small tambourine, tenor drum, 2 bongos, 5 temple blocks, woodblocks, claves, maracas, triangle, cymbals, and gong.
Difficulty: Voice: very difficult; Instruments: difficult
Vocal range: $G^{\#}$ - $g^{b\prime}$
Language: French
Duration: 10:00
Comments: Some rhythmic difficulties in I.

580
Cooke, Arnold (b. 1906)
The Seamew (© 1982)
I. The Swallows
II. The Seamew
III. The Empty Cage
Text: Francis Loring
Publisher: London: Anglo-American Music
For: Baritone: flute, oboe, violin I, violin II, viola, and cello.
Difficulty: Voice: moderately difficult; Instruments: moderately difficult
Vocal range: B - g'
Language: English
Duration: 22:00

581
Crumb, George (b. 1929)
Songs, Drones, and Refrains of Death (1968)
I. La Guitarra (The Guitar)
II. Casida de las Palomas Oscuras (Casida of the Dark Doves)
III. Canción de Jinete, 1860 (Song of the Rider, 1860)
IV. Casida del Herido por el Agua (Casida of the Boy Wounded by the Water)
Text: Federico García Lorca
Publisher: New York: Peters 66463
For: Baritone, *electric guitar, *electric double bass, *electric piano (*electric harpischord), and percussion (2 players).
Percussion instrumentation: (I) glockenspiel, xylophone, tubular bells, 3 tom-toms, bongo drums, 3 Chinese woodblocks, claves, tambourine, 4 antique cymbals, sleigh bells, very small triangle, large suspended cymbal, large tam-tam, small Jew's harp, and 3 tuned Austrian cowbells; (II) vibraphone, marimba, lujon [bass metallophone], 2 timbales, 2 tenor drums, bongo drums, bass drum, 4 antique cymbals, tambourine, 3 temple blocks, large tam-tam, large suspended cymbal, Chinese temple gong, sleigh bells, 3 triangles (large, small, very small), flexatone, large Jew's harp, and plectrum with metal or glass rod; (double bassist)

pair of finger cymbals, and large suspended cymbals; (pianist) 2 guitar plectra.

Difficulty: Voice: extremely difficult; Instruments: very difficult

Vocal range: E - f′

Language: Spanish with English translation by J.L. Gili and Stephen Spender

Duration: 30:00

Comments: *Amplified; the baritone and pianist are required to use a cardboard speaking tube (megaphone) at various points in the piece. Many rhythmic and vocal difficulties; singer must have well tuned ear; a number of vocal effects required such as whispers and shouting.

582

Davies, Peter Maxwell (b. 1934)

Eight Songs for a Mad King, George III (1969)

I. The Sentry
II. The Country Walk
III. The Lady-in-Waiting
IV. To Be Sung on the Water
V. The Phantom Queen
VI. The Counterfeit
VII. Country Dance
VIII. The Review

Text: Randolph Stow & King George III

Publisher: New York; London: Boosey & Hawkes HPS 1170

For: Male voice (bass with good falsetto range), flute (doubling piccolo), clarinet in B^b, piano (harpsichord and dulcimer), violin, cello, and percussion.

Percussion instrumentation: railway whistle, side drum, suspended cymbal, large suspended cymbal, foot cymbals, large and small woodblocks, very large bass drum, chains, small ratchet, tom-tom, tam-tam, tambourine, roto toms, toy birdcalls, 2 temple blocks, wind chimes, crotales, very small bells, glockenspiel, small steel bars (non-resonant), and crow.

Difficulty: Voice: extremely difficult; Instruments: very difficult

Vocal range: E^b - a

Language: English

Duration: 33:00

Comments: This piece was written for Roy Hart who has an extended vocal range and can sing the required "chords" (multiphonics).

583

Dispa, Robert (b. 1929)

Ode, Aan het Kind (1976)

I. Dour onze Handen!
II. Kleine Mensen
III. Wegwerp Kinderen
IV. Gebed

Text: Francesco-Ebo

Publisher: Amsterdam: Donemus

For: Bass, flute, friction drum, xylophone, violin I, violin II, viola, cello, and bass.

Difficulty: Voice: moderate; Instruments: moderately difficult

Vocal range: A^b - $f^{\#\prime}$

Language: Dutch

584

Dittrich, Paul-Heinz (b. 1930)

Kammermusik III with Epilog for Baritone and Woodwind Quintet (1974)

Text: Pablo Neruda

Publisher: New York: Peters 9716a
For: Baritone and woodwind quintet.
Difficulty: Voice: very difficult; Instruments: very difficult
Vocal range: G - g′
Language: German
Comments: 4 movements of quintet alone before Epilog.

585
El-Dabh, Halim (b. 1921)
The Eye of Horus (1967)
Text: Composer
Publisher: New York: Peters
For: Bass, piano, and percussion (2 players).
Percussion instrumentation: medium and large cymbals, cowbell, temple blocks, suspended cymbals, 3 tom-toms, triangle, bracelets of bells, xylophone, marimba, metal tube with metal stick, timpani, deep conga drum, and tam-tam.
Difficulty: Voice: moderately difficult; Instruments: moderately difficult
Vocal range: E - g′
Language: English
Comments: A multi-media work with slides and staging; optional sections; composer's manuscript is difficult to read.

586
Feldman, Morton (1926-1987)
Intervals (1961)
Text: none
Publisher: New York: Peters P6908
For: Bass-baritone, cello, trombone, vibraphone, and percussion.
Percussion instrumentation: tubular bells, antique cymbals, tenor drum, and bass drum.
Difficulty: Voice: moderately difficult; Instruments: moderate
Vocal range: G# - f#′
Language: Singer repeats "Ah Ha Va" or other sounds at his discretion.
Comments: The duration of each sound after simultaneous beginning is left to singer and each instrumentalist.

587
Feldman, Morton (1926-1987)
The O'Hara Songs (1962)
I. (repeated text)
II. (repeated text)
III. (repeated text)
Text: Frank O'Hara
Publisher: New York: Peters P6949
For: Bass-baritone, violin, viola, cello, tubular bells, and piano.
Difficulty: Voice: moderate; Instruments: moderate
Vocal range: G - f′
Language: English
Comments: Duration of each sound after simultaneous beginning is left to singer and each instrumentalist within mm = 66 - 84.

588
Forbes, Sebastian (b. 1941)
Crete Songs (1966)
I. Dawn: From his home among dark rocks
II. Mid Morning: Sharp calls of children in the trembling air
III. Afternoon: Trees etched in immobility

IV. Evening: The old man and the endless sea together
Text: Michael Beckwith
Publisher: London: International Music
For: Baritone or mezzo-soprano, viola, and piano.
Difficulty: Voice: moderately difficult; Instruments: difficult
Vocal range: G# - g′
Language: English
Duration: 6:30

589
Gentilucci, Armando (b. 1939)
Canti da "Estravagario" (1965)
I. La Desdi Chada
II. Punto
II. Con Ella
Text: Pablo Neruda
Publisher: Milan: Casa Musicale
For: Baritone, oboe, violin, viola, and cello.
Difficulty: Voice: difficult; Instruments: moderately difficult
Vocal range: A - f#′
Language: Spanish
Duration: 11:00

590
Gentilucci, Armando (b. 1939)
Siamo prossimi al risveglio (1968)
Text: Anonymous
Publisher: Milan: Ricordi 131483
For: Baritone, piano, double bass, timpani, and tam-tam.
Difficulty: Voice: difficult; Instruments: difficult
Vocal range: B^b - $g^{b\prime}$
Language: Italian

591
Ginastera, Alberto (1916-1983)
Serenata, Op. 42 (1973)
I. Poetico
II. Fantastico
III. Drammatico
Text: Pablo Neruda: Love Poems
Publisher: New York: Boosey & Hawkes
For: Baritone, cello, flute, oboe, clarinet in B^b, horn, bassoon, harp, cello, double bass, and percussion (2 players).
Percussion instrumentation: (I) 4 suspended cymbals, 3 tom-toms, 3 woodblocks, 2 mangoli, claves, sandpaper, tambourine, glass chimes, and flexatone; (II) 2 bongos, 2 congas, 2 tom-toms, bass drum, 3 temple blocks, 3 cowbells, 2 suspended crotales, small maraca, sistrum, güiro, bamboo chimes, flexatone, and toy tin frog.
Difficulty: Voice: difficult; Instruments: difficult
Vocal range: G - f′ (also lowest pitch possible)
Language: Spanish

592
Goldman, Friedrich (b. 1941)
Sing' Lessing (1978)
1.1 An die Leyer
1.2 Auf eine lange Nase
1.3 Auf einen gewissen Dichter
1.4 Auf den Tod eines Affen
1.5 Grabschrift auf ebendenselben
2.1 Die Gewissheit
2.2 Die Diebin
2.3 Der Faule
2.4 Die Türken
2.5 Das Paradies
3 Trinklied
Text: Gotthold Ephraim Lessing

Publisher: Leipzig: Peters 5669
For: Baritone, flute (alto flute, piccolo, maracas), oboe (English horn, cinelli), clarinet in B^b (claves), horn (tambourine), bassoon (flexatone, güiro), and piano (maracas).
Difficulty: Voice: difficult; Instruments: difficult
Vocal range: G - $f^{\#\prime}$
Language: German
Duration: 15:00

593
Groot, Rokus de
Skimbleshanks: The Railway Cat (1985)
Text: T. S. Eliot: from *Old Possum's Book of Practical Cats*
Publisher: Amsterdam: Donemus
For: Baritone, bass clarinet, and trombone.
Difficulty: Voice: difficult; Instruments: difficult
Vocal range: d - f′
Language: English
Duration: 3:15

594
Heider, Werner (b. 1930)
Commission (1972)
Text: Ezra Pound
Publisher: New York: Peters © 1974 8208
For: Baritone, flute (piccolo), clarinet in B^b, trombone, violin, cello, double bass, grand piano, electronic organ, and percussion (2 players).
Percussion instrumentation: 4 cardboard boxes varying in size (2 quasi bongos; 2 quasi tom-toms), 4 bottles varying in size, 2 suspended cymbals played with a bow, 4 auto brake drums, 2 double-sided castanets (sistrum if available), 4 temple blocks, cabaça [large maraca-like gourd], 2 pea-whistles, heavy chains on sheet metal, toy metal xylophone, 2 mouth organs (Hohner - No. 40 piccolo), 2 metronomes, 2 typewriters and paper to insert into them, 2 cassette recorders and pop music tapes, electric shaver, frog (sheet metal, huge, as loud as possible), güiro, toy carousel, and emery paper; the vocalist plays claves or woodblock or metal block.
Difficulty: Voice: very difficult; Instruments: difficult
Vocal range: b^b - $g^{b\prime}$
Language: German or English
Duration: 8:00 - 10:00
Comments: Several vocal effects employed including falsetto and Sprechstimme.

595
Hekster, Walter (b. 1937)
Gesang auf dem Strom (1979)
Text: Li-T'ai-Po
Publisher: Amsterdam: Donemus
For: Baritone, piccolo (alto flute), oboe d'amore, clarinet in B^b (bass clarinet), horn, and bassoon.
Difficulty: Voice: difficult; Instruments: difficult
Vocal range: F - $f^{\#\prime}$ (g′ falsetto)
Language: German
Duration: 7:00

596

Hekster, Walter (b. 1937)

3 Haiku Songs (1977)

Text: Haiku

Publisher: Amsterdam: Donemus

For: Baritone, oboe (English horn), and guitar.

Difficulty: Voice: difficult; Instruments: difficult

Vocal range: G - g′

Language: English

Comments: Score is reproduced from sloppy manuscript and is difficult to read.

597

Henze, Hans Werner (b. 1926)

El Cimarrón: Biographie des geflohenen Sklaven

Esteban Montejo: Rezital für 4 Musiken (1970)

Part I 1. Die Welt (The World)
2. Der Cimarrón (The Cimarrón)
3. Die Sklaverei (Slavery)
4. Die Flucht (The Esacpe)
5. Der Wald (The Forest)
6. Die Geister (Ghosts)
7. Die falsche Freiheit (The False Freedom)

Part II 8. Die Frauen (Women)
9. Die Maschinen (The Machines)
10. Die Pfarrer (The Priests)
11. Der Aufstand (The Rebellion
12. Die Schlacht von Mal Tiempo (The Battle of Tiempo)
13. Der schlechte Sieg (The Red Victory)
14. Die Freundlichkeit (Friendliness)
15. Das Messer (The Machete)

Text: Miguel Barnet: El Cimmarrón

Publisher: Mainz: Schott © 1972 6327; 6454 © 1976

For: Singer (baritone), flute (piccolo, alto flute, bass flute, mouth organ, trill whistle, Jew's harp); guitar, and percussion.

Percussion instrumental low: 3 bongos (small, medium and large), 13 tam-tams (C to c′ chromatic), 4 log drums, 8 bamboo drums, Afro-Cuban marimbula [instrument with plucked tongues of metal or wood on a wooden resonator], drum, bass drum (with foot pedal), 2 tam-tams (high and low), 3 suspended cymbals (high, middle, low), maracas, güiro, and 3 temple bells (high, middle, low).

Difficulty: Voice: extremely difficult; Instruments: very difficult

Vocal range: F# - f#″ (falsetto)

Language: German translation by Christopher Keene; or English translation by Hans Magnus Enzelberger

Duration: 76:00

Comments: Singer, flutist, and guitarist also play percussion instruments; use of quarter tones, Sprechstimme; some graphic notation; vocal effects including shouting, whistling.

598

Henze, Hans Werner (b. 1926)

Der langwierige Weg in die Wohnung der Natascha Ungeheuer (1971)

(The Tedious Way to the Place of Natascha Ungeheuer)

I. Planimetry
II. Attempts at Molestation

III. The Veiled Messengers
IV. The Listless Spy
V. Introduction to the Difficult Bourgeoisie
VI. Attempted Return to the Bourgeoisie
VII. (no title)
VIII. German Song
IX. Geodesy
X. Speech practice (song under the gallows)
XI. Metapenthis

Text: Gastón Salvatore: Der langwierige Weg in die Wohnung der Natascha Ungeheuer
Publisher: Mainz: Schott 43-118
For: Baritone, flute (piccolo), clarinet in B^b (clarinet in E^b, bass clarinet), violin (viola), cello, piano, Hammond organ, horn, 2 trumpets in C, 2 trombones, tenor tuba, bass clarinet (flute), ocarina [globular flute], vibraphone, and small percussion, saxophone (various saxophones and clarinets), double bass, and percussion (mouth organ, charmonica or harmonetta), and tape.
Difficulty: Voice: very difficult; Instruments: difficult
Vocal range: D - $g^{\#\prime}$
Language: German (English translation by Christopher Keene)
Duration: 55:30 - 58:00
Comments: A theater piece; percussion instruments come from a junked car and must consist of steel, aluminum, rubber, wood, glass, and felt. Lighting is desirable; costuming is suggested; the players are divided into a piano quintet, brass quintet, jazz group, and a percussionist. Use of quarter tones in vocal part; also indications for change of vocal register.

599

Iglesias, Raul

DC-8 (© 1981)
Text: Josefina Calcagno
Publisher: Budapest: Editio Musica Z.12 029
For: Baritone, flute, oboe, clarinet in B^b, horn, and bassoon.
Difficulty: Voice: moderately difficult; Instruments: moderately difficult
Vocal range: c - $g^{\#\prime}$
Language: Spanish

600

Kagel, Mauricio (b. 1931)

Fürst Igor, Strawinsky (1982)
Text: Aleksandr Borodin, from Act II of *Prince Igor*
Publisher: Frankfurt: Peters, New York: H. Litolff 8601
For: Bass, English horn, horn, tuba, viola, and percussion (2 players).
Percussion instrumentation: 2 lion's roar with 2 meter-long rope, bass drum, 3 wood pieces, light metal chain, hi-hat and 2 Chinese cymbals; tam-tam (at least 75 cm.), anvil, woodblock (large as possible), sleigh bells, 2 coconut shells, heavy wooden block with handle to be struck on carpet, metal pail with 14 large and heavy stones, claves, saw with double bass bow, deep bell, and sementerion (Greek Orthodox).

Difficulty: Voice: very difficult; Instruments; difficult
Vocal range: E - a′ (falsetto)
Language: Russian with German translation
Duration: 18:00
Comments: Vocal effects required such as tremolo, laughing, falsetto.

601
KAPR, JAN (1914-1988)
Symčcový Kvartet VI (String Quartet No. 6) (1963)
I. Do výsěk
II. Jedina
Text: Renata Pandula
Publisher: Prague: Statni Hudebni Vydavatelstrie H 4044
For: Baritone and string quartet.
Difficulty: Voice: difficult; Instruments: difficult
Vocal range: c - e′
Language: Czechoslovakian (English translation by John Clapham).

602
KOBASHI, MINORU
Ki jo (A Demon Woman) (1975)
Text: Shinpei Kusano
Publisher: Tokyo: Japan Federation of Composers © 1978 JFC-7810
For: Baritone and percussion (5 players).
Percussion instrumentation: (I) Japanese bell, small tom-toms (5), vibraphone, xylophone, ancient cymbals (8); (II) cymbal, bongo, bell, side drum, large cymbal, water gong, glockenspiel, marimba; (III) timpani (2), lions roll [sic], flexatone, woodblock; (IV): timpani (2), 5 large tom-toms, Japanese woodblock; (V) gong, bass drum.
Difficulty: Voice: difficult; Instruments: difficult
Vocal range: A - e′
Language: Japanese (characters and romanized)
Duration: 10:00
Comments: Theatrical effects requested but not required.

603
KOELLREUTTER, HANS-JOACHIM (B. 1915)
Acht Haikai des Pedro Xisto (1962)
Text: Pedro Xisto
Publisher: Munich: Edition Modern M1207 E
For: Bass, flute, electric guitar, piano, and medium size gongs, Turkish cymbal, woodblock, and tam-tam.
Difficulty: Voice: moderate; Instruments: moderately easy
Vocal range: F - e′
Language: Portuguese (German translation by Klaus Wolff provided for performance).
Comments: White score.

604
KURTÁG, GYÖRGY (B. 1926)
Four songs to Poems by János Pilinszky, Op. 11 (1973-75)
I. Alkohol
II. In Memoriam F.M. Dosztojevszkij
III. Hölderlin
IV. Verés
Text: János Pilinszky
Publisher: Vienna: Universal Edition UE 16841

For: Bass and four groups of instruments. Group I: bass guitar. Group II: violin and cello. Group III: violin, viola, and cello. Group IV: cimbalom 1, horn, clarinet in A, bass guitar, violin, viola, cello, and cimbalom 2.

Difficulty: Voice: very difficult; Instruments: difficult

Vocal range: $D^{\#}$ (spoken) C (full voice) - e′ (full voice) - a′ (falsetto)

Language: Hungarian with singable German and English translations.

Comments: Some vocal effects required.

605

Laneri, Robert (b. 1945)

Esorcismi 1

Text: none

Publisher: New York: Seesaw Music

For: Voice (baritone), clarinet in B^b, viola, trombone, and percussion.

Percussion instrumentation: vibraphone, other instruments of percussionist's choosing.

Difficulty: Voice: difficult; Instruments: difficult

Vocal range: f - $d^{b\prime}$ plus highest note possible.

Language: Phonemes

Comments: An aleatoric piece. Read performance notes; use of graphic notation.

606

Lassen, Robert

Dream Variations, Op. 1 (1961)

I. Dream Variation
II. Winter Moon (A Blues)
III. Poème d'automne
IV. Fantasy in Purple
V. Interlude (voice tacet)
VI. Joy

Text: Langston Hughes

Publisher: New York: Independent Music Publishers

For: Baritone, flute, clarinet in B^b (alto saxophone), trumpet in B^b, string quartet, and percussion.

Percussion instrumentation: glockenspiel, 3 timpani, snare drum, bass drum, deep tom-tom, medium ride or suspended cymbal, and high gong.

Difficulty: Voice: moderately difficult; Instruments: moderately difficult

Vocal range: G - $g^{b\prime}$

Language: English

Duration: 14:15

607

Łuciuk, Juliusz (b. 1927)

Wiatrowiersze (1971)

I. Gwiazdy
II. Wędrowiec
III. Kometa
IV. Poezja
V. Wiatr

Text: Wladyslaw Broniewski

Publisher: Cracow: P.W.M.

For: Baritone, flute, clarinet in B^b, horn, bassoon, trombone, and bass clarinet.

Difficulty: Voice: moderately difficult; Instruments: moderately difficult

Vocal range: A - $f^{\#\prime}$

Language: Polish (French translation by Maria Cieszewska provided for performance).

608

Manassen, Alex (b. 1950)

And Death (1974)

Text: Dylan Thomas
Publisher: Amsterdam: Donemus
For: Baritone, flute, and guitar.
Difficulty: Voice: moderately difficult; Instruments: difficult
Vocal range: F - $a^{b'}$
Language: English
Duration: 4:30
Comments: Long unaccompanied section for the voice at beginning of the piece; Note extreme range.

609

Matthews, Colin (b. 1946)

The Great Journey Of Alvar Nuñez Cabeza de Vaca (1988)

I. Shipwreck
II. Landing
III. Flight
IV. Return

Text: Adapted from Alvar Nuñez Cabeza de Vaca's 1542 narrative. Translation by Richard Hakluy Posthumus, or: Purchas His Pilgrims, (1625), Book VIII, Chapter I.
Publisher: London: Faber Music
For: Baritone, flute (piccolo and alto flute), clarinet in B^b (bass clarinet), horn, piano, viola, cello, double bass, and percussion.
Percussion instrumentation: 5 tom-toms, 4 roto-toms, 2 tam-tams, boobams (or marimba), 7 crotales, vibraslap, suspended cymbal, sizzle cymbal, cabaça, and waterphone (or large bowed cymbal).
Difficulty: Voice: very difficult; Instruments: very difficult
Vocal range: A - $a^{b'}$
Language: English.

610

Matuszczak, Bernadetta (b. 1933)

Norwid's Triptych (1983)

I. Solitude
II. Not I to your Song
III. Aerumnarum Plenus

Text: Cyprian Norwid
Publisher: Warsaw: Wydawnictwo Muzyczne Agencji Autorskiej
For: Baritone, bass clarinet, and cello.
Difficulty: Voice: difficult; Instruments: moderate
Vocal range: A^b - d'
Language: Polish
Duration: 11:00
Comments: White score.

611

Méfano, Paul (b. 1937)

Lignes (1968)

Text: Composer
Publisher: Paris: Heugel H.31920
For: Bass, three horns, 3 trombones, bassoon, tuba, amplified double bass, and percussion (6 players).
Percussion instrumentation: (I) marimba, wooden chimes, and maracas; (II) marimba, 2 African tam-tams, maracas, and crotales; (III) tubular bells, suspended medium-low cymbal, 2 tam-tams, 2 crash cymbals, snare drum, and maracas; (IV) xylophone, small bell, whip, woodblock, güiro, African tam-tam, and maracas; (V) 4 bongos, 5

tom-toms, bass drum, crotales, and 2 crash cymbals; (VI) vibraphone, sand block, sizzle cymbal, 5 Thailand gongs, and claves.
Difficulty: Voice: very difficult; Instruments: very difficult
Vocal range: E - g′
Language: French
Comments: White score, some graphic notation.

612
Merku, Pavle (b. 1929)
Qui od Altrove (1973)
I. Il Tempo rallenta
II. Per i sensi Profondi
III. Tra nascita e morte, un poeta
Text: Carlo Betocchi
Publisher: Milan: Suvini Zerboni S.7700Z.
For: Baritone and string quartet.
Difficulty: Voice: moderately difficult; Instruments: moderate
Vocal range: F - f′
Language: Italian

613
Moore, Douglas (1893-1969)
The Ballad of William Sycamore (© 1974)
Text: Stephen Vincent Benet
Publisher: New York: King's Crown Music Press/Sole Agent: New York: Galaxy Music 1.2554.7.
Series: Columbia University Press Music Publications
For: Bass, flute, trombone, and piano.
Difficulty: Voice: moderate; Instruments: moderate
Vocal range: A - d′
Language: English
Comments: Possibly written before 1960.

614
Moss, Piotr (b. 1949)
Garść lisci Wierzbowych (1979) (A Handfull of Willow Leaves)
I. Introduction
II. O sosno jakżeś...
III. Pod tymi pniami...
IV. Na górach Harzu...
V. Jaki może być las wiezb
VI. Ptaki w wierzbach...
VII. Ból serca gaśnie...
VIII. (voice tacet)
IX. Gołe drzewo...
X. Wierzby jak klawiatury
XI. Struny na ziemi...
XII. Trzy baby rankiem...
Text: Jarosław Iwaszkiewicz
Publisher: Crakow: P.W.M. PWM 8526
For: Baritone, three cellos, and 3 double basses.
Difficulty: Voice: difficult; Instruments: moderately difficult
Vocal range: A - $e^{b\prime}$
Language: Polish

615
Nelhybel, Vaclav (b. 1919)
The House That Jack Built (© 1973)
Text: Traditional
Publisher: Hastings-on-Hudson, NY: General Music Publishing
For: Baritone, piccolo, clarinet in B^b, horn, bassoon, harpsichord, and percussion.
Percussion instrumentation: xylophone, temple blocks, bells, and tubular bells.
Difficulty: Voice: moderately difficult; Instruments: moderately difficult

Vocal range: B^b - c′
Language: English

616
OHANA, MAURICE (B. 1914)
Stream (1970)
Text: Phonemes and scattered words and phrases
Publisher: Paris: Salabert E.A.S. 17.073
For: Bass, violin, viola, and cello.
Difficulty: Voice: very difficult; Instruments: difficult
Vocal range: Contra B^b - $c^{b\prime\prime}$
Language: phonemes, French and English.
Duration: 16:30
Comments: One other bass voice serves as an accompaniment for a short duration. Singer must use various accents (ex. Russian, Spanish, etc.). Note extreme range.

617
OLTHUIS, KEES (B. 1940)
L'almanach aux images (1976)
I. Les Marionnettes
II. Le Pastour
III. Chanson de l'escarpolette
Text: Tristan Klingsor
Publisher: Amsterdam: Donemus
For: Baritone, 2 violins, viola, cello, double bass, clarinet in B^b, horn, bassoon, and piano.
Difficulty: Voice: difficult; Instruments: difficult
Vocal range: G - $f^{\#\prime}$
Language: French
Duration: 18:00

618
OSBORNE, NIGEL (B. 1948)
I Am Goya (© 1982)
Text: Andrei Voznesensky
Publisher: London: Universal Edition UE16208L
For: Bass-baritone, flute, oboe, violin, and cello.
Difficulty: Voice: extremely difficult; Instruments: extremely difficult
Vocal range: G - f′ (full voice) - $b^{b\prime}$ (falsetto)
Language: Russian with English translation
Duration: 12:00
Comments: Use of quartertones.

619
PENNISI, FRANCESCO (B. 1934)
Fossile (1966)
Text: Composer
Publisher: Milan: Suvini Zerboni S.6824Z.
For: Male voice (baritone), flute, clarinet in B^b, bass clarinet, horn, harpsichord (celesta), viola, and percussion (2 players).
Percussion instrumentation: (I) 3 suspended cymbals, snare drum, bongos, 2 timpani, and crotales; (II) gong, 3 Chinese blocks, marimba, and glockenspiel.
Difficulty: Voice: difficult; Instruments: difficult
Vocal range: B^b - d′
Language: English
Duration: 10:00

620
PINKHAM, DANIEL (B. 1923)
Eight Poems of Gerard Manley Hopkins (1964)
I. Jesus to cast one thought upon
II. Spring

III. Heaven-Haven
IV. Pied Beauty
V. Strike, churl
VI. Spring and fall
VII. Christmas Day
VIII. Jesu that dost in Mary dwell

Text: Gerard Manley Hopkins
Publisher: Boston: Ione Press/Sole agents: E. C. Schirmer Music 132; E.C.S. 2013
For: Baritone and viola.
Difficulty: Voice: moderately difficult; Instruments: moderately difficult
Vocal range: F - f#′
Language: English
Duration: 15:00

621

Presser, William (b. 1916)

Five Rural Songs (1981)

I. Quaking Aspen
II. Return to the River
III. I Walk in the Woods Tonight
IV. The Mountain
V. Here at Night

Text: John Gracen Brown
Publisher: Bryn Mawr, PA: Tenuto/Sole agent: Theodore Presser T249
For: Baritone, clarinet in B^{b}, and cello.
Difficulty: Voice: moderate; Instruments: moderate
Vocal range: A - f#′ (see Comments)
Language: English
Duration: 7:09
Comments: Contains numerous optional notes for lower voices.

622

Presser, William (b. 1916)

Six Songs of Autumn (1981)

I. There on the Slopes
II. Listen to the Wind
III. On the Fall Wind
IV. Late Autumn
V. Moving Shadows
VI. Autumn Is Turning Now

Text: John Gracen Brown
Publisher: Bryn Mawr, PA: Tenuto/Sole agent: Theodore Presser T250
For: Baritone and viola.
Difficulty: Voice: moderately difficult; Instruments: moderately difficult
Vocal range: A - f′
Language: English
Duration: 8:00

623

Ramous, Gianni (b. 1930)

Lettera alla Madre (1963)

Text: Salvatore Quasimodo
Publisher: Milan: Suvini Zerboni S.6060Z.
For: Baritone, violin I, violin II, viola, cello, double bass, and harpsichord.
Difficulty: Voice: moderately difficult; Instruments: moderate
Vocal range: G# - e′
Language: Italian
Duration: 6:00
Comments: Accompaniment is a bit pointillistic.

624

Redel, Martin

Epilog (1971)

Text: Andreas Gryphius
Publisher: Berlin: Bote & Bock B&B 22410 (1152)
For: Bass-baritone, flute (alto flute), and guitar.

Difficulty: Voice: difficult; Instruments: difficult
Vocal range: F - e′
Language: German

625
Reimann, Aribert (b. 1936)
Unrevealed: Lord Byron to Augusta Leigh (1980)
I. Stanzas to Augusta I
II. Stanzas to Augusta II
III. Letter to Augusta
IV. Epistle to Augusta
Text: Lord Byron: Letters
Publisher: Mainz: Schott ED6941
For: Baritone and string quartet.
Difficulty: Voice: difficult; Instruments: very difficult
Vocal range: G$^{\#}$ - g′
Language: English with German translation.
Duration: 40:00

626
Reutter, Hermann (1900-1985)
Ein kleines Requiem (1961)
I. Trockne Erde
II. Spottverse auf Don Pedro zu Pferd
III. Tanz im Garten der Petenera
IV. Tod der Petenera
V. De Profundis
Text: Federico García Lorca
Publisher: Mainz: Schott E.S.5190
For: Bass, cello, and piano.
Difficulty: Voice: moderately difficult; Instruments: moderate
Vocal range: G - e$^{b\prime}$
Language: German

627
Reutter, Hermann (1900-1985)
Tre Notturni (1975)
I. Das trunkne Lied
II. Venedig
III. Zarthustras Nachtgesang
Text: Friedrich Nietzsche
Publisher: Mainz: Schott ED6651
For: Baritone, piano, flute, oboe, clarinet in A, horn, and bassoon.
Difficulty: Voice: moderately difficult: Instruments: moderately difficult
Vocal range: B - f$^{\#\prime}$
Language: German

628
Rochberg, George (b. 1918)
String Quartet No. 7 (1979)
I. The Beast of Night
II. Floating in a Dream
III. Cavalry
IV. And When the Dream Had Faded
Text: Paul Rochberg
Publisher: Bryn Mawr, PA: Theodore Presser
For: Baritone and string quartet.
Difficult: Voice: difficult; Instruments: difficult
Vocal range: A - g′
Language: English

629
Rorem, Ned (b. 1923)
The Santa Fe Songs (1980)
I. Santa Fe
II. Opus 101
III. Any other time
IV. Sonnet
V. Coming down the Stairs
VI. He never knew
VII. El Musico
VIII. The Wintry-mind
IX. Water-Hyacinths
X. Moving Leaves
XI. Yes I hear them

XII. The Sowers
Text: Witter Bynner
Publisher: New York: Boosey & Hawkes © 1980 VAB 0189
For: Baritone, violin, viola, cello, and piano.
Difficulty: Voice: difficult; Instruments: difficult
Vocal range: G - g′
Language: English
Duration: 25:00

630

RUZICKA, PETER (b. 1948)

"...der die Gesänge Zerschlug": Stele für Paul Celan (1985)

I. Alle die Schlafgestalten
II. Zwei Sehwülste
III. Wonderstaude
IV. Im Glockigen
V. Du wirfst mir
VI. Mandelne
VII. Canto

Text: Paul Celan: from *Zeitgehöft*
Publisher: Hamburg: Hans Sikorski © 1985 H.S.1803
For: Baritone, flute (bass flute), bass clarinet (clarinet in B^b), trumpet in B^b, piano, harp, violin I, violin II, viola, cello, double bass, and percussion (2 players).
Percussion instrumentation: (I) bass drum, vibraphone, and large, medium, and small cymbals; (II) large cymbal, large, medium, and small tam-tam, 3 timpani, and 2 Javanese bucklegongs.
Difficulty: Voice: very difficult; Instruments: very difficult
Vocal range: A - f#′
Language: German
Duration: 20:00
Comments: Some graphic notation.

631

STRAVINSKY, IGOR (1882-1971)

Elegy for J.F.K. (1964)

Text: W. H. Auden
Publisher: New York: Boosey & Hawkes B&H 19267
For: Baritone or mezzo soprano, 2 clarinets in B^b, and alto clarinet in E^b
Difficulty: Voice: difficult; Instruments: difficult
Vocal range: c - e′
Language: English
Duration: 2:00
Comments: Also published for mezzo soprano (B&H 1926).

632

SUTERMEISTER, HEINRICH (b. 1910)

Vier Lieder für Bariton nach Texten Schweizerichen Minnesänger (1968)

I. Walter von Klingen
II. Konrad von Landegg
III. Taler von Rheineck
IV. Bruder Eberhard von Sax

Text: Swiss Minnesingers
Publisher: Mainz: Schott © 1970 5968
For: Baritone, violin, flute, oboe, bassoon, and harpsichord.
Difficulty: Voice: moderately difficult; Instruments: moderately difficult
Vocal range: B^b - f′
Language: German

633

TAKAHARA, HIROFUMI

Yoru (Night) (© 1978)

Text: Composer
Publisher: Tokyo: Japan Federation of Composers JFC-7812

For: Voice (baritone), cello, clarinet in B^b, and percussion (1 player).
Percussion instrumentation: marimba, glockenspiel, 3 tom-toms (1 medium, 2 large), 1 gong, 3 woodblocks, and 1 suspended cymbal.
Difficulty: Voice: difficult; Instruments: difficult
Vocal range: F$^\#$ - f$^{\#\prime}$ (falsetto)
Language: Japanese
Comments: Some Sprechstimme.

634
ŢĂRANU, CORNEL (b. 1934)
Le Lit de Procuste (1970)
I. Felie de noroi e ciclulmeu
II. Zborul de u liu
Text: Camil Petrescu
Publisher: Paris: Editions Salabert M.C.562
For: Baritone, clarinet in B^b, viola, and piano.
Difficulty: Voice: difficult; Instruments: difficult
Vocal range: A^b - f′ (also highest note possible)
Language: Romanian and French
Duration: 6:00
Comments: Some use of graphic notation.

635
TESTI, FLAVIO (b. 1923)
Cantata Quarta, Op. 31 (1974) (Viens, mon beau chat)
Text: Charles Baudelaire
Publisher: Milan: Ricordi 132297
For: Baritone and 2 clarinets in B^b.
Difficulty: Voice: moderately difficult; Instruments: difficult
Vocal range: A^b - e′
Language: French
Duration: 7:00

636
TESTI, FLAVIO (b. 1923)
Cantata Terza, Op. 28 (1973)
Text: Rafael Alberti
Publisher: Milan: Ricordi 132138
For: Baritone, flute, clarinet in B^b, horn, guitar, celesta, harp, and double bass.
Difficulty: Voice: difficult; Instruments: difficult
Vocal range: A - g′ (a$^{b\prime}$ falsetto)
Language: Spanish

637
THOMSON, VIRGIL (1896-1989)
The Feast of Love (1964)
Text: *Pervigilium Veneris* (2nd or 4th century a.d.), freely translated by the composer.
Publisher: New York: G. Schirmer 126
For: Baritone, flute, oboe, clarinet in A, bass clarinet (clarinet in B^b), bassoon, glockenspiel, cymbal, harp, violin I, violin II, viola, cello, and double bass.
Difficulty: Voice: difficult; Instruments: moderately difficult
Vocal range: e - g′
Language: English
Duration: 8:00

638
VOSTŘÁK, ZBYNĚK (1920-1985)
Tři Sonety ze Shakespeara, Op. 33 (1963)
I. Sonnet CXXVII (In the old age...)
II. Sonnet CXXIX (The expense of spirit...)

III. Sonnet LV (Not marble, nor the guilded monuments...)
Text: William Shakespeare: Sonnets 127, 129, and 55.
Publisher: Prague: Státní Hudební Vydavatelství H4205
For: Bass, flute, clarinet in B^b, horn, trumpet in B^b, trombone, harp, violin, viola, cello, and double bass.
Difficulty: Voice: difficult; Instruments: difficult
Vocal range: G - e′
Language: English
Duration: 10:00
Comments: Piece is pointillistic; white score.

639

Weisgall, Hugo (b. 1912)

Fancies and Inventions (1970, rev. 1972)

I. To Criticks
II. Soft music
III. To Daffodils
IV. To his Mistresse objecting to him neither Toying or Talking
V. To Cherry-Blossoms
VI. To the Detracter
VII. The Voice and Violl
VIII. The Frozen Heart
IX. I call and I call
X. To Musick. A Song

Text: Robert Herrick: *Hesperides*
Publisher: Bryn Mawr, PA: Theodore Presser © 1974 442-41006
For: Baritone, flute, clarinet in B^b, viola, cello, and piano.
Difficulty: Voice: difficult; Instruments: difficult
Vocal range: B^b - a′
Language: English
Comments: 7 is particularly difficult; most songs have a high tessitura.

640

Wellesz, Egon (1885-1974)

Ode an die Musik, Op. 92 (1965)

Text: Pindar
Publisher: Vienna: Doblinger D.12.290
For: Baritone or alto, flute, oboe, clarinet in B^b, trumpet in C, horn, bassoon, harp, violin, viola, cello, and double bass.
Difficulty: Voice: moderately difficult; Instruments: moderately difficult
Vocal range: B^b - e′
Language: German
Duration: 5:00

641

Wuorinen, Charles (b. 1938)

A Message to Denmark Hill: made into a Cantata (1970)

Text: Richard Howard: Untitled subjects: "1851"
Publisher: New York: Peters 66384
For: Baritone, flute, cello, and piano.
Difficulty: Voice: very difficult; Instruments: difficult
Vocal range: F$^\#$ - f$^{\#\prime}$
Language: English
Duration: 26:00
Comments: Use of recitative and aria in a contemporary context.

Medium Voice

642
Albright, William (b. 1944)
Father, We Thank Thee (1973)
Text: from the *Didache* (teachings of the Twelve Apostles) translated by F. Bland Tucker
Publisher: Bryn Mawr, PA: Elkan-Vogel 362-03179
For: Voice (medium), piano or organ, and at least three of the following instruments: harp, glockenspiel, celesta, vibraphone, piano (poss. 4-hand), chimes, organ chimes, glass harmonica, handbells, carillon, acoustic guitar (harmonics), antique cymbals (tuned), tuned goblets (arco), toy piano (chromatic), prepared tape (bell or bell-like sounds), and electric piano.
Difficulty: Voice: moderately easy; Instruments: moderately easy
Vocal range: d′ - c″
Language: English
Comments: Some aleatoric elements; can also be sung by unison choir or congregation.

643
Aslamazov, Alexandr Georgievich (b. 1945)
From Armenian Lyrics (1974)
Publisher: Leningrad: State Publishers "Soviet Composer" c410K
For: Medium voice and two clarinets in B^b.
Difficulty: Voice: difficult; Instruments: difficult
Vocal range: b - $a^{b''}$
Language: Russian
Comments: Use of unsual meter.

644
Banks, Don (1923-1980)
Tirade (1968)
I. We're in a permanent museum
II. This land is marked with an ochre line
III. Our future suits computers
Text: Peter Porter
Publisher: London: Schott 11073
For: Voice (medium), piano, harp, and percussion (3 players).
Percussion instrumentation: 2 timpani, 2 gongs, 2 tam-tams, 2 glass wind chimes, 2 wood chimes, 3 maracas, 6 temple blocks, 2 tumbas [Afro-Cuban drum], glockenspiel, 3 bongos, 3 high pitch cymbals, 2 low pitch cymbals, 6 tom-toms, güiro, bass drum, vibraphone, 2 cowbells, hi-hat, snare drum, knife, marimba, 2 crotales, 1 tubular bell ($e^{b'}$), and foot operated siren (for conductor).
Difficulty: Voice: moderately difficult; Instruments: moderate
Vocal range: a^b - $a^{b''}$
Language: English
Comments: Some aleatoric elements.

645
Beeson, Jack (b. 1921)
A Creole Mystery: A Short Story (1970)
Text: Lafcadio Hearn adapted by composer
Publisher: New York: Boosey & Hawkes © 1979 BH.BK.789
For: Medium voice and string quartet.

Difficulty: Voice: moderately difficult; Instruments: moderate
Vocal range: a - $g^{b''}$
Language: English
Duration: 9:00 - 10:00

646
BEESON, JACK (B. 1921)
The Day's No Rounder Than Its Angles Are (1971)
I. Why Can't I Live Forever
II. Dance of the Haemophiliacs
III. The Day's No Rounder Than Its Angles Are
Text: Peter Viereck
Publisher: New York: Boosey & Hawkes BH.BK.784
For: Medium voice and string quartet.
Difficulty: Voice: difficult; Instruments: difficult
Vocal range: a - $a^{b''}$
Language: English
Duration: 12:00

647
BEHREND, SIEGFRIED (1933-1990)
Requiem auf Hiroshima (1970)
Text: none
Publisher: Cologne: Hans Gerig
For: Voice (medium), solo mandolin (with contact microphone), solo guitar (with contact microphone), various percussion instruments which must include glockenspiel, vibraphone, xylophone, marimba, and a plucked "orchestra" of various instruments which must include 2 mandolins, dola [mandola - larger mandolin of the 17th century], guitar, and double bass.
Difficulty: Voice: moderate; Instruments: moderate
Vocal range: no definite pitches
Language: phonemes and German
Duration: 9:50
Comments: Score is difficult to decipher; not enough explanation of meanings; see *Tabulator für Schlaginstrumente* by Siegfried Fink, Hamburg: Musikverlag Simrock.

648
BERGER, JEAN (B. 1909)
Five Songs (© 1965)
I. Pour lui j'ay mes prisé
II. Car c'est le seul désire
III. Sans cesse mon coeur sent
IV. Vous m'estimez légère
V. O Domine Deus!
Text: Mary Stuart, Queen of Scots
Publisher: Denver: John Sheppard Music Press 3001
For: Medium voice, flute, viola, and cello.
Difficulty: Voice: moderate; Instruments: moderate
Vocal range: b - $f^{\#''}$
Language: French, V is in Latin; English translation is provided.

649
BERGER, JEAN (B. 1909)
Messianic Songs (© 1988)
I. Why do the Nations so furiously rage Together?
II. Comfort Ye my People
III. Glory be to God
Text: George Frideric Handel's *Messiah*
Publisher: Denver: John Sheppard Music Press
For: Voice (medium) and string quartet.

Difficulty: Voice: moderately difficult; Instruments: moderately difficult
Vocal range: d′ - g″
Language: English

650

Berger, Jean (b. 1909)

Tres canciones (© 1968)

I. Ninguno cierre las puertas
II. Ay, triste, que vengo
III. Ya cantan los gallos

Text: Anonymous poems from the court of Ferdinand and Isabella
Publisher: Denver: John Sheppard Music Press
For: Medium voice, viola, and cello (or piano).
Difficulty: Voice: moderately difficult; Instruments: moderately difficult
Vocal range: c′ - g″
Language: Spanish

651

Bergsma, William (b. 1921)

Four Songs (1981)

I. This is the Key to the Kingdom (Traditional)
II. The Head from the Well of Life (George Peele)
III. Frolic's Song (George Peele)
IV. Hokey Pokey, Whiskey, Thum (Traditional)

Publisher: New York: Galaxy Music 1.2941
For: Medium voice, clarinet in B^b, bassoon, and piano.
Difficulty: Voice: moderate; Instruments: moderate
Vocal range: a - f″
Language: English

652

Birtwistle, Harrison (b. 1934)

La Plage (1972)

Text: none
Publisher: Totowa, NJ: Universal Edition/European American Music
For: Voice (medium), 3 clarinets in B^b, piano, and marimba.
Difficulty: Voice: moderately easy; Instruments: moderate
Vocal range: $d^{b\prime}$ - c″
Language: None; however, the voice is to imitate a bell.
Comments: Use of microtones; also aleatoric and improvisatory elements.

653

Birtwistle, Harrison (b. 1934)

Ring a Dumb Carillon (1969)

Text: Christopher Logue
Publisher: London: Universal Edition UE 14192L
For: Voice (medium high), clarinet in B^b, and percussion.
Percussion instrumentation: 5 suspended cymbals, 4 timbales, 4 woodblocks, 4 temple blocks, 5 cowbells, 1 maraca, 1 pair of claves, and 1 pair of bongos.
Difficulty: Voice: moderately difficult; Instruments: moderately difficult
Vocal range: a - a″
Language: English

654

Bujarski, Zbigniew (b. 1933)

Kompozycja Kameralna (1963)

I. Wola ku niebu wielkie... (Sigedzi Tsuboi)
II. Na cienistym wzgórzu... (Kisiro Tanaka)

Publisher: Warsaw: P.W.M.
For: Voice (medium), flute, harp, piano, 2 microphones, amplifier, loudspeakers, and percussion.
Percussion instrumentation: xylophone, bells, timpani, 2 bongos, 2 tom-toms, 4 cymbals (SATB), and tam-tam.
Difficulty: Voice: difficult; Instruments: difficult
Vocal range: b - g″
Language: Polish
Duration: 8:15
Comments: White score; some Sprechstimme.

655
Corghi, Azio (b. 1937)
Symbola (1971)
Text: none
Publisher: Milan: Suvini Zerboni S. 7396 Z.
For: Voice (medium), flute, cello, piano, percussion, tape, and synthesizer.
Percussion instrumentation: triangle, cowbell, 3 suspended cymbals, Chinese gong, 2 tubular bells (pitched a and g#′), glass chimes, wood chimes, castanets, woodblock, 3 temple blocks, bongos, tambourine, snare drum, 3 tom-toms, bass drum with pedal, and maracas.
Difficulty: Voice: moderately difficult; Instruments: moderate
Vocal range: Notations are not exact; pitches range from low to high
Language: phonemes
Comments: There are 3 versions for different combinations of instruments. Carefully read the instructions provided; use of graphic notation.

656
Crosse, Gordon (b. 1937)
Corpus Christi Carol, Op. 5 (1961)
Text: Anonymous 16th century
Publisher: London: Oxford University Press
For: Voice, clarinet in A, horn, violin I, violin II, viola, and cello.
Difficulty: Voice: moderately easy; Instruments: moderately easy
Vocal range: c′ - a″
Language: English

657
Dávid, Gyula (1913-1977)
A rózsalángolás (1966)
I. A rózsalángolás
II. Mikor a rózsák nyílni Kezdtek
III. Idegen virág
Text: István Vas
Publisher: Budapest: Zenemükiado Z. 5528
For: Voice (medium), flute, and viola.
Difficulty: Voice: moderately difficult; Instruments: moderately difficult
Vocal range: b♭ - g#″
Language: Hungarian

658
De Bohun, Lyle (b. 1927)
Slumber Song (© 1975)
Text: Composer
Publisher: Washington, D.C.: Arsis Press
For: Voice (medium) and melody instrument.

Difficulty: Voice: moderate; Instruments: moderate
Vocal range: c′ - e″
Language: English

659

Dessau, Paul (1894-1979)
Begrüssing (1974 version)
I. (Voice tacet)
II. Plubberum, dudo rumdum (unaccompanied)
III. Wenn du in einer Kutsche gefahren kämst
IV. "Die Freunde," 1. Fassung (voice & piano)
Text: Bertolt Brecht: Die Freunde
Publisher: Berlin: Bote & Bock © 1979 B&B22567 (1347)
For: Voice (medium), flute, string quartet, and piano.
Difficulty: Voice: moderately difficult; Instruments: moderate
Vocal range: b - e″
Language: German

660

Feldman, Morton (1926-1987)
I met Heine on the Rue Fürstenberg (1971)
Text: none
Publisher: Vienna: Universal Edition UE 15470
For: Voice (medium), flute (piccolo), clarinet in B♭ (bass clarinet), piano, violin, cello, and percussion.
Percussion instrumentation: vibraphone, tenor drum, tubular bells, temple block, glockenspiel, timpani, woodblock, and triangle.
Difficulty: Voice: moderately difficult; Instruments: moderate
Vocal range: b♭ - g″
Language: none - no phonemes given
Duration: 10:00
Comments: Voice is treated as an instrumental part; vocal tremolo.

661

Flothuis, Marius (b. 1914)
Hommage á Mallarmé, Op. 80 (1980)
Text: Composer
Publisher: Amsterdam: Donemus
For: Voice (medium), flute, cello, and piano.
Difficulty: Voice: moderately difficult; Instruments: difficult
Vocal range: c♯′ - e″
Language: French
Duration: 4:00

662

Françaix, Jean (b. 1912)
Déploration de Tonton: chien fidèle (© 1980)
Text: Georges Ravon
Publisher: Paris: Éditions Musicales Transatlantiques E.M.T. 1217
For: Voice (medium), 3 violins, 3 violas, cello, and bass.
Difficulty: Voice: difficult; Instruments: moderately difficult
Vocal range: c′ - f♯″
Language: French
Duration: 7:30

663

Gideon, Miriam (b. 1906)
The Adorable Mouse: A Fable (1960)
Text: based on Jean de la Fontaine's La Souris Métamorphasée
Publisher: New York: Joshua Corporation © 1975 855/Sole agent: New York: G. Schirmer

For: Voice (medium), flute, clarinet in B^b, bassoon, horn, timpani, and harpsichord.
Difficulty: Voice: moderate; Instruments: moderate
Vocal range: c′ - g″
Language: English

664
Gideon, Miriam (b. 1906)
Creature to Creature (© 1985)
I. The Fly
II. Spider
III. Snake
IV. Firefly
V. Hoot Owl (Interlude)
VI. L'envoi
Text: Nancy Cardozo: An Animalculary
Publisher: Hillsdale, NY: Mobart Music Publications © 1985/Sole agent Hackensack, NJ: Jerona Music
For: Voice (medium), flute, and harp.
Difficulty: Voice: difficult; Instruments: difficult
Vocal range: a - g″
Language: English

665
Gideon, Miriam (b. 1906)
Questions on Nature (1964)
I. How the earth moves
II. Why the planets...
III. Whence the winds arise
IV. Whether the stars fall
V. Whether beasts have souls
VI. Why we hear echoes
VII. Why joy is the cause of weeping
Text: Adelard of Bath
Publisher: Hillsdale, NY: Mobart Music
For: Medium voice, oboe, piano, glockenspiel, and tam-tam.
Difficulty: Voice: difficult; Instruments: difficult
Vocal range: c#′ - g″
Language: English
Duration: 9:30

666
Gideon, Miriam (b. 1906)
Rhymes from the Hill (1968)
I. Bundeslied
II. Wiegenlied
III. Zwei Uhren:1
IV. Zwei Uhren:2
V. Der Seufzer
Text: Christian Morgenstern: Galgenlieder
Publisher: Hillsdale, NY: Mobart Music 106
For: Voice (medium), clarinet in B^b, cello, and marimba.
Difficulty: Voice: moderate; Instruments: moderately difficult
Vocal range: c′ - f″
Language: German; English translation by Max Knight

667
Gideon, Miriam (b. 1906)
Spirit above the Dust: A Song Cycle on American Poetry (1980)
I. Prologue (Anne Bradstreet)
II. Know the World (Archibald MacLeish)
III. The Two Trees (Archibald MacLeish)
IV. The Linden Branch (Archibald MacLeish)
V. Black Boy (Norman Rosten)
VI. Caliban (Norman Rosten)

VII. Interlude (voice tacet)
VIII. The Snow Fall (Archibald MacLeish)

Publisher: New York: Peters 66852
For: Voice (medium), flute, oboe, bassoon, horn, violin I, violin II, viola, and cello.
Difficulty: Voice: very difficult; Instruments: difficult
Vocal range: c#′ - f#″
Language: English
Duration: 15:00

668

GRUNDMAN, CLARE (B. 1913)

Zoo Illogical (© 1974)

Text: Composer
Publisher: New York: Boosey & Hawkes Oct. 5855 (parts B. Ens. 201)
For: Voice (medium), flute I (piccolo), flute II, clarinet in B♭ I, clarinet in B♭ II, bass clarinet, bassoon, trumpet in B♭, trombone, and percussion.
Percussion instrumentation: finger cymbal, large and small tom-toms, bells, xylophone, temple blocks, triangle, timpani, woodblock, cymbals, and piano (optional).
Difficulty: Voice: easy; Instruments: moderately easy
Vocal range: c′ - d″
Language: English

669

HAAN, RAYMOND H. (B. 1938)

Benediction (© 1986)

Text: Numbers 6:24-26
Publisher: Minneapolis: Art Masters Studios V-9
For: Voice (medium), organ, and C instrument.
Difficulty: Voice: easy; Instruments: moderately easy
Vocal range: b♭ - e♭″
Language: English

670

JOHNSTON, BEN (B. 1926)

Five Fragments (© 1975)

Text: Henry David Thoreau: *Walden*
Publisher: Baltimore: Smith Publications
For: Medium voice, oboe, cello, and bassoon.
Difficulty: Voice: very difficult (see comments); Instruments: very difficult (see Comments)
Vocal range: f - g″ (unadjusted) (see Comments)
Language: English
Comments: To be performed in just intonation.

671

KAGEL, MAURICIO (B. 1931)

Tango Alemán (1978)

Text: none
Publisher: Frankfurt: Henry Litoff; New York: Peters 31127; 8412
For: Voice (medium), violin, bandoneon [an accordion may be substituted for the bandoneon], and piano.
Difficulty: Voice: difficult; Instruments: difficult
Vocal range: c′ - f♭″
Language: Performer sings exclusively in an incomprehensible, imaginary language.
Comments: Singer required to whistle.

672

Kingsley, Gershon (b. 1922)

Three Sacred Songs (1969)

I. Prepare to Meet Thy God (Amos 5:24)

II. Rise Up My Love (Song of Songs 2:10-12)

III. I Will Give Thanks unto the Lord (Psalm 9:2-3)

Publisher: New York: Transcontinental Music TV545

For: Voice (medium), cello, and keyboard.

Difficulty: Voice: moderate; Instruments: moderate

Vocal range: b^{b} - f″

Language: English and Hebrew

673

Koch, Frederick (b. 1923)

Trio of Praise (© 1972)

Text: Joseph Joel Keith

Publisher: New York: Seesaw

For: Medium voice, viola, and piano.

Difficulty: Voice: moderate; Instruments: moderate

Vocal range: a - f$^{\#}$″

Language: English

674

Lacerda, Osvaldo (b. 1927)

Hiroshima meu amor (1968, rev. 1976)

Text: Augusto de Campos

Publisher: São Paulo: Editora Novas Metas 77002

For: Voice (medium) and percussion (4 players).

Percussion instrumentation: (I) atabaque, snare drum, and tam-tam; (II) bombo, suspended cymbal, and vibraphone; (III) suspended cymbal, and timpani; (IV) bombo, caixa de madeira, tam-tam, and xylophone.

Difficulty: Voice: moderately difficult; Instruments: difficult

Vocal range: b - f″

Language: Portuguese

675

Lacerda, Osvaldo (b. 1927)

Losango Cáqui No. 6 (1970, rev. 1976)

Text: Mario de Andrade

Publisher: São Paulo: Editora Novas Metas 77003

For: Voice (medium) and percussion (4 players)

Percussion instrumentation: (I) caixa clara; (II) bombo, caixa de madeira, castanets, glockenspiel, pair of cymbals, and vibraphone; (III) bomba, glockenspiel, suspended cymbal, snare drums, and vibraphone; (IV) tamborine, tam-tam, 2 timpani, vibraphone, and xylophone.

Difficulty: Voice: moderately difficult; Instruments: moderately difficult

Vocal range: c′ - e^{b}″

Language: Portuguese

676

Láng, István (b. 1933)

Kamarakantáta (1962)

I. Miben Hisztek

II. Kopogtatás Nélkül

Text: Attila József

Publisher: Budapest: Editio Musica Z.4533

For: Voice (medium), clarinet in B^{b}, cello, piano, and percussion.

Percussion instrumentation: chimes, vibraphone, bongos, gong, and suspended cymbals.
Difficulty: Voice: moderately difficult; Instruments: moderate
Vocal range: c′ - g#″
Language: Hungarian; German translation
Duration: 10:00
Comments: Convenient piano reduction along bottom of score.

677

Le Douarin, Alain

Hymne a Sept Temps (© 1976)
Text: Maxime Le Forestier
Publisher: Paris: Editions de Misère E.50 M.
For: Voice (medium), guitar, and double bass.
Difficulty: Voice: moderate; Instruments: moderately difficult
Vocal range: c#′ - d″
Language: French

678

Level, Pierre-Yves (b. 1937)

Ce que j'aime (© 1970)
Text: André Massepin
Publisher: Paris: Heugel H.32024
For: Voice (medium), flute I and II, xylophone ad lib., and tambourine.
Difficulty: Voice: easy; Instruments: very easy
Vocal range: d′ - d″
Language: French

679

Łuciuk, Juliusz (b. 1927)

Sen Kwietny (Floral Dream) (1960)
I. Dzieńwyznania
II. Obraz
III. Oczy
IV. Świt kwietniowy
V. Nokturn trzeci
Text: Julian Przyboś
Publisher: Cracow, P.W.M. PWM-4688
For: Voice (medium), flute (piccolo), clarinet in B♭, bass clarinet, alto saxophone, horn, trombone, vibraphone, piano, harp, violin, viola, and cello.
Difficulty: Voice: moderately difficult; Instruments: moderately difficult
Vocal range: b - a♭″
Language: Polish (French translation by Allan Kosko)
Duration: 9:00

680

Maros, Rudolf (1917-1982)

Sirató (Lament) (1969)
Text: Composer
Publisher: New York: Southern Music Publishing/Peer Musikverlag
For: Voice (medium), alto flute, oboe, clarinet in B♭, bassoon, bells, harp, violin I, violin II, viola, cello, double bass, and marimba.
Difficulty: Voice: difficult; Instruments: difficult
Vocal range: c′ - f″
Language: Hungarian (German and English translations)

681

Muldowney, Dominic (b. 1952)

The Duration of Exile (1983)
I. Prelude: Alles wandelt sich (Everything changes) (translated by John Willett)

II. Der Lautsprecher (The Wireless) (translated by Michael Morley)
III. Der Rauch (The Smoke) (translated by Derek Bowman)
IV. Über die Unfruchtbarkeit (On Sterility) (translated by John Willett)
V. Wechsel der Dinge (Things Change) (translated by John Willett)
VI. Finland 1940 (translated by Sammy McLean)
VII. Tannen (Fir-Trees) (translated by Derek Bowman)
VIII. Die Maske des Bösen (The Mask of Evil) (translated John Willett)
IX. Postlude, Alles wandelt sich (Everything changes) (translated John Willett)

Text: Bertolt Brecht
Publisher: London: Universal Edition UE 17653L
For: Voice (medium), flute, oboe, clarinet in B^{b} (alto saxophone), harp, violin, viola, and trombone.
Difficulty: Voice: moderately difficult; Instruments: moderate
Vocal range: a - e″
Language: German; singable English translation
Duration: 22:00

682
Pablo, Luis de (b. 1930)
Canción (1979)
Text: Juan Gil-Albert
Publisher: Milan: Suvini Zerboni S. 8634 Z.
For: Voice (medium), oboe, trumpet in B^{b}, celesta, and harp.
Difficulty: Voice: difficult; Instruments: difficult (extremely difficult celesta part)
Vocal range: b - g$^{\#}$″
Language: Spanish

683
Reveyron, Joseph
Le Chant des noces (Bridal Song) (© 1966)
Text: Yehuda Halevy (Juda ha-Levy)
Publisher: Tel Aviv: Israeli Music Publications #I.M.P. 219
For: Voice (medium), flute, harpsichord, triangle, and high and low tambourine.
Difficulty: Voice: difficult; Instruments: difficult
Vocal range: d$^{\#}$′ - g″
Language: Hebrew (romanized); German translation by R. G. Wolfsohn; English translation by Rachel Vernon; French translation by the composer.

684
Riley, Dennis (b. 1943)
Summer Music (1982)
I. Praeambulum
II. Capriccio
III. Canzona
IV. Finale

Text: Thomas Campion
Publisher: New York: Peters © 1987 67057
For: Medium voice, flute, and guitar.
Difficulty: Voice: moderately difficult; Instruments: moderately difficult
Vocal range: c′ - e″

Language: English
Duration: 8:00
Comments: Also published for mezzo soprano: New York: American Composers Alliance, © 1979.

685

Schafer, R. Murray (b. 1933)

Arcana (1972)

I. I have become an enchantress
II. The poison of the serpent...
III. I purify my God...
IV. I search for the formula...
V. I have closed the passage...
VI. One of us is a phantom...
VII. You will eat no opium tonight
VIII. Questions for midnight
IX. I am dreaming...
X. The more the seekers...
XI. Whomever deciphers...
XII. When the labyrinth...
XIII. Many sacred fires are profane
XIV. He comes with a sword...

Text: Middle Egyptian hieroglyphs translated by D.B. Redford
Publisher: Toronto: Universal Edition Canada UE16016
For: Voice (medium), flute (piccolo), clarinet in B^b, trumpet in B^b, trombone, violin, cello, harp, piano (electric organ), and percussion (one player).
Percussion instrumentation: glass chimes, tam-tam, glockenspiel, bass drum, vibraphone, suspended cymbal, woodblock, metal block or anvil, tom-tom, claves, temple blocks, 4 bongos, wrist bells or small ring of sleigh bells, maracas, small brass chimes, sizzle cymbal, two temple bells, medium gong, cymbals, tubular bells, Japanese tree bell, timpani, crotales, wood or bamboo chimes, and small nipple gong.
Difficulty: Voice: very difficult; Instruments: very difficult
Vocal range: a - $a^{b''}$ plus highest note possible
Language: Phonemes (I.P.A.)
Duration: 17:30
Comments: White score; vocal effects required including affected scream.

686

Sharlin, William (b. 1920)

V'shamru (© 1987)

Text: Be-Shaaray Tefilu: Gates of Prayer
Publisher: New York: Transcontinental Music 991219
For: Voice (medium), keyboard, clarinet in B^b, horn, and bassoon.
Difficulty: Voice: moderately difficult; Instruments: moderate
Vocal range: d′ - e″
Language: Hebrew

687

Sharvit, Uri (b. 1939)

Divertissement (1964)

Publisher: Tel Aviv: Israeli Music Publications I.P.M. 220
For: Medium voice, flute, bassoon, Arabic drum, and piano.
Difficulty: Voice: moderate; Instruments: moderate
Vocal range: c′ - c″
Language: only the sound "Hah"

688
SIMONS, NETTY (B. 1913)
Songs for Wendy (1975)
I. The Fly (William Blake)
II. A Centipede (Anonymous)
III. On the Grasshopper and Cricket (John Keats)
IV. The Caterpillar (Christina G. Rossetti)
V. Was Worm (May Swenson)
Publisher: Bryn Mawr, PA: Merion Music/Sole Agent Theodore Presser #441-41011
For: Voice (medium) and viola.
Difficulty: Voice: difficult; Instrument: difficult
Vocal range: b - f#″
Language: English
Duration: 8:50

689
SOMERS, HARRY (B. 1925)
Twelve Miniatures (1965)
I. Springtime Sea
II. The Skylark
III. The Visitor
IV. Night Lightning
V. The Portent
VI. September Voices
VII. Autumn Nightfall
VIII. The Scarecrow
IX. Lament
X. Winter Night
XI. Loneliness
XII. The River
Text: from Japanese Haiku
Publisher: Don Mills, Ontario: BMI Canada
For: Medium voice, soprano recorder or flute, viola da gamba or cello, and spinet or piano.
Difficulty: Voice: moderately difficult; Instruments: moderate
Vocal range: b - f#″
Language: English; English words taken from a translation by Harold G. Henderson in *An Introduction to Haiku.*
Duration: 15:00
Comments: Use of quarter tones.

690
STAEPS, HANS ULRICH (1909-1988)
Das Lied tönt Fort: Spielmusik (1963)
I. Es Springt ein heller Brunnenstrahl
II. (voice tacet)
III. (voice tacet)
IV. (voice tacet)
V. Ein Brunnen steht...
Text: from a North German folk melody
Publisher: Vienna: Doblinger D12.349
Series: Flautario, 2
For: Voice (medium) ad lib., soprano recorder (or violin), alto recorder (or violin), and tenor recorder (or viola).
Difficulty: Voice: easy; Instruments: moderate
Vocal range: c′ - c″
Language: German
Comments: Can be performed with or without the voice.

691
STEINER, GITTA (B. 1932)
Three Poems (1969)
I. Wend to me...
II. Shore dry, lost, sea tossed...
III. What am I...
Text: Composer
Publisher: New York: Seesaw
For: Medium voice and percussion (2 players).

Percussion instrumentation: (I) vibraphone, glockenspiel, wind chimes, and antique cymbals; (II) tom-tom, Chinese temple blocks, cymbals, snare drum, bass drum, hi-hat, gong, 2 bongos, xylophone, and wind chimes.
Difficulty: Voice: difficult; Instruments: difficult
Vocal range: b^b - a″
Language: English
Duration: 8:00

692
Terzakis, Dimitri (b. 1938)
Die Tore der Nacht und des Tages (1987)
Text: Composer, based upon Parmenides and Jan Kochanowski
Publisher: Bad Schwalbach: Edition Gravis EG130
For: Medium voice (soprano or tenor), clarinet in B^b, and piano.
Difficulty: Voice: very difficult; Instruments: difficult
Vocal range: b - $b^{b''}$
Language: Polish
Comments: The tessitura is quite high; therefore this author recommends high voice rather than medium voice. Use of quarter tones.

693
Trimble, Lester (1923-1986)
Petit Concert (1969)
I. Introduction (voice tacet)
II. Arioso (William Shakespeare)
III. Intermezzo (voice tacet)
IV. Arioso (William Blake)
V. Finale con Arioso (William Blake)
Publisher: New York: Peters 66069a
For: Medium voice, violin, oboe, and harpsichord (or piano).
Difficulty: Voice: moderate; Instruments: moderate
Vocal range: $d^{b'}$ - $a^{b''}$
Language: English
Duration: 12:00

694
Wienhorst, Richard (b. 1920)
I Will Sing the Story of Your (Thy) Love, O Lord (1978)
Text: from Contemporary Worship 3 (Psalm 89:1, Jeremiah 33:11, Psalm 100:5)
Publisher: Springfield, OH: Chantry Music Press VOS 8012
For: Voice (medium), flute, and organ.
Difficulty: Voice: moderate; Instruments: moderate
Vocal range: $c^{\#'}$ - e″
Language: English
Comments: Can also be sung by unison choir.

695
Wooldridge, David (b. 1927)
Night Canticle, Op. 34 (© 1980)
I. I saw eternitie... (Henry Vaughan)
II. Appon the midsummer evin (Sir William Dunbar)
III. Wostron wind (Anonymous 14th century Cornish)
IV. They flee from me (Sir Henry Wyatt)
V. A Lament for the Innocents (Anonymous 5th century Celtic)
VI. Le petit cordonnier (Anonymous 13th century Provençal)

VII. In Darkness let me dwell (John Dowland)

Publisher: Bridgewater, CT: Hinchinbroke Music

For: Medium voice, flute (alto flute and piccolo), oboe (English horn), clarinet in A (alto saxophone and bass clarinet), vibraphone, crotales, high gong, tabor, tambourine, harp, violin I, violin II, viola, cello, and double bass.

Difficulty: Voice: difficult; Instruments: difficult

Vocal range: f - $A^{b''}$

Language: English and French

Duration: 15:00

Comments: Scordatura tuning for harp; optional male chorus.

Countertenor and Miscellaneous

696

Bank, Jacques (b. 1943)

Lied: hommage aan Franz Schubert (1976)

Text: Composer

Publisher: Amsterdam: Donemus

For: Countertenor or mezzo soprano, clavichord, piano, and percusion (2 players).

Percussion instrumentation: 2 wood blocks, 2 temple blocks, slit drum, 2 bongos, 2 tom-toms, snare drum, bass drum, triangle, 3 suspended cymbals, cowbell, tam-tam, wood chimes, glass chimes, wind chimes, jingling johnny, 4 maracas, timpano, flexatone, and marimba.

Difficulty: Voice: difficult; Instruments: moderately difficult

Vocal range: g - b″

Language: Dutch

697

Boyd, Anne (b. 1946)

Cycle of Love (1981)

I. Was it yesterday...
Interlude I
II. Winter night, winter night
III. So much love piled...
IV. The sudden, sudden gust last night
Interlude II
V. Is love a dream...

Text: Korean Sijo translated by Don'o Kim

Publisher: London: Faber

For: Countertenor, alto flute, cello, and piano.

Difficulty: Voice: difficult; Instruments: difficult

Vocal range: g^{b} - $f^{\#}$″

Language: English

698

Crosse, Gordon (b. 1937)

Verses in Memoriam (1978)

Text: David Munrow

Publisher: New York: Oxford University Press

For: Countertenor or alto (two bells), recorder, cello, and harpsichord.

Difficulty: Voice: moderately difficult; Instruments: difficult

Vocal range: $g^{\#}$ - d″

Language: English

Duration: 8:30

Comments: Some graphic notation.

699

Goosen, Jacques G. (b. 1952)

Georg-Trakl-Lieder (1978)

I. An den Knaben Elis
II. Elis 1
III. Elis 2

Text: Georg Trakl

Publisher: Amsterdam: Donemus

For: Countertenor, 7 violins, 4 violas, 2 cellos, double bass, harp, and percussion.

Percussion instrumentation: 3 tam-tams (high, medium, low), antique cymbals, 2 vibraphones.

Difficulty: Voice: very difficult; Instruments: very difficult

Vocal range: a - b″

Language: German

700

Kopytman, Mark (b. 1929)

October Sun (1974)

Text: Yehuda Amichai

Publisher: Jerusalem: Israeli Music Publications IMP 34-1
For: Countertenor, flute, viola, cello, piano, and percussion.
Percussion instrumentation: 3 woodblocks, 3 tom-toms, cymbal, tam-tam, and vibraphone.
Difficulty: Voice: difficult; Instruments: difficult
Vocal range: a - $a^{b''}$ plus highest and lowest notes possible
Language: Hebrew (with singable English translation)
Duration: 8:30
Comments: White score; some graphic notation.

701
Roper, Ramon
The Jackdaw (© 1978)
Text: William Cowper
Publisher: Paigles, England: Anglian Edition ANMS49
For: Countertenor, oboe, cello, and harpsichord.
Difficulty: Voice: moderately difficult; Instruments: moderately difficult
Vocal range: g - $e^{b''}$
Language: English

702
Finnissy, Michael (b. 1946)
Mr. Punch (© 1986)
Text: Composer
Publisher: London: Universal Edition UE16193
For: Voice, flute (piccolo), clarinet in E^b, violin, cello, piano, and percussion (one player).
Percussion instrumentation: triangle, güiro, car horn (klaxon), bass drum, large Chinese block, side drum, and tambourine.
Difficulty: Voice: difficult; Instruments: very difficult
Vocal range: none
Language: English
Duration: 21:00
Comments: Singer must portray nine characters; most of voice part is spoken but in strict rhythm; some pitch approximations.

703
Renosto, Paolo (1936-1988)
Ah, l'amarvi, cari oggetti (1972)
Text: none
Publisher: Darmstadt: Tonos
For: Female voice and two or more instruments.
Difficulty: Voice: moderately difficult; Instruments: moderately difficult
Vocal range: left up to singer
Language: left up to singer
Duration: no less than 10:00; no more than 20:00.
Comments: This work is aleatoric and contains seven "sheets." On each sheet is a system of symbols that represents sounds and/or actions to be performed. Performance notes must be read carefully.

704
Schwartz, Elliott (b. 1936)
Septet (© 1972)
Text: Composer
Publisher: New York: Carl Fischer
For: Voice (no vocal range), any woodwind, any *other* woodwind, any brass, violin, any *other*

bowed instrument, and percussion (2 players).

Percussion instrumentation: (I) 2 instruments of tuned pitch and 2 groupings (4 in one, 5 in the other) of untuned but relatively pitched instruments; (II) Same as percussion I but different instruments; groupings are 4 in one and 3 in the other.

Difficulty: Voice: moderate; Instruments: moderately difficult

Vocal range: none specific

Language: phonemes and English

Duration: 12:00

Comments: The piece is aleatoric. Read instructions carefully. Numerous vocal effects are required. Speaker/singer is called for.

705

Yun, Isang (b. 1917)

Gagok (Song) (1972)

Text: Traditional Korean

Publisher: Berlin: Bote & Bock

For: Voice (any), guitar, and percussion.

Percussion instrumentation: 2 triangles, 4 gongs, glockenspiel, 2 handbells, bak [Korean multiboard whip], 2 small cymbals, 4 cymbals, 5 temple blocks, 5 tomtoms, and 2 jingling johnnies.

Difficulty: Voice: difficult; Instruments: difficult

Vocal range: e′ - f″ (if read as treble clef)

Language: Korean

Duration: 7:00

Comments: No clef indicated; several vocal effects (tremolo, vibrato control, slides, etc.).

Index of Composers

Index of Literary Sources

Index of Music Publishers

Index of Instruments

1. "Keyboard" may include one or more of the following: piano, celesta, harpsichord, and organ (and their electronic counterparts) in various combinations. The entry for a work will usually make it clear how many keyboard players are required.
2. "Percussion" may require from one to many percussionists. The entry usually, but not always, indicates how many.
3. Items with an asterisk (*) call for resources besides the instruments indicated, for example, tape, amplification, or the playing of percussion instruments by other instrumentalists.
4. [Order of listing of instruments] Harp, guitar, and other listed instruments are included in the instrument count. Woodwinds are listed by family only: thus flute, piccolo, alto flute, and bass flute are all represented by "fl."

For more detailed information, including doublings, consult the individual entries in the annotated bibliography.

1 Instrument + Keyboard + Percussion

2 INSTRUMENTS

2 Instruments + Keyboard

2 Instruments + Percussion

2 Instruments + Keyboard + Percussion

3 INSTRUMENTS

3 Instruments + Keyboard

3 Instruments + Percussion

3 Instruments + Keyboard + Percussion

4 INSTRUMENTS

4 Instruments + Keyboard

ENSEMBLES OF 6 OR MORE INSTRUMENTS

Winds and strings except as noted. Guitar, harp, unusual instruments, and some exceptional instrumental combinations are noted.

6 INSTRUMENTS

6 Instruments + Keyboard

6 Instruments + Percussion

6 Instruments + Keyboard + Percussion

7 INSTRUMENTS

7 Instruments + Keyboard

7 Instruments + Percussion

7 Instruments + Keyboard + Percussion

8 INSTRUMENTS

8 Instruments + Keyboard

8 Instruments + Percussion

8 Instruments + Keyboard + Percussion

9 INSTRUMENTS

9 Instruments + Keyboard

UNUSUAL PERCUSSION AND CURIOSITIES

OTHER RESOURCES